W9-ALJ-762

Jumping the Broom

THE AFRICAN-AMERICAN WEDDING PLANNER

HARRIETTE COLE

An Owl Book

HENRY HOLT AND COMPANY

NEW YORK

◆

*With great love and respect I dedicate this book
to Gurumayi Chidvilasananda*

◆

Henry Holt and Company, Inc.
Publishers since 1866
115 West 18th Street
New York, New York 10011

Henry Holt® is a registered trademark
of Henry Holt and Company, Inc.

Copyright © 1993, 1995 by Harriette Cole
All rights reserved.

Published in Canada by Fitzhenry & Whiteside Ltd.,
195 Allstate Parkway, Markham, Ontario L3R 4T8.

Library of Congress Cataloging-in-Publication Data
Cole, Harriette.
Jumping the broom : the African-American wedding planner
Harriette Cole—1st ed.
p.   cm.
Includes bibliographical references and index.
1. Weddings—United States—Planning.
2. Afro-Americans—Marriage.   I. Title.
HQ745.C64   1993   92-38458
395'.22' 08996073—dc20   CIP

ISBN 0-8050-2143-4
ISBN 0-8050-2142-6 (An Owl Book: pbk.)

Henry Holt books are available for special promotions
and premiums. For details contact: Director, Special Markets.

First published in hardcover in 1993 by
Henry Holt and Company, Inc.

First Owl Book Edition—1995

Designed by Eric Baker Design Associates

Printed in the United States of America
All first editions are printed on acid-free paper. ∞

9   10   8
5   7   9   10   8   6
(pbk.)

All photographs copyright © 1993 by George Chinsee, except the
ones used by permission on the following pages: page 12, courtesy of
the Toone Family; pages 17, 18, courtesy of Ellen Howard; page 22,
courtesy of the Cole Family; page 42, courtesy of the Oliver Family;
pages 64, 172, 174, courtesy of Bill Boyd; page 114, courtesy of
Greg Miller; page 148, courtesy of James Van Der Zee; first page of
color insert, courtesy of Jackie Nickerson. Special thanks to Eric
Robertson African Arts for cultural art pieces used on cover
and in African-American Wedding Album.

A NOTE OF THANKS

THE OUTPOURING OF SUPPORT for this project has been tremendous. So many have offered their insight, assistance, contacts, legwork, patience, and, above all, love, to make *Jumping the Broom* a book that I hope you will treasure. I would like to say a special thank-you to a few of the many people who have contributed to its birth.

Throughout all of my pursuits, I have had the support of my family. I could never have completed such a massive undertaking without them: The Honorable Harry A. Cole and Doris Cole, Stephanie Cole Hill and Corey Hill, Susan Cole Hill and George Hill, and my partner, George Chinsee, whose careful camera and overall calm saved the day.

Essence Communications, Inc., has nurtured me over the years, and supported me through this project. Thanks to Edward Lewis, Clarence Smith, Susan L. Taylor, Stephanie Stokes Oliver, Marlowe Goodson, Mikki Taylor, and Michaela Angela Davis.

Many businesses, individuals, bridal and fashion designers, and artists wholeheartedly embraced this project, including: Chuck Olbricht, Pam Kueber, Al Falk, and the impeccable cars from the Ford Motor Company; the Reverend Wendell Phillips and the Reverend Marion C. Bascom; clinical psychologist Brenda K. Wade; E. Ethelbert Miller, director of the Afro American Resource Studies Center at Howard University, and Charles Blockson, curator of the Charles Blockson Book Collection at Temple University; Franklin Hokett, the deceased menswear designer whose work appears on the cover and throughout the book; Lydia Allotey, Aziza, Lois Barrett, Kevin Edwards, FIXIT Records, Arline Burks Gant, Camille Howard, Montego Joe, Janice McKnight-Magona, Flo McAfee, Dianne McIntyre, Patrice McLeod, George Preston, Josh Rose, Patricia Hall Sadoun, Klare Shaw-Moss, Alexander White; and culinary couples Wanda Malone Deramus and Paul Carter Harrison, Mattie L. Jordan and Roger Allen Gaye, Mildred C. Stevenson and Charles Dewitt Stevenson, and Carol Hall and Cliff Holliday.

Artists of all measure offered tremendous support, including: Alitash Kebede; African art dealers Eric Robertson and Bill Karg; artists Bill Pajaud, Lloyd Toone, Lynn Wilder, Cynthia Janet White, Mathew Thomas, and Jimmy James Greene.

Without its faithful core group, *Jumping the Broom* would not be the resource that it is today. Special thanks to the untiring creative team of this project (listed separately on the following page); Una Mulzac at the Liberation Bookstore in Harlem who sparked the idea; Mark Levine from Henry Holt who passed it on; my steadfast attorney, Kervin Simms of Simms & Walters; my hardworking agent, Madeleine Morel; my dedicated editor, Theresa Burns; my patient designers, Eric Baker and Kate Thompson; and most of all my teacher and guide, Gurumayi Chidvilasananda.

THE CREATIVE TEAM

Harriette Cole—Author
Sadia Graham—Assistant to Author

RESEARCH
Doris Cole
Katherine Cooke
Eric Easter
Gina Ross
Ipeleng Kgositsile
Sandra Martin
June Kelly
Alitash Kebede
Peggy Dillard Toone

PHOTOGRAPHY
George Chinsee—Photographer
Giovanni DeMoura—Assistant

ART
Alitash Kebede—Curator

FASHION
Sandra Martin—Fashion and Shoot
   Coordinator
Patricia Arrington—Stylist
Rick Ramsey—Assistant Stylist
Jeffrey Woodley for Zoli Illusions; Annu for
   Khamit Kinks; Diane Da Costa for
   Turning Heads—Hair Stylists
Roxanna Floyd for Zoli Illusions—
   Makeup Artist

FOOD
Jonell Nash—Food Editor
Charmaine Jones—Cake Designer
Janice Ervin, Patricia Arrington—
   Prop Stylists
Roscoe Betsill—Food Stylist
Paula Sanchez—Assistant

MODELS
Patricia Arrington
Leon Craig for Zoli Illusions
Melanie Landestoy for Elite Model
   Management
Lynn Matthew for Grace Del Marco
Arielle Tracan McKoy
Phina Oruche for Bethann Management
Rashid Silvera for Zoli Model
   Management, Inc.
Marie St. Victor
Bunita Tilley for Bethann Management
Brett Walker for Storm
Roshumba Williams for Bethann Management

FLORIST
The Daily Blossom, NYC

BOOK DESIGN
Eric Baker, Eric Baker Design Associates
Kate Thompson

TRANSPORTATION
Ford Motor Company

RESEARCH ASSISTANTS
Tonya Adams
Regina Robertson
Sala Patterson
Djassi Johnson

LOCATIONS
Cover, courtesy of Virginia and Earl
   Arrington, Brooklyn, NY
Food, courtesy of Lou Willard,
   Kerhonkson, NY

CONTENTS

An African-American
Wedding Album appears
after page 96.

INTRODUCTION

GETTING MARRIED may just be the most exciting—and sacred—moment a couple can share. As countless married folks can testify, walking toward that altar is surely a march that requires carefully directed steps. What can make your walk more memorable is including our African-American heritage, which amplifies and celebrates who we are. As a reminder of those deep roots that define *who we are* as a people, and that direct our development into family and, in turn, pillars of our community, I wrote *Jumping the Broom: The African-American Wedding Planner.*

When first published back in 1993, this book's goals were twofold: to help couples identify whether they were ready to make the sacred commitment before them and, if so, to help them prepare for this enormous step. The response has been tremendously gratifying, with enthusiastic letters and phone calls pouring in from all over the country. One couple in Oakland, California, Keith and Yolanda Patterson, shared an extraordinary story about how they used this book as a creative launchpad: The spiritual highlight of their wedding was a majestic wooden altar, draped with Masai fabric, that they designed in honor of their families uniting. Altar treasures included a basket of fruit to represent bounty and nourishment; West African *chiwaris*, or antelopes; libation bowls to invite their ancestors to come and bless the wedding; West African fertility dolls; photographs of their family lineage; and a Bible. That they were allowed to place their precious altar in their church and make a prayer before it during the ceremony represented a true melding of African traditions with Western conventions. These newlyweds were so inspired that they started their own business, Heritage Altars in Oakland, California, designing altars for other couples who want to honor their own union in a similar way.

Today many Black-owned businesses across the United States, like the Pattersons', can be instrumental in helping couples organize culturally rich wedding ceremonies. For this reason, I have expanded the resource guide in this new edition by nearly 200 businesses. Let it be your jumping-off point. A telephone number may change; your hometown may not be included. But a look through the Yellow (and Black) Pages, a call to your local African-American resource center, library, art gallery, dance class, or friend, will lead you to members of our community who *can* fulfill your needs.

When my husband George and I sealed our union in May 1993, I witnessed firsthand the magic of getting married *our style*. By the time of the ceremony, I had described the power and purpose of jumping the broom at least a hundred times, in conjunction with the promotion of this book. Yet on our sacred day, the depth of that single act came alive with greater fire. Toward the end of the ceremony, our minister, Dr. Eugene Callendar, asked our family members to stand and join hands. He then offered a prayer of unification, in African tradition, to acknowledge that our two families had become one. After we declared our vows to each other, we turned toward the congregation. Two drummers started slowly beating. Dr. Callendar began to speak about how our ancestors, who were brought to this country involuntarily by slavery, were not allowed legally to marry. About how they didn't consider union without ritual and proper sanctioning to be conceivable. He said that every time an African-American couple jumps the broom it makes our ancestors proud. As the drums reached a full roar, the great white tent under which we all found shelter raced with African calls. George and I clasped hands and jumped high in the air and over our broom. In that instant, time stopped. I later fell to my knees and offered a prayer of gratitude for the abundant strength that comes from our own homes, our every generation.

Within these pages is all you need to know to plan a wedding of any size. Keep track of your ideas by using the new companion to this book, *Jumping the Broom Wedding Workbook*, which has pages for your thoughts and worksheets to help you organize and keep the information and inspiration you gather.

Most of all, don't allow the various stresses and complications of what can be one of the most challenging *and* euphoric periods of your life to distract you too much. Remember, if you work together to plan your wedding and share responsibilities along the way, the going will be a lot easier.

Please accept my deepest wish for your majestic and fruitful union!

*E ku ori ire o.**

Harriette Cole

* *"Wish you luck" in the Nigerian language of Yoruba*

PART I

Will You Marry Me?

⊙⊙⊙⊙⊙⊙⊙⊙

CHAPTER I

MARRIAGE VIA THE ANCESTORS

I remember riding on the back of a motor scooter in 1987 on the small island of Tobago, sister island to Trinidad just off the coast of Venezuela, when I happened upon a wedding. My friend and I had ridden into a large, open field, one half of which was empty, the other half alive with a soccer game in full motion. Surrounding the field on three sides was a small village. Neat little houses lined the streets. Beyond the field, with the backdrop of an old fort framed by the setting sun, rushed the vivid blue ocean.

After a few minutes passed, we heard the unmistakable sound of happiness. There was laughter in the air, the rise and fall of intimate conversation—with a Caribbean accent—and a group of about twelve or so teenagers moving across the field. The young men wore dark jackets and light pants with colorful boutonnieres; the young women sashayed in pastel-painted ankle-length dresses with delicate portrait collars. Couples were forming. Young brothers worked to impress their female companions as the sisters blushed and experimented with their newly discovered charm.

A wedding had just ended in this village, and the youth were there to celebrate it. Together they walked and skipped and enjoyed one another as they passed by each family home announcing the good news before their day was complete.

The memory of that moment has stayed with me. The joy in those chocolate-brown faces, the responsibility being fulfilled of sharing the good fortune with the community, the beauty of the surroundings, all reminded me of what a rich cultural heritage Black people share, no matter where we live.

⊙⊙⊙⊙⊙⊙⊙

Crossing sticks was one way Black couples at the turn of the century chose to show their commitment to one another. Symbolizing the strength and vitality of trees, the staff-like sticks were crossed to honor and bless the new life that was about to begin.

THE ROOTS OF TRADITION: FAMILY

Respect for ritual and ceremony resounds from Tobago to Washington, D.C., like a deep-bellied gong amplifying, purifying, and forever reconnecting the soul of the diaspora. You can almost hear the ancestral drumbeat when you sit back and reminisce with family elders, leaf through vintage photo albums, listen to tales of life gone by. The beat is profound, ever pulsing and uniquely ours. How each of us interprets it creates the depth and diversity that defines us all.

Especially today, when couples prepare to marry, we look for that perfect melding of all that represents our culture. In the Black community, what does this mean? What are the wedding rituals our ancestors and parents followed when they experienced this moment in their lives?

The common denominator for our people the world over is *family*. In some African societies a marriage is not official until a libation has been poured and a prayer offered requesting grace from those family members who have passed. In countless African tribes from the east, the west, and the southernmost points, inclusion of nuclear and extended family members throughout the process of marriage has been a given. Even today parents in some African societies still arrange marriages for their children. It is customary in Ghana for aunts and other elders to play private detective, running what amounts to a background check on a future spouse to determine that person's reputation, health and wealth status, family heritage, and other vital information. Aunts, cousins, and older female relatives throughout West Africa often take on the role of "wedding consultant," helping to secure all the details of the courtship and ceremony.

Family elders impart detailed counseling once a couple has received the requisite permission from both sets of parents. For young women the messages come both in whispered tones and in group meetings when female elders share insights on the duties of a wife—everything from how to cook food and clean house to how to make love. In Liberia there is even a special school, called Sande Society, to which young girls between ages six and ten go for several years to learn the art of homemaking. Many African societies tend to be male-centered, and young men surely don't get off the hook when it comes to marital duty. Their fathers, mothers, and community elders teach them the ways of providing for their families. Lessons vary depending upon the nature of the group's income, and whether it is based on agriculture, mining, hunting, or other means. African communities commonly practice rituals through which boys must pass to reach manhood and during which they receive all of the lessons that they need to function as adults. If a generalization can be made about a continent of people, it is that African families tend to be close-knit even today, though they may be sewn together a bit differently than their African-American counterparts.

Beneath the Surface

Yet all isn't rosy in the African family, at least as far as women go. A pervasive sentiment is that women are essentially governed by their husbands, something that women in America of all races have fought against—for better and for worse—with some measure of gain. African women tend to experience greater difficulty exercising their independence than their African-American sisters. And in the event of divorce, historically and in the present, it is extremely difficult for them to share in the dissolution of family assets. Years ago, in fact, there was what amounted to a binding prenuptial agreement in which the bride's family would be held accountable for *all* gifts given to her and her family since the beginning of the courtship, even if that meant from before she was born. Until *all* gifts were returned to the groom's family, no divorce would be granted. I have found no mention of women getting money, gifts, or even the children returned to them at the end of a marriage.

Another tradition that is endured by many African women and largely accepted throughout the Motherland is the practice of polygamy. Right now in many African communities, men are allowed to have many wives, while women are likely to be considered disgraceful if they are not virgins on their wedding night. (Followers of Islamic tradition are limited to four wives.) Some sisters here in America argue that the situation may not be substantially different, except that in African societies men are held responsible for the livelihood of each of their wives, whereas here extramarital companions aren't respected (or provided for).

It must be acknowledged that there are groups of people in the United States, from the Mormons to several African-centered spiritual communities, who also believe in polygamy and encourage its existence. One sister explained that her spiritual leader justifies the practice by saying that there are not enough single brothers compared to the number of sisters. Since building families is the foundation of the Black community, he explained, he encourages growing the family through polygamy. Clearly polygamy is a topic of heated debate in the Black community, with men and women taking both sides.

What's less likely to get the female vote is the centuries-old practice of female circumcision. Although largely illegal, even today women along the desert plains and beyond continue to receive *clitoridectomies*, painful operations that mutilate their genitals, often making them unable to experience sexual pleasure. Much like other rites of passage, this operation is usually celebrated with song, dance, and feasting. Ironically, it often occurs just before the wedding ceremony. (One account indicates that the goal was not one of pain or discomfort at all. Instead, it was to make the woman more open to receive her husband.) Alice Walker recently wrote a book exploring the subject, *Possessing the Secret of Joy*, and has been speaking on the tragedy of the tradition, while at the same time recognizing that it links women to their cultural heritage. Anthropological studies dating back to the early 1900s discuss how missionaries made desperate pleas against the practice and imposed costly fines on "offenders," hoping to end this activity—with only marginal success.

A further tension comes from the magnetic draw of industrialization that has helped to split up family units by separating many couples, as one partner travels from his or her rural homeland to the city for work. In the past, divorce was a difficult and relatively rare action for a couple to take in many African countries; today the numbers are increasing as families live under the stress of lengthy separation.

Even with the sometimes severe rituals of the wedding process, the unbalanced nature of the marriage bed, and the contemporary stresses that African families face, they still appear to be staying together and building strong family units.

RITUAL ON THESE SHORES

In America customs among people of color had to be re-created. When West Africans were brought forcibly to these shores some four hundred years ago they were stripped of much of what was theirs—their homeland, their

ⓞⓞⓞⓞⓞⓞⓞ

Like many of our ancestors, attorney George Henry Rosedom and educator Ruth Victoria Tignor, both from Baltimore, chose elegant Western attire for their wedding in 1944.

community structure, their freedom, even, in some cases, their sometimes sexist ways. Not long after the beginning of slavery, Africans were also denied the right to marry in the eyes of the law. Slaveholders apparently thought that their captives were not real people but were, instead, property to be bought and sold. As such, they had no rights. Further, if allowed formally to marry and live together, slaves might find strength in numbers that could lead to revolt. Adding to their trauma, these early friends to white settlers were quickly and brutally forbidden by law to marry their white counterparts—a situation that remains a sore spot for inter-racial couples today.

Yet the enslaved were spiritual people who had been taught rituals that began as early as childhood to prepare them for that big step into family life. How could they succumb to this denial?

They could not. So they became inventive. Out of their creativity came the tradition of jumping the broom. The broom itself held spiritual significance for many African peoples, representing the beginning of homemaking for a couple. For the Kgatla people of southern Africa, it was customary, for example, on the day after the wedding for the bride to help the other women in the family to sweep the courtyard clean, thereby symbolizing her willingness and obligation to assist in housework at her in-laws' residence until the couple moved to their own home. During slavery, to the ever-present beat of the talking drum (until drums too were outlawed, since they were considered a dangerous means of communication), a couple would literally jump over a broom into the seat of matrimony. Today, this tradition and many others are finding their way back into the wedding ceremony.

Slave narratives and other early nineteenth-century documentation reveal the ways in which slave couples did their jumping. With the master's permission, a couple was allowed to stand before witnesses, pledge their devotion to

Born shortly after Emancipation, the late Starke Littleton Tignor, a ship's steward, and Mary Louise Davenport, a housewife, married in Northumberland County, Virginia, in 1892. When Mary passed away, she was buried in her wedding dress.

each other, and finally jump over a broom, which would indicate their step into married life. Below is a slave marriage ceremony supplement, found in the sheet music—dated Sunday, September 9, 1900—to the song "At an Ole Virginia Wedding":

Dark an' stormy may come de wedder;
I jines dis he-male an' dis she'male togedder.
Let none, but Him dat makes de thunder,
Put dis he-male and dis she-male asunder.
I darefor 'nounce you bofe de same.
Be good, go 'long, an' keep up yo' name.
De broomstick's jumped, de world not wide.
She's now yo' own. Salute yo' bride!

Following are two versions of jumping the broom from *Bullwhip Days: The Slaves Remember* by James Mellon. What's especially revealing is that in both instances the master of the plantation encouraged and blessed the union of "his" slaves. In the first passage the slave Joe Rawls reminisces about his wedding at the turn of the century.

Well, dey jis' lay de broom down,
'n' dem what's gwine ter git marry'
walks out 'n' steps ober dat broom bofe
togedder, 'n' de ole massa, he say, "I now
pronounce you man 'n' wife" 'n' den
dey was marry'. Dat was all dey was t'it
—no ce'mony, no license, no nothin',
jis' marryin'.

The second passage is a description of the wedding ceremony of a woman named Tempie Durham. What is particularly disturbing is that the master also had fun at the expense of his slaves and that after an elaborate wedding, complete with food, drink, and formal ceremony, the groom had to leave to go back to his owner's plantation nearby. The couple was never allowed to live together. They did have eleven children, which prompted Tempie to write, "I was worth a heap to Marse George, 'kaze I had so many chillun." Here's her version of jumping the broom:

After Uncle Edmond said de las' words
over me an' Exter, Marse George
got to have his little fun. He say,
"Come on, Exter, you an' Tempie got
to jump over de broomstick backwards.
You go to do dat to see which one gwine
be boss of your househol'." Everbody come
stan' roun' to watch. Marse George hold
de broom 'bout a foot high off de floor.
De one dat jump over it backwards an' never
touch de handle gwine boss de house, an' if
bofe of dem jump over widout touchin' it,
dey ain't gwine be no bossin'; de jus'
gwine be 'genial.

I jumped fus', an' you ought to seed
me. I sailed right over dat broomstick,
same as a cricket. But when Exter jump, he
done had a big dram an' his feets was so big
an' clumsy dat dey got all tangled up in dat
broom, an' he fell headlong. Marse George,
he laugh an' laugh, an' tole Exter he gwine
be bossed till he skeered to speak less'n I
tole him to speak.

The practice of jumping the broom is the most widely known wedding ritual born in the African-American community, thanks to Alex Haley's epic family saga *Roots*, in the dramatic scene in which Kunta Kinte and Bell took their step into married life. Since the 1970s countless African-American couples have incorporated this tradition into their weddings with the intention of creating a bridge between them and their cultural heritage. Photography professor Gary Kirksey and college counselor Shirley Williams jumped the broom outdoors after passing under a wicker trellis when they married in Ohio in 1991. Marketing executive Reginald Oliver and magazine editor Stephanie Stokes made their leap in church, right after they were pronounced husband and wife back in 1979 in Seattle, Washington. Before cutting the cake at their reception in New York City in 1992, Heather Bond and Samuel C. Bryant, Jr., jumped together into wedded bliss. And the list goes on and on. No matter how

Western or cultural African-American ceremonies may be, that one act binds thousands of couples together in solidarity.

The use of traditions that have been either borrowed from African shores or from the Caribbean, or that were born anew here, span much farther than this one practice. In many cases, Black couples don't even realize they are part of our own tradition. Take, for instance, the lesser-known tradition of crossing sticks. Artist Lloyd Toone unearthed an early-1900s family wedding portrait from Chase City, Virginia, featuring a couple crossing two strong sticks, one more sign of holy matrimony. Among the Samburu of Kenya, sticks were also used during wedding celebrations by the groom to brand the beloved cattle that he would give his wife to finalize their vows.

Cultural links can be found throughout the process of getting married, from the food we eat, to the way we dress, to the rituals we perform at the ceremony. For example, just the thought of preparing West Indian Black Cake, not to mention eating it, whets an African-American palate. Along with plain old delicious pound cake, it is a remnant of our Caribbean and African legacies that frequently finds its way onto wedding dessert tables today. Our current desire to decorate our hair with vibrant dyes of burnished red and braids adorned with cowrie shells dates back centuries to the custom of covering hair with a mixture of red ochre and animal fat on special occasions, and of wearing the plentiful cowrie shells to encourage fertility. The revived practice of pouring libation to the ancestors and offering a prayer of supplication to them dates back possibly to the beginning of time and has been incorporated into many contemporary ceremonies.

As you turn the pages of *Jumping the Broom*, savor the many stories of ethnic wedding touches that appear throughout. Take note of the ways in which contemporary couples have authentically translated African rituals into their weddings as well as how they have created unique interpretations of their own. The journey begins in the next chapter with information on the nature of commitment that is necessary for every successful marriage.

Richard Cole, of
Washington, D.C.,
met Myrtle White, of
King and Queen
County, on a catering
job in Baltimore. A
year later, in 1937,
they married at her
home. Myrtle made
the gown for her
big day.

CHAPTER 2

THE ELEMENTS OF COMMITMENT

The act of getting married both here and throughout Africa and the Caribbean is brimming with much more meaning than a simple "I do." First, it requires truly understanding and accepting the solemn oath of those two words. As couples inch closer to that final moment of crossing the invisible threshold into familyhood—whether it's by reciting vows, pouring a libation, jumping a broom, drinking a ceremonial wine, or sharing a huge feast—elders from both shores agree that it is crucial that the two become fully aware of the path before them.

Many African historians and scholars have said that by the hour of the final marriage ceremony, an African couple—whether Christian, Islamic, or of local religious faith—is essentially already married. The road has been carefully paved from engagement to the requisite celebrations. The families have offered their blessings, and, in many cases, the couple has been spending a great deal of time together getting to know each other. The same basic steps are followed here in the United States: The family is queried, an engagement secured, a date set, and the parties begin. And as with African unions, the wedding itself comes anywhere from a few months to more than a year after the engagement.

Yet, across both continents our marriages seem to be unraveling rather than being fortified. As a nation more than 50 percent of our marriages end in divorce. What that means is that literally millions of people are throwing in the towel, giving up on their commitment—quite often before they have given it a fair chance.

WHEN THE GOING GETS TOUGH

In order to cement your commitment *before* you marry, it may do you good to take a look at the history of Blacks in this country, and at some of the particular difficulties we have faced in our unions. Certain Afrocentric historians argue that the demise of the Black family has everything to do with racism. From the dawn of American slavery, Black families have been weakened, first not permitted to become legal partners for life, and then not allowed even to live together, in some cases for fear of revolt. Black men were feared and revered, in both cases for their strength. As this nation has grown, movement to improve the plight of Black people has been in baby steps. Affirmative action has helped and hindered us. Welfare has proved to be a double-edged sword, by requiring that families be separated in order to be eligible for resources.

In the first half of this century our communities and neighborhoods were fortresses that fostered closeness out of necessity; we were not allowed to live, work, or be educated anywhere else. Integration has actually splintered our strength in some respects, helping to create divisions among our people and subsequently diluting the glue that was once our lifeblood. What this means for contemporary marriages is that we usually don't have the greater community to nurture us during hardship. As with other Americans, the hard meaning of "for richer or poorer" has been driven home during this nineties flirtation with depression, which has resulted in both partners spending more time outside of the home working than at home cultivating their family. Finally, our extended families are often far away and unable to fortify us when we need them most.

Beyond racism is another possibility for the weakening of the marriage bond. Couples of all ethnic backgrounds in America today can and do get caught up in the event that they are planning—often the most elaborate they've experienced in their lives—and lose sight of the bigger picture, the life awaiting them. There's the tug-of-war that often ensues between the mother of the bride and the bride-to-be about what style of wedding the couple will have. This fiery issue can become one of control, making the question for the bride, "Whose wedding is this, anyway?" Instead of the focus remaining on nurturing the embryonic relationship, many couples experience tension over planning details that, in some cases, leaves the groom on the outside not fully participating in the process.

Responsibility in the Motherland

These circumstances simply don't play out in such dramatic detail in traditional African cultures for two reasons: The Continent was not ravaged by slavery and its aftereffects in the same way, and African wedding and marriage rituals are steeped in traditions that provide unwritten codes of behavior that must be honored, leaving little room for interpretation.

Take the role of men, for instance. Whereas in America it is possible for men to have a rather secondary role in the wedding process, in African communities the young man often takes a very active role, fulfilling a detail of duties in order to meet his obligation. For the Samburu of Kenya, according to Nigel Pavitt's book, *Samburu*, the groom-to-be must be between twenty-five and thirty-five and be inducted into warrior status, called *moran*, before he is eligible for marriage. When the elders agree that he can marry, he—with his family, or in certain cases, his family instead of him—must conduct a search for his bride in a neighboring village. On the wedding day, he must make a day's journey to reach his intended's family home, with specific gifts in hand. During the first day of festivities he is responsible for killing the wedding ox that will be served at the meal. Following two celebratory days with his "best man" and close friends, he must bring his bride back to his family residence within one day.

Even more responsibility lies on the shoulders of family elders. Among the Akan and throughout sub-Saharan Africa, once a young man notices a young woman and expresses interest, the process begins, explains Lydia Allotey, an import/export specialist of Ghanaian and Jamaican heritage who has lived and worked extensively throughout the Continent. An entire delegation of family members, composed of elders, parents, aunts, and uncles, visits the home of the intended's family to express interest in the young woman. A series of questions will be asked about who the intended is, what she has accomplished or failed at in her life, the status of her family's reputation. Meanwhile, a delegation from the young woman's home has already been engaged in the background check of the groom. Sometimes it takes up to a year to get family members on both sides to agree to the proposed marriage. Once an agreement is reached, the formal delegation again visits the bride's family, making note that they request a union. This meeting results in an engagement. A formal marriage ceremony will normally be held within three months. That ceremony actually represents a culmination of several parties over a week's time.

Similarities prevail regardless of the degree of modernization that some African nations have experienced. Today among the Akan, for example, a couple is not truly married until after the traditional wedding—which requires a meeting of family elders, giving gifts, and sharing drinks—has occurred, whether a Western church ritual takes place or not. For many nations, even if the couple is abroad, they are expected to follow certain steps to "tie" their marriage. With all of the delicate footwork required even prior to an engagement, the likelihood of divorce in many African unions is quite low compared to that of Americans.

The American Sensibility

Things are a bit different in the United States. It could be that the wonderful gift of freedom that we enjoy is a mixed blessing. On the one hand, couples are able to marry in whatever manner they choose. They can just as easily take a trip to City Hall in jeans and T-shirts to be married before the justice of the peace as they can opt for all-out religious or secular fanfare. Although the steps leading to marriage aren't usually as elaborate in America, those leading out of it can be equally tedious and expensive, both emotionally and economically. Some religious officiates as well as psychologists argue that America's relaxed "rules" of sexuality, the increased number of couples who live together prior to marriage, and the growing numbers of individuals who become independent before marriage all add to the weakening of the marriage bond. Of course, there are others who rally just as strongly on the other side, saying that each of these factors contributes to the greater awareness in both partners of their own needs as well as the commitment involved in becoming husband and wife.

In any case, what many people seem not to grasp is that with freedom comes incredible responsibility. That responsibility in marriage, according to all spiritual traditions, encourages that the couple unite with the blessing and support of their family, and further requires that the two enter into this holy union in the presence of God. As the Reverend Wendell Phillips, longtime pastor of Heritage United Church of Christ in Baltimore, Maryland, puts it, "In a successful marriage, there is a triangle—the two people and God, that other Presence, Allah, Jehovah, whatever you wish to call the higher power. It's that other Presence that sustains you when you run into difficult experiences in married life."

One of my intentions in writing *Jumping the Broom* is to encourage couples to think long and hard about marriage before entering into it. Why? So that as African Americans we can take responsibility for ourselves, our families, and our communities. So that we can strengthen rather than diminish our powerful heritage.

KNOW YOUR PARTNER

One of the most effective ways to lay the foundation for your relationship *before* the big day is to spend time alone and with your partner, carefully contemplating the meaning of the relationship you are about to enter. A good way to do this, especially if you have a spiritual home, is to engage in premarital counseling. Such counseling can help to clarify the issues that are most important in the building of a marriage.

Having counseled couples over the past thirty years, the Reverend Wendell Phillips offers here a number of critical issues that you need to address before you marry, preferably under the tutelage of a spiritual adviser.

Is premarital counseling required for couples to get married?

Legally it is not. You should ask your spiritual leader about whether it is required in order to marry in your place of worship. Counseling is recommended in many Christian churches.

How many counseling sessions are recommended?

A minimum of three sessions, including private meetings with each partner as well as a joint meeting. If there are deep-set issues that need to be resolved, such as family disputes or interfaith issues, the number of sessions should be increased.

Who does the counseling?

Normally the counselor is the leader of the spiritual community. When neither partner has a spiritual home, the counseling can be sought from a psychologist who specializes in family issues.

What kinds of questions should you expect to answer in these meetings?

In the individual sessions you will talk about your family background and your own personal history, how you see that you have developed into the person you are today, your marital and religious histories.

In the group session the focus of discussion will be primarily on finances and sex. The big question regarding money is, "How do you intend to handle your finances?" Phillips strongly recommends that couples pool their resources into joint accounts, which will force them to sit down and discuss what they're spending and why. He further paraphrases Matthew, saying, "'Where your treasure is, there also is your heart,' so why would you trust your partner with your life but not your money?" The one who's most capable of managing the money should accept that responsibility, he says.

Regarding the hot topic of sex, Phillips encourages couples with this advice: "Think along the lines that there is no other experience in marriage that has the healing quality of the sexual experience." He further adds that when sex is needed to heal the relationship, it's often refused because one partner is angry at the other.

How can you resolve family matters, especially when they include divided families with remarried parents who don't get along?

Many people today are the product of single-parent households. In some cases the parents may be remarried or still bitter about their break up and the events that have played out over the years. A wedding brings many of these issues to the surface, particularly when family members who don't normally spend time together now have to consider whom they want to invite to the wedding, where they will sit, who they have to see, and so on.

More important is what the family relationship will do to the health of the budding union. What Phillips helps couples do is explore the nature of their family relationships, with the focus on discovering how the young man and woman got to be the people he and she are today. To help avoid the pitfalls that have plagued an individual's family, he physically charts out and diagrams the family relationships so that there is a clear, tangible record to be studied. When family matters are particularly troubling, counseling should be extended until the issues are resolved enough for the couple to experience a nurturing bond that will not be harmed by outside influences.

How can you come to terms with being of different religious backgrounds?

Seek counseling to get to the heart of how you feel about the situation. Again, individual counseling is advised in the beginning, allowing each partner the opportunity to express his or her views on the other's spiritual practice. A spiritual counselor can normally tell whether there is acceptance or competitiveness in play on this issue. You should not make the mistake of taking the matter lightly, especially if you plan to have children. Phillips strongly advises that couples decide on the faith their children will be reared in prior to having them to avoid forcing the children to pay the high price of living in spiritual confusion.

How can you have your wedding ceremony in a spiritual center if you are of two different faiths?

Consult your wedding officiate when you reserve your date. In many cases, clergy will allow interfaith marriages to be performed in their house of worship. You may be able to invite a wedding officiate from your betrothed's faith to share in the ceremonial duties. (See Chapter 13 for more ideas.)

What are the best tools you can develop now to nurture a loving and lasting relationship?

There are several. Develop the discipline of listening. Listening requires paying attention to the whole person so that you can see beyond the words. Words can sometimes be concealing rather than revealing, but a good listener should be able to pick up cues and see the pain or joy, hurt or happiness beyond what is simply said. At the same time, you can't expect your partner to be a mind reader! Yet paying attention to your partner's everyday habits and idiosyncrasies is part of listening.

Piggybacking here is the age-old wisdom that couples should *never* go to sleep angry with each other—because you might not wake up. Instead, you should attempt to work through your problems to reach a resolution. If no agreement is in sight, you should be able to agree to disagree and still be able to love each other and nurture your relationship.

Another tremendous healer is the art of humor. Couples who learn to infuse humor into their relationship tend to fare well. Learning to laugh at yourself, and not at your partner, will help you to move through problems and disappointments more smoothly.

Of equal importance is nurturing a prayerful life. You may ask, "What happens if only one partner is actively involved in spiritual practice?" The worst thing a mate can do is to badger the other about being more spiritually active—this will only alienate him or her further. Instead, the one who is already involved should pray by him or herself on behalf of the other. In turn, the partner who is not involved in church or prayer needs to be willing to give the other person that space or time needed to participate in his or her chosen discipline.

Once you're married, how can you handle problems that seem to be out of your control?

Go to your spiritual adviser *before* you go to your in-laws or the lawyer. Phillips makes an agreement with each couple he marries, not for a fee, but for the first opportunity to help them work through difficulties. As important as he knows the family to be to the success of a relationship, Phillips argues that it will probably be easier for a counselor to identify the real problem and help the couple address it before it has your mother's, brother's, sister's, and aunt's interpretations clouding the view.

What can you learn from your African brothers and sisters that will fortify your relationships?

Remember first and foremost that a marriage will do one of two things: uplift the community or lower it, because it is a community spiritual experience. As our

African forebears knew, we need to understand that we are basically and primarily spiritual beings. Phillips says, "It's a part of our heritage, and I think the Motherland understands that better than we do. The majority of our problems today are a result of a cutting off from our spiritual heritage." He further urges couples to seek guidance when they need it. Quoting the Swiss psychiatrist Carl Jung, he says that people's problems over age thirty-five are basically of a spiritual nature, which is why they are seldom addressed. It's up to us to change that.

An Exercise in Discovery

By the time they are engaged, most couples feel that they truly *do* know each other well. What happens in many cases, however, is that there are many aspects of each of your personalities that you have yet to reveal to each other—some that you may not even know yourself. San Francisco–based clinical psychologist Brenda K. Wade has written a wonderful resource book, *Love Lessons*, that can be a great best friend to couples as they start their married life. To help the two of you explore your thoughts about your impending union, Wade has created the following questionnaire. The purpose of this exercise is simple: to assist you and your mate in getting to know each other. Even if you have lived together for a few months or even a few years, these questions can help to clarify your thoughts and feelings about important issues in preparation for the next step.

The rules are basic:

1. Write all of your answers down.

2. Remember that there are no wrong or right answers.

3. Give the most complete, detailed answers possible. Don't say, for instance, "I want respect." Instead, say exactly what that means to you.

Maybe, "I need you to praise me," or, "I want to have the final word on things."

4. Be honest. Manipulation doesn't work. Sooner or later your partner will be furious with you if you hide your true motives.

5. Be certain you understand your partner's answers. Ask for clarification if necessary. Discuss the answers.

6. Thank your partner for sharing his or her answers with you.

Physical Needs and Desires

1. What kind of sexual relationship do you expect to have with your partner?

2. What is your ideal frequency of intercourse?

3. What is your favorite sexual fantasy?

4. What do you feel uncomfortable with sexually?

5. What sexual behaviors are off-limits for you?

6. What birth control will you use?

7. Do you expect your partner to be monogamous?

8. Do you want to have children in this marriage? If yes, when?

9. Is there anything else in the sexual arena that you want to share with your partner?

10. Do you have any special needs for touching or physical affection? Be specific.

11. How do you like to wake up in the morning (quietly, to music, in your partner's arms, etc.)?

12. How do you like to sleep at night (on which side of the bed, wearing what, in silence, etc.)?

Emotional Needs and Desires

1. What is your favorite way to have your partner demonstrate his or her love for you (words, touch, gift, etc.)?

2. How do you like to show your love for your partner?

3. When you feel upset or hurt, what would you like your mate to do to comfort you?

4. If the two of you have a problem that you can't resolve together, what would you be willing to do to move forward (talk with friends, seek marital counseling, read books together, etc.)?

5. Is there any particular emotional need that you have that your partner

should know about (something that lingers from childhood, for example)?

6. Do you have any fears about your marriage that you haven't shared?

7. What do you feel will be your greatest emotional difficulty as a spouse?

8. What do you feel will be your greatest emotional strength as a spouse?

9. Why are you getting married?

Money

This is a tricky area for most couples. Again, remember that there are no wrong or right answers.

1. Will you have a joint checking account?

2. Will you have a joint savings account?

3. How will you share or divide bills and expenses?

4. How much will you save each month?

5. What investment and retirement plans do you have?

6. If you plan children, how will they be provided for?

7. If either of you (or both) already has children, how will they be provided for?

8. How much money do you have?

9. How much indebtedness do you have?

10. What property do you bring to your marriage?

11. Will you have a prenuptial agreement drawn up legally?

12. What kind of financial contribution or support do you expect from your partner?

Intellectual

1. What intellectual pursuits do you most enjoy (books, museums, music, art, etc.)?

2. What is your favorite form of entertainment?

3. Do you want to further your education during your marriage?

4. Do you plan to change professions?

5. What career path do you see before you?

6. How would you like your partner to assist or support you in reaching your goals?

Spiritual

1. What kind of spiritual beliefs do you hold?

2. What is God to you?

3. What holidays do you want to celebrate and how?

4. What spiritual practices do you want your partner to participate in?

5. What daily spiritual ritual can you do together to build family unity?

6. What spiritual beliefs do you want to teach your children?

7. What service do you think you can give as a couple to help others?

Cultural

1. How do you envision the religious and spiritual life that we share together?

2. If we have children, how would you like our children to be raised? Spiritually, culturally, etc.?

3. How will we resolve cultural differences when they arise? (Bearing in mind that there is no right or wrong answer; you simply need to find a way that works for both of you.)

4. What holiday traditions are important to you?

5. Are there new cultural traditions you would like us to create together?

6. What are your family's commitments and expectations for me as a spouse? (In some cultures, a son- or daughter-in-law has a specific role.)

Marriage is an experience that is unique for every couple; knowing some of the pros and cons should help the two of you come to a heartfelt and realistic commitment. There truly is no formula for a successful marriage, other than that you must learn to love and respect each other at all times, especially when you disagree. As this quiz illustrates, you will have many challenges ahead as your life unfolds. Cherish the moments in the beginning that will lay the foundation for your life together.

CHAPTER 3

YOUR ENGAGEMENT

Tradition in America has it that the nervous groom-to-be comes calling to the bride's house to ask her stern father for her hand in marriage. At that meeting, the father firmly quizzes him on his intentions, after which he either gives his blessing or expresses his unwavering disapproval. Similarly, the Kwangari tradition required the bridegroom to come to the bride's father asking for her hand in marriage only to be sent away three times before receiving her father's approval. Among the Ibo of Nigeria, the Twifo of Ghana, and many other West African peoples, an entire contingent of family comes to the bride's home asking for permission for their son to marry the young woman in question. In each case the underlying reason for what appears to be extreme paternal intervention is the search for true commitment on the part of the potential husband.

MAKING THE ANNOUNCEMENT

More common today in the United States is that couples first come to an agreement together that they want to be married. In light of the American population's escalating divorce rate, this step takes on tremendous significance. However the two of you come to a mutual agreement about your future, let the notion simmer inside—silently (at least to the public)—for a while. Contemplate the meaning of "for the rest of your life," honestly committing your very being to that notion. Only after you both agree that you want to take the big step should you make your announcement.

And, yes, the first to know should be your parents. As much as you may want to spread the word to all of your friends and colleagues, take heed. Marriage is a joining of two into one, an extension of the lifeblood of the families that brought the two of you into this world. Respect them by telling them first.

Telling Your Parents

Organize a meeting, preferably with both sets of parents, where you make the announcement together. Both of you can help break the ice by sharing warm insights from your experiences—including childhood tales and stories about your life as a couple.

For the Akan of Ghana in West Africa, according to Dr. Kwasi Ohene-Bekoe, pastor of the International Church of the Metroplex in Dallas, the proposal begins with the father of the young man handling all of the negotiations. "The man's father would go to the wife's father, talk to him, tell him what he wants," he explains. "Then the woman's father would say that he will get back in touch with him. In a couple of weeks, her family would respond saying 'It's okay. We give our blessings.' Then the woman's father and the man's father get together with friends for a drink, provided by the young man's father." This act declares the official engagement. Although the actual steps to getting engaged may vary from region to region, Ohene-Bekoe assures us that parental involvement is a given throughout the Continent.

The way to organize your engagement announcement here in America should entail just as much respect, if less ceremony. When you live in the same city as your families, it's likely that your intended has already met your parents. So your announcement meeting will be just that—a formal acknowledgment of your future plans. When M. Keith Rawlings sought approval to marry Illona Sheffey back in 1978, everybody was from Baltimore, and Keith knew Illona's family quite well. Naturally, the two thought that "getting permission" would be a cinch. Keith likes to tell the story of how it didn't actually turn out that way. First of all, Keith and Illona were young, twenty-two and twenty-one respectively. He was in medical school; she in law school. The last thing Illona's parents wanted to hear, Keith says, was that they were making wedding plans. When Keith told Illona's father, "I want to marry your daughter," her dad's response was, "What exactly does that mean?" So Keith spent the next few hours explaining in detail what he thought was obvious, including how he intended to support his wife and their young life together. Now, with two children and more than fifteen years of marriage under their belt, the couple say they knew they were ready for their betrothal, but now they understand why Illona's parents pressed them to articulate their plans.

If your families have not already met, and you live in different towns, don't just call them up and announce your intentions. Treat your announcement as you treat your upcoming union. One of the sweetest things you can do is write a note to your parents letting them know that you want to bring your beloved home "to meet the family." Your letter can read something like this:

Dear Mom and Dad:

I'm as happy as you always wanted me to be, and I've found a wonderful man, Reggie Johnson, with whom I can share my happiness. I can't wait for you to meet him. We'd like to come to visit on the weekend of the 16th.

Please let me know soon if this is okay.

Love you,

Janice

His letter should read similarly.

Notes are wonderful because they later become keepsakes. If you simply are not a letter writer, do call your parents and ask them if you and your friend can come to visit at a specific time. Of course they will want to know why. Do your best to keep the specifics concealed. Make sure you let them know that everything is all right, though, so that they don't worry every day leading up to your arrival!

If your parents are unaware of your relationship, during your visit give them a chance to warm up to the idea of a special new person in your life. Spend time with one another, and then let them know your intentions.

In the unlikely event that your parents disapprove, you must then decide together on your next course of action. It is best for you to continue working at building a loving relationship between them and you. Give it some time. Though some couples choose not to acknowledge it, parental approval *is* significant in a marriage. Especially during the tough times it is essential to have a loving family on whom you can depend. If, however, you ultimately decide to marry against your family's wishes, be clear in your decision, *and* be ready to absorb the wedding costs alone. No matter what, do inform your family of your wedding date and send them an invitation.

THE FAMILY MEETING

The time that you and your families spend getting to know one another should be considered most sacred. Your parents, siblings, and relatives will most likely be the ones who reinforce the glue when times get tough. They may also become sources of conflict.

The Reverend Clarence Glover from Shreveport, Louisiana, and Sybil Pruitt from Athens, Texas, both previously married, paid particular attention to their family meetings. They were advised by Ghanaian minister Ohene-Bekoe that if there was something in either of their families about which they disagreed or that caused them discomfort, they were to talk it out with each other. Should there be a problem, their spiritual adviser told them that in the Ghanaian tradition, usually the father or the brother of the bride would go to talk to the groom's family to see if they could iron things out before the wedding. Clarence and Sybil found that taking such care helped them to establish even stronger bonds with their family members.

Even if your marriage is not your first, you should tell your parents your plans and ask for their blessing.

If You Have Children

In all cases, it's best to introduce your intended to your family *before* you walk down the aisle. This becomes critical when the family means your children. More than 50 percent of adult Black women today have children; 34 percent don't have husbands—yet. When the time comes, remember to be loving and understanding with them. If you live with your children, more than likely they have met your fiancé on several occasions. Take time with them *alone* to share your news. Watch your children's reactions carefully, and be prepared to answer their questions. Reassure them of your love for them, that your fiancé will be an *addition* to your whole family, not a person who will take you away from them. This is true even when your children are teenagers. At that critical stage they may rely on you even more for love and attention. Only after they are comfortable with the idea should you bring your fiancé to them to discuss your new family structure together. Later you can decide how and if they will participate in your wedding. Clarence and Sybil included Sybil's ten-year-old son, Mondre, in their African-inspired wedding ceremony. All three members of the newly formed Glover family received a wedding band during a ceremony at the church.

Tell Everyone Else

It's finally time to share your good fortune with your extended family of colleagues and friends, whether you've set a date or not. Be mindful that if you do not intend to invite many colleagues, you shouldn't give blow-by-blow details of your planning as you go along. If you sense that your boss is wondering if you will continue working there, especially if your fiancé lives in another city, be up front with him or her. Talk about your plans with your fiancé first, of course, and then share them with your employer; it's best to have your boss on your side during your engagement. On those days when you need extra time to make phone calls or go to important appointments, you will need his or her support. Staying focused throughout the process should help you to keep a constant gauge on your performance at work and on your employer's comfort.

Once you have set a date and confirmed a location for your wedding and reception, send an announcement to your local newspaper and the newspapers from each of your hometowns (if different), including the Black media. Your announcement can appear anywhere from three months to one year before your wedding day. Send your announcement to the society page editor, and include a black-and-white glossy 5" x 7" or 8" x 10" photograph of yourselves either separately or together, along with details about yourselves and your upcoming wedding. Contact the newspaper for specifics on the format to follow; details may vary.

WITH THIS RING. . .

Ornamentation of both bride and groom at the wedding ceremony is as customary among many African peoples as it is in America. Whereas couples here often exchange rings and small items of jewelry, such as pearls for women and watches for men, it is often the groom's responsibility in African homelands to offer his bride gold pieces, earrings, or neck rings, as well as beaded necklaces on their wedding day. According to Angela Fisher's *Africa Adorned*, among the Dinka people of East Africa, ivory and Venetian glass beads are considered valuable gifts that are presented to the bride by the bridegroom's family. To announce a young woman's engagement, elders of the East African nomadic Turkana and Pokot people wear aluminum leaf pendants suspended from their noses. For the Ndebele of Zimbabwe and South Africa, husbands are known to give their betrothed weighty necklaces that symbolize their step into united life.

Tradition in America romanticizes the groom's going out all alone to search for the perfect diamond and the ideal setting for his bride-to-be. At a candlelit dinner for two in the most posh restaurant he can *almost* afford, the nervous beau presents his sparkling treasure to the woman of his dreams.

Although this scene can and does turn out fine for some, it just may be sending the wrong message. Marriage is not a fairy tale that spins out in elegant detail. It is a

BANDS OF COMMITMENT
For centuries throughout the Motherland, African couples have exchanged treasured jewelry, particularly gold pieces, to celebrate their marriage. Today, rings represent an eternal bond between you and your partner. Select them with great care, and do consider bands with cultural symbols.

partnership that takes many moments of shared decision making. For this reason—and the fact that making changes in an engagement ring can be quite costly—it may be wise for couples to consider selecting their engagement and wedding rings together. (A note: Remember not to make assumptions. Men don't always wear wedding bands, so women should check to see if their fiancés are planning on wearing a ring. If a ring isn't under consideration, decide how you feel about it and discuss it.)

If your fiancé does surprise you with a ring of his choosing, whether it's your dream ring or not, do remember that it represents a gift of love from him that most likely took many hours of contemplation, not to mention money, on his part. Accept it with love. Later, you may be able to add a ring to your wedding set that more closely reflects your taste.

A Joint Decision

Suppose the two of you decide to join forces on the ring question. Sit down and talk about what you want your rings to convey, what materials you prefer, and how much money you want to spend. Experts recommend spending no more than three weeks' salary on your jewelry investment for both engagement and wedding rings.

Next, it's a good idea to discuss your views on diamonds. Precious gems that they are, diamonds are now the preferred wedding stone. They capture light magnificently, are incredibly durable, and are traditionally symbolic of love and commitment in the United States. Folks spend hours poring over books and display cases trying to ascertain their four *c*'s: cut, clarity, color, and carat. Some Black couples, however, are still debating whether they should purchase them or not. When my husband and I were planning our wedding, apartheid was still in full swing, and so we considered carefully the gem we would use to represent our union. Diamonds are mined in huge quantities in South Africa, as well as other parts of the world, and we, like many other American Blacks, did not want to support the exploitation of our African brothers and sisters. For this reason, we chose the yellow sapphire for our engagement rings. Now that apartheid has come to its end, the pressure is relieved about selecting a diamond. Some African-centered spiritualists remind us that diamonds are crystallized from carbon, one of life's most fundamental elements. Although we question the way that they have been harvested, they are presumed to have tremendous healing powers. Even more interesting is that although diamonds were used in jewelry hundreds and even thousands of years ago in India and different regions on the continent of Africa, it was not until the twentieth century that they became popularized as wedding ring treasures.

Some couples who are not willing to *purchase* diamonds still wear them when they are family heirlooms, since they then have taken on ancestral value. Whenever a family ring is offered to a couple, it represents a sweet gesture of love and family commitment. In such cases, know that it is acceptable to have the stones reset into a more contemporary or otherwise appealing setting. Do discuss the details with your fiancé before making the changes, though!

Working with a Jeweler

Shopping for a ring requires more than simply walking into a jewelry store, selecting a ring, and walking out. Even if you skip over diamonds and thereby avoid the search for the four *c*'s, you will need to make a number of important decisions to find the right ring.

A good first question is, "What type of metal do you want?" Gold is by far the most popular metal for rings. Historically, gold was one of the essential gifts offered to a bride among a wide variety of African tribes. Gold comes in several karats, which basically means the ratio of pure gold, which is 24 karats, to gold plus alloys. Eighteen-karat gold is the standard for gold used in wedding rings, although specialty stores may offer a higher karat, up to 22, that is still hard enough to endure daily wear. Gold also comes in several colors, most often in white and yellow. At specialty jewelers, the range may be broader and quite interesting as you search for a color that will complement your skin. At Reinstein/Ross, a New York–based fine jewelry design company, for instance, gold is blended

◆

BEYOND DIAMONDS

Engagement rings and decorated wedding bands can be ornamented beautifully without diamonds and have been for centuries in Europe and Asia. Many couples choose their birthstones, although any precious or semiprecious stone you love is appropriate. Below is a listing of traditional birthstones.

JANUARY: *garnet or hyacinth*

FEBRUARY: *amethyst*

MARCH: *aquamarine, bloodstone, or jasper*

APRIL: *diamond*

MAY: *emerald*

JUNE: *pearl, moonstone, or agate*

JULY: *ruby or onyx*

AUGUST: *sardonyz, peridot, or carnelian*

SEPTEMBER: *sapphire*

OCTOBER: *opal or tourmaline*

NOVEMBER: *topaz*

DECEMBER: *turquoise or lapis lazuli*

◆

into a variety of colors, including apricot, peach, and chartreuse.

The second most popular metal is platinum. As more and more brides use white diamonds in their settings, platinum frequently serves as a neutral base, since it does not add color to diamonds or any other inlaid stone. Although prices do fluctuate, platinum in 1992 was virtually on par with gold.

Silver is less commonly used for wedding rings today for two reasons. In the United States it is not considered as precious as gold or platinum. Moreover, it is not as durable, being a much softer metal from which stones may readily become dislodged. It can serve beautifully, however, in a band form.

After you have selected the metal for your rings you must answer another question: Will there be stones set in your engagement ring? In one or both of your wedding bands? If so, what stones will they be? As you make your decision, take several factors into consideration: how often you intend to wear the ring; how durable the stone is; what your color preferences are.

Diamonds are the hardest, most durable stones on the market. They wear well in everyday use and reflect light beautifully. Small diamonds, even chips, can also be used to frame other stones to create exquisite settings.

The next hardest precious stone is the *sapphire*. Majestic in its common coloration of nearly indigo blue, the sapphire also comes in other colors, including peach, orange, purple, chartreuse, apricot, magenta, and lavender.

A stone often found in family heirlooms is the *ruby*, which actually is a member of the sapphire family. Brilliant red rubies can cast a royal glow on burnished skin.

Emeralds are the next hardest stones. Although they are frequently seen in a crystal-clear, light green color, they too come in other shades of green, from aquamarine to a yellow that is called heliodor.

Following these in order of hardness are other beautifully colored stones, including *garnet, amethyst, peridot, citrine,* and *tourmaline.*

Brian Ross, co-owner of Reinstein/Ross, assures clients that most precious and semiprecious stones are durable enough to be used in wedding ring settings for both men and women. But since these rings are made to wear forever—and maybe every day forever—you must realize also that no stone is invincible. Even diamonds chip and scratch. The good news, according to Ross, is, "A stone is only a rock. No matter what happens to it, it can usually be polished and fixed."

When you have made your final selections, your last question will be, "How do we pay?" Many jewelers request that you give 50 percent of the total cost when you place your order, the balance upon receipt of your jewelry. For rings with any custom detailing, allow at least four weeks for completion, preferably longer.

An African Message

When Abdel and Dyane Salaam, of Forces of Nature Dance Theatre Company in New York City, decided to celebrate their tenth anniversary, they knew where to go for their rings—to Khamitic elder and jewelry designer Sen-Ur Semahj. As a practitioner of the ancient spiritual Khamitic tradition, Abdel explains that for him and his wife, "It would only be fitting that we would utilize symbols of regeneration that come from our highest and most profound mind-set in the ancient world." Following the religious philosophy of ancient pre-Egyptian peoples of the Nile Valley, the Khamites, which dates back to 4240 B.C., Semahj says he makes jewelry based on "the elegance, beauty, and memory of the sovereignty of the Nile culture." Cast primarily in gold and silver, the rings that are made by Semahj's business, The Shrine of Ptah, bear carvings that symbolize love, fertility, and truth. The rings that Abdel and Dyane chose are 18-karat gold with ancient carvings of *ankhs*, which signify life; *lotuses*, which symbolize beauty emerging, transformation, and things working themselves out; and *ra*, which has the generative energy of the sun, the power of light. Each wedding band conveys in Metu-Neter or hieroglyphic language, "living in truth." Some of the symbols used are as follows:

Nubian Khamitic Symbols

Ankh: eternal life and love, respect of life, the man/woman/child principle

Djed Column: stability and strength, fortitude

Ert or Art (the Cobra): intuitive, discerning principle of achievement

Eye of Heru: all-seeing eye, true vision, of the Creator

Feathers of MAAT: law, balance, truth, justice, reciprocity

Mer-Khut (pyramid): power and strength, permanence

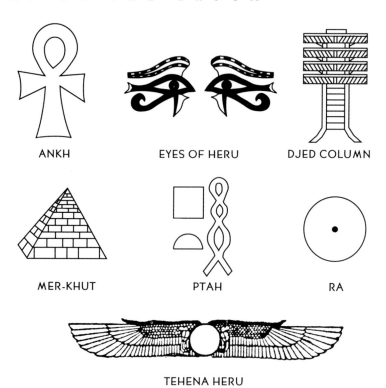

ANKH　　　EYES OF HERU　　　DJED COLUMN

MER-KHUT　　　PTAH　　　RA

TEHENA HERU

MARRYING THE KHAMITIC WAY

There's more to Semahj's craft than symbolic rings. He also has been ordained by his spiritual community to officiate over weddings. Just as premarital counseling and the meeting of families is traditional throughout Africa and America, so is it a requirement in the Khamitic faith. Each couple is also asked to enter into a fourteen-day cleansing process where they learn of the records of their ancestral story. During the two-week period, they eat in a strictly vegetarian manner and consume large quantities of water and vegetable juices that aid in clearing out their systems. They also take various herbal compounds, all preparing them for their new life together.

Ptah: deity of foundation, creative principle, the beginning, the earth

Ra: the hidden sun, principle of energy manifesting macrocosmically as mother space and microcosmically as melanin (or Kham-Ur, as in, the great black)

Tehena Heru (wings of the falcon): spiritual ascension, Christ consciousness, enlightenment

Tyet (the buckle of Est [Isis]): the divine mother or the Khamite Eve, symbol of reproductive organs of the mother principle

Caring for Your Ring

Think of your engagement and wedding rings as investments in your future. Take special care of them while you're wearing them *and* when you're not.

◆ Clean your rings with a mild household detergent regularly, using a small nylon brush—a toothbrush will do—to remove environmental film and debris.

◆ Have your rings checked for fit and security of stones once a year by a professional jeweler.

◆ Don't wear your rings when you're doing work that could scratch or otherwise damage them, including heavy housework. Chlorine bleach may wreak havoc on your mounting.

◆ Develop a habit of storing your rings in a cloth-lined case when you're not wearing them. Create a special place for them other than your jewelry box or a display case where they will be the most safe.

◆ Keep your rings off kitchen and bathroom counters. Too many down-the-drain disasters have occurred to risk this one.

◆ Get proper insurance. Have your rings professionally appraised, and buy a rider on your home owner's or renter's insurance specifically for them. If you don't have personal property insurance, now's the time to look into purchasing some.

CHAPTER 4

THE GIVING OF GIFTS

New York historian and Ford Foundation fellow George Preston's archaeological expedition to Ghana back in 1968 transformed his life. It was there, in the town of Twifo-Hemang, that he took a fancy to a local woman, Akosua, whom he married two years later. For George, entering into the dance of courtship and marriage in a tiny African village was a delicate process. From the moment he noticed Akosua, who was part owner of her family's cocoa plantation, he learned that he had to be introduced in a circuitous fashion. It wasn't proper for him to meet her directly. "The guys in the village had to arrange for us to meet," he explains, "as if by accident." Once the two became friends and began to spend time together, he says, they naturally entered into what we know as engagement. George says, "The guys asked me at a certain point if I knew what I was doing. Because we were spending so much time together, it meant that we had to 'make custom,' which essentially meant get married." Along the road to getting married, George was informed that the couple were supposed to give small gifts to each other. He learned that he needed to go to Akosua's family with an ombudsman who would formally express his desire to marry her. The couple subsequently began to spend more time with Akosua's family, a must in Ghanaian marriages where the joining of families is the essence of the new union.

Invite a family member or trusted friend to help you keep track of your gifts as they arrive. Record all gifts in a book specifically for that purpose. Number each box and envelope, identify the sender, and then get your thank-yous out right away.

When the actual marriage ceremony occurred, it was without the pomp and circumstance that we know as tradition in America. What happened was quite simple. A small group of family members and close friends gathered at Akosua's family home. George wore an antique toga with *kente* detailing. Akosua wore a traditional long skirt with a white shirtwaist lace top, sash, and head wrap. In "making custom" George brought a number of specific gifts to her family—what has been termed as "bride price," but is essentially a dowry. Included in the gifts were money, a bolt of cloth, and clear liquor. He offered the gifts to the family elders; what followed was a pivotal sanction—the pouring of libation to the ancestors. The family chief, who was Akosua's uncle, poured the clear local liquor, called *akpateshie*, repeating the following words in his native language, Twi: "Almighty God, on whom we lean and do not fall, take this wine. Ancestors, all of you, come and take this drink." At this point, had the two been in America, the minister would be saying, "You may now kiss the bride!"

REMEMBER THOSE SPECIAL TO YOU

Ghanaian customs resemble a number of rituals in America. One is in the giving of gifts. Couples in America usually give each other small presents during their period of courtship, although it's not required. They also often give gifts to each other's parents—small tokens of love, such as household items, even flowers—when they come to visit for the first time.

Although not characteristic of Western weddings, a tradition worth adopting is the giving of gifts to parents as part of the wedding ritual. In Ghana, Nigeria, and other places in West Africa, the gift to the bride's family symbolizes a token payment in exchange for the groom's taking the woman out of her family home, thereby removing an able worker from the present family structure. Here the translation could be for couples to give presents to both families, symbols of thanks and welcome that make wonderful markers for the beginning of the new union.

For Your Bridal Party

However you come to your final mutually agreed-upon selection of attendants, do remember them with lasting tokens of your appreciation and love. In America, it's common for the bride to give her maid or matron of honor and the bridesmaids jewelry, a picture frame engraved with the date of the wedding (for a photo of the bridal party), or a delicate writing instrument engraved with the attendant's initials. The groom customarily presents his attendants with an engraved picture frame similar to the one offered to the bridesmaids, an engraved wallet, or bow ties and cummerbunds for the event.

These standard gifts become more precious when they bear a cultural reference. For your bridesmaids, for example, look for cultural treasures such as amber, marcasite, or malachite earrings (that can double as adornment for the ceremony), cowrie-covered necklaces or bracelets, a strip of *kente* cloth, an ethnic picture frame, an elegantly designed incense burner. The men in your party may appreciate their wedding accessories (cummerbund and bow tie), or even umbrellas in *kente*, mud cloth, or other cultural fabrics. Many African and Caribbean textiles are being reproduced on cotton, which makes the prices more reasonable than authentic hand-loomed or -dyed originals on cotton or silk. What about small ceramic decorative items made by Black designers? Sometimes these can be personalized with the date of the wedding and initials of the attendant. Visit Black museum shops and cultural bookstores for other creative ideas.

From Your Bridal Party

One extra-special responsibility of the bridal party is the giving of gifts to the couple. The male attendants customarily offer the groom a collective gift, such as a briefcase, electronic equipment, or a silver memento engraved with their signatures and the wedding date. Similarly, the female attendants chip in to present the bride most traditionally with engraved silver or crystal. Don't feel that you have to select from these narrow choices. Let your understanding of the bride's and groom's personalities be your guide, and agree on a gift that best reflects their interests. Since it is also customary for the members of the bridal party to give the couple separate wedding gifts, make that choice your opportunity to consider the couple as a team. Check their registry for ideas.

For Each Other

The kinds of gifts you can offer each other today cover a broad range. Most traditional are wedding rings and precious jewelry for her, a silver picture frame, a watch, cuff links, or leather goods for him. You don't have to stop with these ideas, though.

Gina Gray and Albert Granger did share rings with each other when they married in Baltimore in 1989. But there was more. Instead of getting one big present for her honey, Gina went all out, presenting an assortment of gifts, beginning on her wedding day and continuing on each day of their honeymoon. The gifts included all sorts of small items, including an adapter for their personal stereo that would allow the two of them to listen to the same sounds as they lounged on the sparkling beaches in Puerto Rico. Albert's final gift represented Gina's way of keeping the honeymoon fires burning. It was an invitation to go on a "date" at their favorite restaurant back home a week after they returned.

Creativity was at an all-time high during the gift giving between Vimilakshi Archer, a reflexologist and hatha yoga instructor, and Baaba Archer, a plumber, when they got married in 1981 in the backyard of their rural home in Richmond, Virginia. First of all, the two declared their vows barefoot—in a symbolic gesture of uniting their spirits with the core of their environment. When it came time to offer each other wedding gifts, it was only fitting that they exchange shoes. "For us, it meant that we would always walk together," Vimilakshi explains.

LET THE PARTIES BEGIN!

Once you announce your engagement, it's time for celebration. Sometimes there are so many parties it can make your head swim. Couples have told stories about old friends they haven't seen in years who have shown up to celebrate their joy, and about the memories of childhood and other long-past experiences that have been shared round-robin as the group assembled to swap tales of the engaged couple.

The many celebrations surrounding your wedding are really the only occasions that you do not govern. They are hosted by people who care about you—your parents, dear friends, and co-workers—with your happiness, and sometimes surprise, in mind. Most often they are moments when your loved ones shower you with gifts.

Your Engagement Party

In Western tradition the official announcement of your wedding is made at this party, which is normally hosted by your parents shortly after you and your fiancé have secured "permission" to take that next giant step. Although many African-American couples have skipped this event over the years, it truly is a joyous way to share your happiness with your family and close friends. For some it may also be the first time that both families have met. That was one of the main reasons that Alyce Bates-Lipkin and her husband, Leonard, decided to organize an engagement party when their daughter Tracee's longtime companion asked their permission to marry. Says Mrs. Lipkin, "Tracee and Hosea had been knowing each other all their lives, from grade school. But their families didn't know each other." Because Hosea's family members were not all located in Detroit proper, Mrs.

Lipkin says hosting a formal party was the only way they could get everyone together.

And what a party they had. From soup to nuts—literally—they held a magnificent feast for their families. Nearly as involved as a wedding, their engagement party required formal printed invitations, a catering staff and a professional photographer. Since some of the family members had never met, Mrs. Lipkin even created an interactive game for everyone to play at the beginning to break the ice. While she and her husband were mingling, caterer Jan Goffney's crew from Ruth's Kitchen were serving hors d'oeuvres and cocktails, followed by a sit-down dinner and dessert—for a mere 150 guests who were family. As the evening's high point, Tracee's dad gave a toast to the couple, and their family priest blessed her engagement ring and the couple.

The Lipkin event is nothing new for members of the diaspora. In fact, Ghanaian chef Bill Odarty explains how in his country there is even a special name for the engagement party, *Yoheniifeemor*. At this event, lavish food and drink are served, toasts are made, and the blessing of the union is ensured by the local elder.

If you want to have an engagement party to announce your wedding plans, you will need to get started just as soon as you decide to marry. Talk to your parents to see if they are interested, willing, and able to host. Although the Lipkin affair was quite a magnificent event, yours can be scaled to fit your personal budget. And even if you chip in, if you want the party to be hosted by your parents, make it so. Where the money originates shouldn't be the deciding factor.

It's Shower Time

Bridal showers are traditionally small, informal parties hosted by the bride-to-be's close friends where the guests bring personal and household gifts, tell stories, and basically have a good time. Long ago, they used to be reserved solely for womenfolk. More and more showers today are unisex, where married or engaged couples, male and female friends *and* their children are invited to participate in the festivities. Originally the purpose of the shower was to help pave the way for the young woman's life ahead by stocking her with the things she needs most. Topping the list is lingerie for her trousseau. Years ago the family actually made trousseau items by hand, either over the years or in the months leading up to the wedding. Today the world of fine lingerie is available for the buying. One sister told me that wealthy Cuban families send their daughters all the way to Paris to shop for those little luxuries! What often happens is that good friends get together and send out invitations (although they are not mandatory) to a lingerie shower including appropriate sizes and styles when applicable. This information generally comes via Mom or the bride herself.

Planning a bridal shower can be fun, especially if the hostess allows enough time to pull it all together—usually one to two months before the wedding itself. The party works best when it is centered around one theme. Choices range from lingerie to linens, kitchen necessities to garden supplies—and for some, cultural treasures. The point is to give the bride and groom practical things that they can use and always treasure. A round-the-clock shower is also a great idea. Guests are sent invitations listing a specific time of day, and they are asked to bring a gift that would be most appropriate for that hour. For Atlanta-based Angela Dawson's shower, her friends gave her everything from a coffee maker with a timer for 7:00 A.M. to lingerie for 9:00 P.M.

Bridesmaids' Luncheon

Separate from a bridal shower, a bridesmaids luncheon is an informal party hosted by the bride-to-be on a weekend afternoon or even at a dinner on a week night. The small group gets a chance to talk about the upcoming event, make plans for picking up dresses and accessories, or just has a good time. Both mothers should be welcome at this affair. Although not a requirement, if you have time to host a special luncheon for your bridesmaids, it's the perfect time to offer them gifts. Depending upon your budget, the party can be as simple or elaborate as you prefer.

For the Boys

A groom once said that "a bride has more fun." Not necessarily. Beyond the couple shower is the traditional bachelor dinner or party. Rumor has it that this is the party where the groom-to-be has a wild night one last time before committing to his wife. In reality, the scene is more likely to be a gathering of the guys with food and drink where they roast the bridegroom and swap stories about him from over the years. There are times when the boys will hire a female dancer or have some exotic element included. Rest assured, sisters, they tell me that even under those conditions, he's looking from a distance. (For friends who plan a party with spice for a man or a woman, it's best to get a gauge on whether it will be appreciated in fun or considered distasteful.) If gifts are given, they normally reflect traditional male interests such as sports, electronics, or other hobbies. A cultural party for a man could be a refreshing change, when guests bring household items such as ethnic patterned coasters, mugs, and cocktail napkins or personal items such as *kente* and other African or Caribbean print ties, cummerbunds, or cuff links. This party is often hosted by the man's brother(s) or the groomsmen and ushers in the wedding.

YOUR OWN GIFT REGISTRY

When photographer John Gairy and prop stylist Janice Ervin got married in 1980, they were thirty-something adults. They had already established themselves independent of their families, had both been previously married, and had maintained individual residences for a number of years. The last thing they needed was to sign up with a traditional gift registry for china, flatware, linens, and so on. Instead, they sat down together and listed the items that they most wanted and needed to enhance their new life. Lovers of the great outdoors, they decided on a canoe and hiking gear. They identified the retailers who carried what they wanted and informed their guests.

Only the two of you know what items you need to establish your home together and whether the services of a traditional bridal registry will offer you what you need. If you are starting from scratch and moving into a new home with few personal possessions, a registry may be of tremendous assistance.

It is often through the powerful combination of a bridal registry and the bride's mother that word gets out to guests about what the couple wants. Leading department stores across the country offer seasoned bridal consultants who can and do attend to the couple's myriad needs. Typically, a bridal registry enables you to select all of the home furnishings you want—from a broad selection of styles and prices— and then put your choices on a computerized listing that is accessible at stores throughout the country. Often this free service includes notification cards to wedding guests that you are registered with the store. Many department stores hold annual and semiannual bridal fairs where they offer information on how to put your wedding and your home together, with experts presenting suggestions on everything from photographers and florists to pots and pans.

Sometimes even all of that assistance is not enough. The problem with many gift registries is that they do not have an extensive selection of ethnic household items. If you are looking for ceramic plates or table linens with Afrocentric motifs, you may be hard-pressed to find them in traditional department stores. Instead of settling for items that are not your first choice, be creative. Don't be afraid to ask the store's wedding consultant to special order a particular item that you want to include on your list.

Be open to doing a little research and remember to look in your own community first. Go shopping for "new" gift registries with a list in hand of the items you most want and need. If you are organized and focused, you will get better results.

Approach ethnic boutiques, museum shops, and independent vendors who carry the items you like. Make it clear to them that you are getting married, that you may or may not have registered with a major department store, but that, in any case, you need to supplement your gift list with specialty items that they carry. Once you see that the store owner or manager is receptive, use the following questions as guidelines for creating your own registry:

1. Have you ever coordinated a gift registry for a wedding in the past? If so, how smoothly did it go? Be specific.

2. Can you guarantee that you will have the items I want in the quantity I need?

3. Can you keep a log, either by computer or manually, indicating which items are already purchased and inform guests when appropriate? Can you contact me periodically with purchase updates?

4. Are you equipped to accept telephone orders from out-of-town guests?

5. Will you deliver packages through an insured service?

Giving Back

All that Carol Hall and Cliff Holliday wanted when they got married were blessings for a long-lasting, loving union. The very thought of signing up with a registry and selecting a vast assortment of household items was out of the question for them. Although this was her first wedding, Carol was forty-three and had already collected all of the essentials she says she could ever need; her forty-eight-year-old fiancé was in the same situation. In fact, the big challenge for the couple was how they were going to pool their individual belongings to create one home together.

Knowing that their friends would want to offer a token of their love, the two decided to include a note in their wedding invitation, requesting that instead of home goods, a check to either Morehouse or Bennett College would be most appreciated. Both schools are historically Black institutions, Morehouse being Cliff's alma mater; Bennett was Carol's mother's college and the school where she attended her freshman year. Giving back to the community to help educate our youth was a cause that Carol and Cliff thought everyone would value.

To collect the gifts, Carol had two boxes decorated in white wedding paper with a school decal demarcating them. When guests arrived at the reception, they simply slipped their gift into the appropriate box. In the end, the newlyweds were able to contribute several thousand dollars to the schools.

If you make the decision to register your wish list, do so with only two businesses to make shopping easy for your guests. The national department store route is great for couples who have family and friends spread across the country and beyond. Smaller retailers can be perfect supplemental resources. If you have found a fantastic art object, say, at a third location, reserve that information as a suggestion to your bridal party or a close relative when you are asked.

Do yourselves a favor and always be mindful of your guests. When you register, select gift items that range in price, so that those with smaller budgets will find items they can comfortably purchase for you.

When You Really Want Money

Asking for money for your wedding is a touchy subject. Most etiquette specialists say it's a no-no for the couple to tell their guests directly of their needs. Usually the bride's mother takes on the responsibility of subtly sharing that bit of news. If you are asked, you may discreetly respond by speaking of imminent plans that require a big outlay of cash—buying a house or a car, for instance. When you truly prefer not to receive an outpouring of household gifts, don't register. You will still be given some tangible items, however, and those should be received graciously—even if you do intend to return them later.

A great tradition still lives on these shores as well as in Nigeria, that of showering the bride with money during the reception. In America, the act is so much a part of the event that elaborately decorated money bags are crafted and sold just for that purpose. (Some artists are making them now with ethnic motifs.) When the bride and groom make the rounds at their reception, greeting their guests, friends and family slip them envelopes with monetary gifts inside. Jamaican-born model Althea Lang learned a new meaning of this tradition when she married a Nigerian-born brother in Washington, D.C., in 1986. At her reception, guests followed the tradition of laying money on her as she made her rounds. By the end of the ceremony, she says, the entire floor was carpeted with cash intended to help start off the couple's new life together.

GIFT IDEAS FOR GUESTS

It is considered good protocol in the United States for any person invited to a wedding to offer a gift to the couple. That gift should be a thoughtful expression of commitment to their union. Think about what they like to do, their style, their plans for the future. With ideas in mind, find out where they are registered to see if any of your ideas match. Even if you decide to give them something else, checking the registry

THE SIGNIFICANCE OF THE STOOL

One of the most precious items in a traditional West African Asante home was historically a wooden stool. Traditionally carved out of one piece of wood, the stool came alive with intricate detail from the collective experience of the particular clan and its ancestors. One account explains that "an Asante stool is supposed to be the repository of its owner's soul, and for this reason the miniature fetters are placed round the central support of the stool 'to chain down the soul to it.'" For the matrilineal Asante, a stool was considered a seat of honor and power for a wife.

will give you a better sense of what *they* like so that you can give them a gift that they will fully appreciate and use. *Do* ask the bride's mother if the couple prefers money. If you can afford it, you may consider giving them a small amount of money along with a gift. A lovely gesture would be to offer couples with children a special gift just for the child.

As you search for the perfect gift, don't get carried away or allow yourself to feel pressured into spending more money than you can afford. Your gift should be one of love that is given freely—without placing a burden on you. This is understood in traditional West African communities where little formal attention is paid to gift giving at the ceremony. In many Senegalese villages, for example, the women of the community often share recipes, advice on keeping marriage alive, as well as fabric and household items with the young woman before the wedding and after—all precious gifts to be sure.

Another way to give the couple what they want and need, even if your budget is tight, is to select a single item from their registry, say a dinner or dessert plate. Since others will also be purchasing some of their china, your gift will be much appreciated and could be the piece that finishes their set. Back in the early 1900s when Black folks in particular had very little means but weren't short on good taste, they followed a similar path. My grandmother, Carrie E. Freeland, a domestic worker all of her life, used to pool her funds with her husband's to give a single sterling silver spoon to relatives and friends who got married. On each anniversary, they would offer another piece of silver to help the couple complete their dinner settings.

Below are additional ideas for original wedding gifts.

For lovers of African-American/Caribbean culture:
   ◆ a coffee-table book on Black art or history

◆ an affordable original work by a Black artist

◆ blank cards featuring Afrocentric images

◆ a subscription to a Black magazine

◆ season tickets to the local Black theater or dance company

◆ a membership to the local Black museum

◆ cultural weavings, tapestries, or precious fabrics

◆ an African stool (see sidebar on pp.56–57)

◆ a pair of Chiwaris (wooden antelope carvings, found plentifully in the Ivory Coast and other points in West Africa, as well as at your local African art boutique)

◆ a bowl of cowrie shells (cowrie shells, found off the coast of West Africa, were historically used for money and are traditionally used for purification and worship. The shell itself is a symbol of power, beauty, and auspiciousness)

◆ language classes in Swahili or another African tongue

◆ a set of ceramic cups and saucers, dessert plates, or vases designed by a Black artist

For those with culinary interests:

◆ cooking or wine-tasting classes for two

◆ a subscription to a culinary magazine

◆ a gift certificate to their favorite restaurant

◆ an African, Caribbean, or Southern cookbook

For outdoor enthusiasts:

◆ bicycle or motorcycle helmets

◆ workout gear

◆ backpacks

◆ a gift certificate from a sporting-goods store

◆ camping equipment

◆ a subscription to an active/outdoor magazine

◆ a summer's supply of bug repellent and other staples

Today many African Americans collect Asante and other tribes' stools and display them as art pieces in their homes. *Essence* editor-in-chief Susan L. Taylor and her husband, writer Khephra Burns, went one step further. With a backdrop of mountains at the end of summer, they planned an intimate wedding with their family and closest friends in August 1989. Just as in a church setting when both families are seated in the front pews to witness the ceremony, at their outdoor event each of the elders in their families was led to a front-row seat of honor— an Asante stool.

For investors:
- ◆ U.S. Savings Bonds
- ◆ their favorite (or your favorite) stocks
- ◆ opening a college savings account for couples with children

For the spiritual:
- ◆ an elegantly bound religious book
- ◆ a book of transporting prose
- ◆ a well-crafted incense burner and incense
- ◆ unusual candlesticks and candles
- ◆ a gift certificate to a weekend spiritual retreat

Other great ideas:
- ◆ enrollment in the local video store
- ◆ gift certificates for at-home massage for two
- ◆ enrollment in tennis, sailing, computer, or artist camp
- ◆ membership in a health club (three months)
- ◆ housecleaning service
- ◆ landscaping or gardening service

For those who need staples:
- ◆ throw pillows that match the bedroom or living room design
- ◆ a stepladder
- ◆ a doormat with a welcoming image
- ◆ an ironing board with an ethnic-print cover
- ◆ a toolbox with all the basics—screwdrivers, a hammer, duct tape, nails, screws, etc.
- ◆ wooden African baskets that can hold objects, such as magazines, books, etc.
- ◆ a set of scented lightbulbs
- ◆ ethnic-print dish towels
- ◆ a laundry basket filled with cleaning supplies (also great for a shower gift)

From You to Your Guests

A wonderful tradition here in the United States is that of giving a memento of sorts to all of the people who attend your wedding and reception. It doesn't have to

◆

FOR GUESTS ONLY

In keeping with Western tradition, know these bits of information about gift-giving:

◆ *If you receive a wedding invitation, custom says that you are supposed to give the couple a gift. Even if you do not attend the wedding, the gift should be forwarded to them as close to the wedding date as possible, definitely within one year.*
◆ *On the other hand, if you receive an announcement of a wedding, you are not obliged to send a wedding gift. A note or card of congratulations would be great, though!*
◆ *When the wedding reception is held at a public hall or other facility, consider sending the couple's wedding gift to their new home or that of the bride's mother where it will be handled less and be secure upon arrival.*

◆

be anything big or expensive, just something to remind them of this special occasion in the years to come. Here are a few ideas from couples who have already gotten married:

◆ fragrant incense wrapped in tissue paper and colorful ribbon
◆ your wedding poem rolled into a scroll and tied with a piece of raffia
◆ a packet of flower seeds wrapped in decorative paper with a message from the two of you
◆ a tiny silver bag filled with heart candy
◆ a sample-size vial of fragrant oil that you both love, wrapped in a tiny box with a message
◆ a small piece of Black memorabilia
◆ an invitation to your fifth anniversary party
◆ ethnic-print pocket square for the men, handkerchiefs for the ladies, handmade by you or a friend and wrapped in a tiny box
◆ lollipops for the children

SAYING THANK YOU

Showing appreciation to the many generous people who offer you gifts should be done formally. To avoid leaving someone out, get a book that you use solely for recording

gift receipts. You should create a chart that indicates the gift received and the date, the name of the giver, the gift itself, and the date that the thank-you note was mailed. Be diligent about sending thank-you notes each week, if not each day that gifts are received, so that they don't pile up. You can enlist the help of your family and your wedding party—preferably someone with legible penmanship!—to get the job done. Make it your business to send thank-you notes no later than three months after receipt—better to send them within two weeks.

Be zealous in your kindness. Your loved ones have extended themselves to make you happy. Write with sincerity and clarity, telling them how much you appreciate their gift. Do mention what it is, unless it's money in which case you may mention what you intend to do with it. Don't tell them that you intend to return their gift, even if it's a duplicate. Above all, never suggest you are unhappy with it—even if that is true. Instead, kindly thank them for thinking of you and search for a way to link the gift with some warm aspect of their love for you.

PART II

Jumping
the Broom

CHAPTER 5

ORGANIZING THE LOGISTICS

I n the not too distant past, couples in America had little to do with their wedding planning. The bride's family took care of everything. The person in charge at most weddings, regardless of ethnic background, was, and sometimes still is, the mother of the bride. Her daughter's big event often represented *her* big day, one she planned using all the resources at her family's disposal. Though her daughter's input may have been considered, it was largely unnecessary. Barring a number of verbal sparring sessions and tearful outbursts, this arrangement has worked fairly well (and continues to) when the bride is young and not yet independent.

But things have changed. The average age of marrying couples in 1990 was well above eighteen, hovering closer to twenty-six for African-American women and nearly twenty-eight for African-American men, according to a noted demographer. (It's about the same for white Americans as well.) Although age doesn't necessarily make a difference in roles for some African tribes—a number of whom actually marry later in life anyway—it has a tremendous impact in this country. Couples over twenty-five here are more likely to have established their own homes outside of their family's, moved to other cities, pursued their own lifestyles, and—most important of all—have their own money. At such a critical juncture in their lives, in a country that not only allows tremendous freedoms but that also has experienced tumultuous household changes since the dawn of the civil rights and women's movements, more and more people, including African Americans, are choosing to make important decisions about their own weddings and are becoming more actively involved in all the details.

Today the concept of sharing financial responsibility for the wedding expenses is becoming more common. This may have evolved simply out of necessity, since the average cost of a wedding today is upwards of ten thousand dollars, with some weddings costing two or even three times that figure. As couples marry later in life, they often have two incomes from which they can contribute to their big day, an offer many parents find hard to refuse.

MAKE PLANS, NOT WAR

To ensure that your wedding is a success will take concentration and focus on your part, regardless of whoever else is contributing to the event. Whether you decide to get married a year or two in advance or within six months of the date, get started on the plan immediately after you announce your engagement. For many, a wedding is the biggest event they have ever organized. It's a time of learning how to follow up on the never ending stream of details as well as how to delegate—all with the greatest respect for everyone involved (including yourself).

Start by purchasing a loose-leaf binder in which you record all the details of your planning. You will use this resource book alongside *Jumping the Broom* to keep track of all your steps along the way. As you gather brochures, price lists, and other materials, either punch holes in them and incorporate them into the book, or place them in a pocket in the front or back. Share your binder with your fiancé, so that basic information is in one place. Look for one with a decorative cover, displaying an ethnic design or some other image that you find appealing. In addition, you may want to keep a purse-size notebook with you at all times to keep notes as you go about each day.

Make wish lists, and write them down. Many women dream for years about how their wedding will unfold. Surprisingly enough, plenty of men have a few hidden thoughts on the matter, too. Both of you should dream big, but be ready to compromise as needed. The last thing you want to do is go into the hole or put your family deep in the red in order to start your new life.

From the outset set up formal meeting times with your fiancé. Especially if you have busy schedules, it is important to carve out regular times to discuss your wedding plans with each other. By creating an appointment hour per week in the beginning and per day as you move closer to the date, you will be able to respect each other's commitments and get the job done.

ESTABLISH A TIMETABLE AND BUDGET

Review your wish lists carefully. Ask yourselves the following questions to help you determine the type of wedding you want and what you can afford:

When do you want to get married?

Undoubtedly a key factor in your planning, your wedding date must be set right away. Most couples get married on Saturdays during the summer months. That means that those dates go the fastest for wedding and reception sites, caterers, cake designers, dressmakers—everyone. If you have selected a Saturday between May and August, you will probably need to book your site at least a year in advance. (See Chapter 9 for more details on location selection.)

Even if you pick a date during the off-season (during the winter months if you're in the United States, summer in the Caribbean), you need to make your selection immediately. All other services hinge on that being secure.

How large do you want your wedding to be?

Decide on this with each other before you talk about any details with your parents. Understand that you may need to be flexible on this number because of budgetary or space concerns.

You may want to have an intimate affair. Determine what intimate means to you. Are you talking about immediate family only? Do both of you have small families? What would be a cutoff number of guests?

Many couples have what is considered a moderate-size wedding—anywhere from 125 to 185 people. If you want a larger wedding with all the trimmings, what number of guests do you have in mind? The numbers can grow as big as you can afford. One young couple in Detroit just had a wedding for 400 guests, primarily because the bride's parents had a long list of friends and family who were all invited—and they could afford to foot the bill!

Whom should you invite?

Forget your ideal number of guests for a minute. Write out rough lists of your family members and friends whom you would like to witness this moment in your lives. Start with a full-blown list, and come back to it in a couple of days. You're bound to have forgotten someone. Consider family and friends who will probably be on your parents' lists and include them. You may want to put their names in a separate notation, though. After her initial listing, one forty-something bride who had lived in many places across the country categorized her suggested guest inventory by state so that she would be sure not to miss anyone important.

Once you feel that you have conducted an exhaustive mental search for potential invitees, start counting. On the first go round you're bound to have too many names. Begin editing. It's a good idea to have two operating lists—one that represents the bottom line and one that includes the people you will invite if all conditions are right.

Neither should include an unrealistic number of people—whatever that means for you.

No matter how large or small your wedding may be, know that you will probably not be able to invite everyone. Determine with your parents how many invitations each of you will get, and stick to that. Often families cut the number in half or in thirds, giving one-third to the couple. Decide what works best for you. (For more information on defining your guest list, see Chapter 6.)

How many people do you want to have in your bridal party?

It cannot be stressed enough that your wedding party should include only those people who truly love you, who have supported you, and who will continue to cherish your union especially during the hard times in the coming years. This special group should consist of those people who will be responsible for helping you to keep the myriad pieces together as your wedding details unfold, so they should be selected carefully. Don't get caught up in conflicts about obligation or the numbers game. If you start asking yourself questions like "Do I have to ask her to be a bridesmaid even though she gets on my nerves?" or "Must we add an extra groomsman just because the balance is off?" stop for a minute. Contemplate seriously the individuals whom you are asking to stand up for you. Do you believe in your heart that they will support you for many years to come? Do they openly welcome you *and* your partner? Does your partner approve of your choice of attendants? Do you approve of his? If the answers are affirmative, whatever the number of attendants you select will be fine. What you want most is for your bridal party to consider their role in your union with tremendous honor.

If even after careful editing, your list is long, you can make it work. Be creative. You can follow the lead of Carol Hall of Los Angeles. As a forty-three-year-old first-time bride, she had made many great friends over the years. She paid tribute to them all by listing them as honorary attendants in her wedding program and playing a recorded message of love and thanks to them all into the actual ceremony. Another sister, Angela Dawson of Atlanta, used a different strategy. With a wedding party of nearly a dozen, she made most of them attendants. Angela had them open the ceremony at her church, each accompanied by an usher. Each couple was responsible for carrying a candle that they placed on the altar; afterward that entire group took their seats, leaving only the bride and groom and four members of the bridal party standing.

How much money do you plan to contribute?

The days when the bride's parents paid for everything are largely over. Today it's more likely that you will be contributing significantly to your wedding expenses.

Review your financial status. How much money have you saved? How much money can you save from now until your wedding day? With pooled resources, how much can you safely offer to the event? An intimate wedding of twenty to thirty guests with a reception at home, catered by family and friends, can cost as little as a thousand dollars (including your clothing), if you plan wisely. A wedding for 150 with a reception held at a catering facility normally runs anywhere from five to eight thousand dollars, based on 1992 prices—not counting all the other expenses. If you plan to go all out, you can spend as much as a million dollars, as Whitney Houston reportedly did when she married Bobby Brown!

With those figures in mind, if it doesn't look like you can afford what your dream wedding will cost, don't panic. You have several options. First you must allow your fantasy to transform into a more realistic picture. Second, know that in many cases parents *do* absorb a substantial portion of the cost. If you feel that your parents will contribute, be ready to illustrate clearly what type of wedding you want to have with a rough approximation of how much you can contribute. They will be grateful for your consideration and understand that you plan to be integral players in the wedding plans. Third, think about your friends and relatives and their talents. You may be able to negotiate reduced prices on musicians, transportation, even a reception site if you know someone who can help. Last, consider pushing back the date to when you will have saved more money. What you shouldn't do is take out a loan to finance your wedding.

BUDGET BREAKDOWNS

Only you will know how to tailor your wedding budget. Below are some traditional expense breakdowns to help you make important decisions more comfortably. Each member of the bridal party is included, along with the financial responsibilities considered appropriate for each.

SUPERSTITIONS

Early African-American superstitions tagged May as an unlucky month to marry. For Muslims, Saturday is considered bad luck, with Thursday being the preferred day to establish a union.

The Bride

- wedding ring for the groom, if a double-ring ceremony
- a gift for the groom (optional)
- gifts for the maid/matron of honor and female attendants
- physical examination and blood test (as needed)
- personal stationery

The Groom

- the bride's engagement and wedding rings
- wedding gift for the bride (optional)
- marriage license and blood test, as required
- bridal bouquet and corsages for mothers and grandmother
- gifts for groom's attendants
- clergy fee
- rental or purchase of formal wear
- bachelor party (optional)
- accommodations for out-of-town guests of groom (optional)
- the honeymoon (optional)

Bride's Family

- wedding dress and accessories
- trousseau: personal clothing for the bride (some of which can be handmade by family members)
- wedding invitations and thank-you notes, printing, postage, etc.
- reception costs: hall, caterer, entertainment, cake, champagne, etc.
- transportation for bridal party (i.e., limousines) to ceremony and reception
- flowers for attendants, families, and flower girl, ceremony and reception sites
- engagement, wedding, and reception photographs and/or video
- church or ceremony site rental and music for ceremony
- attendants' dresses (optional)
- bridesmaids' party (optional)
- wedding-guest book
- accommodations for out-of-town guests of bride (optional)

Groom's Family

- personal traveling expenses and clothing
- wedding gift to couple
- rehearsal dinner (optional)
- liquor at the reception (optional)

Bridesmaids

- ◆ purchase of bridesmaids' dresses and all accessories
- ◆ transportation to and from location of wedding
- ◆ contribution to a gift from all of the bridesmaids to the bride
- ◆ individual gift to the couple
- ◆ shower and/or luncheon for the bride

Groomsmen/Ushers

- ◆ rental of wedding attire
- ◆ transportation to and from location of wedding
- ◆ contribution to a gift from all of the ushers to the groom
- ◆ individual gift to the couple
- ◆ the bachelor dinner, if given by ushers

Call a Family Meeting

Once you have formulated your ideas, sit with both of your families to determine who will pay for what aspects of your wedding and reception. Have with you your general outline of the wedding you wish to have with an estimation of cost. Distribute copies if your parents want to look at the figures. Always remember that it is *your* wedding that you are planning. To keep control over it you must stay organized, calm, and respectful of all parties involved.

Since discussing finances can easily lead to debate, be mindful of the way that you talk to each other—and to everybody else. Make this first big money discussion a positive exchange out of which the two of you can grow to know each other better—and become better money managers. It will also prove an excellent barometer for how you share information with your families.

Once the family group decides on the budget and time schedule, redraft it and provide everyone with copies. This may seem like a lot of work, but it may prove to be your lifesaver in the end. There are countless numbers of people, products, and services involved in planning a wedding, and the two of you are ultimately responsible for keeping the flow of events in check. Pay attention to your family members. Make a mental note of who is willing and able to work with you on big projects and small ones and assign tasks accordingly. Be sure they are comfortable when they agree to their assignment. Check in with everyone individually throughout the planning process to make sure that all is running smoothly. If you feel that you need more help—and your budget allows—hire a wedding consultant to organize the logistics for you.

HIRING A WEDDING CONSULTANT

Sisters in the South talk about how Cousin Lucy and Aunt Hattie helped their niece to get married, and everything turned out just fine! Then there are the church ladies in Arkansas who rallied around the choir leader to help her organize the details for her daughter's upcoming wedding. What about the neighbors in Mali who brought pots and pans, spices, and all sorts of food to help prepare for the wedding of their fellow villager? And, don't forget mothers the world over who may get on our nerves from time to time, but who ultimately get the job done with precision and accuracy.

No matter where you turn there's a vivid tale in our communities about a relative, family friend, or neighbor who has pitched in to make a wedding successful. You will be thrilled to know that many people will offer their love and support—and specific services—to you for your wedding. When people ask what they can do to help, be prepared with specific answers. Keep a record of who will be performing what task, and follow up with them to make sure that they are on the right track.

Beyond the help of family and friends, more and more couples are finding that they can use professional help. A wedding consultant or event planner who also organizes weddings may actually be necessary if you and your fiancé have demanding jobs. If you can afford it, a consultant or coordinator will handle all the details of your wedding, right down to picking up the honeymoon tickets. As Rita Harris Bowers, a consultant in Baltimore explains, "We go and do the research once the bride tells us what kind of wedding she wants to have." Bowers and her partner actually clocked many hours of library time when they were asked in 1991 to organize an Afrocentric wedding. Although the bride had a vague idea of her dream, the concrete information was not at anyone's fingertips. Using a consultant meant that she was able to incorporate many ethnic details into her ceremony.

Working with a wedding consultant can be the perfect complement to your own efforts if you remain clear and focused in all of your communications. It all starts with your initial consultation. At that crucial meeting you must clearly explain your wedding and reception ideas. Ask as many questions as you may have about the services available, and ask for advice on how you can execute your ideas. Have your ideas written down so that you can refer to them during your conference. Whether your preliminary meeting is free or requires a nominal fee (usually no more than fifty dollars), you will want to get the most information for your time. Included in your discussions should be details on:

◆ your lifestyle (meaning, of course, the two of you)
◆ your interests and hobbies
◆ the style of wedding you want
◆ specific cultural or regional requests
◆ your favorite colors for the bridal party
◆ the size of the bridal party
◆ the essentials: where you live, where and when you want the wedding to be, how much money you have to spend

At your initial meeting, it is imperative that you know your total budget, including contributions from parents and other family members. It is only then that the consultant can explore possible ways to execute your ideas. That figure will also determine whether you can afford a consultant to work with you on an ongoing basis. Consultants get paid either a flat fee or a percentage. If your budget does not allow for a consultant throughout your planning, do not despair. Instead, glean as much information from your initial meeting as possible, and consider hiring the consultant just for the wedding day itself.

Having help on the day of your wedding can relieve you of many headaches, primarily because someone else who is experienced in juggling an assortment of details will be fully responsible. Who should take on this role? Many African-American couples call on well-organized, gregarious aunts or friends of their mothers to keep all activities in check. Most churches have wedding coordinators to assist for a small fee. Of course, professionals are available for hire. Whoever you enlist should meet with you a couple of weeks in advance to review your day's plans. The more information you can provide, the better. Prepare a master list of who will be included in the wedding party, what the chain of events will be for the day, and the time frame in which it is all to happen. Los Angeles wedding consultant Lynn Jeter says that wedding day coordinators usually oversee the entire day's events, from morning until the reception is over. Often they run the rehearsal and assist at the rehearsal dinner, thereby getting to know the family and the main players for the following day. They may also handle any confirmations of deliveries, setups and pickups, as well as transporting gifts after the event. The particulars depend upon the needs of the couple—and their budget. The base price for many coordinators for the wedding day itself is five hundred dollars. As you select your coordinator, review all details carefully and have him or her sign a contract of agreement.

COUNTDOWN TO THE BIG DAY

Refer to this countdown as you move through your planning process. It should assist you in keeping track of small details.

Six to Twelve Months Prior

◆ Brainstorm together on what type of wedding you want to have and choose the date.
◆ Set a real budget.
◆ Decide on the size of guest list based on your budget.
◆ Reserve a location for your wedding and reception.
◆ If your ceremony will occur at a religious site, make an appointment with your clergy to secure all details and to arrange for premarital counseling.
◆ If you need a wedding officiant, interview several before selecting yours.
◆ Select members of the bridal party.
◆ Set up gift registry.
◆ Select wedding dress, accessories, color scheme, and bridesmaids' dresses.
◆ Select florist.
◆ Interview and select band or disc jockey for reception.
◆ Review photographers' wedding portfolios and select one.
◆ Consult with travel agency on honeymoon destinations and prices.

Four Months Prior

◆ Check state and local regulations for obtaining marriage license. Be sure to check in the area where your ceremony will be held. In most states you must be at least eighteen years of age to be married without parental consent; you need proof of identity and, if previously married, proof of divorce. And you may need a physical and a blood test. If you intend to marry out of the country, find out the rules well in advance of your trip.
◆ **Order passports, if necessary.** (This can take as long as a month in some states, so plan ahead.)

◆

HOW TO FIND A WEDDING CONSULTANT

Wedding consultants range in experience, availability, and cost. Many consultants in the Black community work part time. Others actually double as corporate event planners, a service that can enable them to build deeper relationships among the vendors they need to serve their clients. Some are experienced in ethnic weddings; many are not. Begin your search using these recommendations:

Consider word-of-mouth as the first route to take. Talk to friends who have recently married and ask for referrals. Ask other wedding professionals, such as caterers, florists, limousine services, and musicians. Even a reputable dry cleaner may offer a good referral.

Check in special bridal newspaper supplements of your local mainstream and Black newspapers for suggestions.

Go to bridal fairs at area department stores and catering facilities. More and more Black bridal fairs are cropping up across the country, featuring a vast assortment of ethnic vendors.

Refer to the Resource Guide for suggestions.

◆

◆ **Shop for your wedding trousseau.** Write out a list of the items you will need for your wedding night and your honeymoon. Take that list with you when you shop. Also, give it to your mother and maid of honor (if she requests it) as reference for your bridal shower.

◆ Finalize guest list.

◆ Select a stationer and order invitations and matching thank-you notes.

◆ If you are personalizing your ceremony, write vows or select readings. (See Chapter 8 for ideas.)

◆ Formally announce your engagement.

◆ Finalize reception site, caterer, photographer, and other services; pay required deposits.

◆ Order wedding attire for men, dresses for both mothers.

◆ Select rings. (See Chapter 3 for more information.)

◆ Finalize honeymoon plans.

Two Months Prior

◆ Mail wedding invitations first class.

◆ Organize transportation for yourselves and the wedding party.

◆ Purchase wedding gifts for each other.

◆ Purchase your attendants' gifts.

◆ Have final clothes fittings.

◆ Make time to get marriage license. Check with City Hall where you plan to marry for the requirements. You will probably have to go together.

◆ Send thank-you notes for gifts as you receive them.

◆ Make hotel and transportation arrangements for out-of-town guests. (Check with your travel agent for group discount fares.)

Three to Four Weeks Prior

◆ Plan ceremony and reception decorations and discuss with proper contacts.

◆ Arrange for a trusted friend or family member to oversee signing of guest book.

◆ Arrange for hair (for both of you) and makeup for the big day.

◆ Have wedding portrait taken. If you need a portrait for your newspaper announcement, have it taken earlier. Consider having a picture made of the two of you together.

◆ Organize name and address change, if any, by getting forms for postal delivery, driver's license, Social Security cards, credit cards, banks, etc.

Two Weeks Prior

◆ Check fittings of all wedding raiment, including groom's.

◆ Give caterer final count for reception.

◆ Plan seating arrangements for reception.

◆ Reconfirm honeymoon plans with travel agent.

One Week Prior

◆ Check fit of wedding rings, and pick them up if you haven't already.

◆ Confirm details with caterer, photographer, florist, musicians or D.J.

◆ Ask a family member or hired consultant to handle all errands on your big day.

◆ Pack for your honeymoon, placing all important documents together.

On Your Big Day

◆ Get up at a leisurely pace and meditate, take a walk, or do some other activity that relaxes you!

Tips for Tight Schedules

Not everyone allows at least six months to plan a wedding. My sister Stephanie, for example, decided in August 1992 to get married in November of the same year! A more than full-time computer engineer, she did not have round-the-clock availability to organize the details. Her fiancé, Corey Hill, an independent contractor, had a little more flexibility and helped as much as he could. To pull it all off in two months is a tribute to great planning—and to our mother who immediately put all of her organizing skills to work and made it happen.

If you find yourselves with only a few months to plan your wedding, don't panic. Just remember that every single day and minute count. You will have to be decisive from the start.

◆ **Plan your theme and stick to it.**

◆ **Find a wedding and reception site immediately.** Secure them with a deposit.

◆ **Keep it simple.** That means everything from the number of people in the wedding party to the food at the reception and the specifics of the ceremony. In this way you will be less inclined to make mistakes.

◆ **Select wedding attire immediately**. Your best bet is to buy a dress off the rack and have it altered, or even rent a dress if you find one you like. If you are ordering a bridal gown from a store that has to order your size, get the delivery date in writing. Go one step further and find out if they have a backup dress in case yours doesn't come in!

◆ **Make daily agendas, and check off each item as you handle it.** At day's end, review your list. Put any unfinished business at the top of the next day's list. Block out your days by the hour so that you can work more efficiently.

◆ **By all means, hire someone to help you if you can afford it.** Of course, if your mother or another relative is willing, she might just be the best helper you can get!

CHAPTER 6

INVITATIONS AND OTHER STATIONERY

Where departure from African tradition in the United States becomes most obvious is when folks start writing things down. On these shores, there are elaborate rules about the kinds of stationery that you should have for your wedding, including engagement announcements (which are separate from wedding announcements), wedding invitations, response cards, reception cards, at-home cards, thank-you formals (for gifts) and informals (for after the marriage). Throughout the dance of marriage, correspondence flows. And it can be expensive. Some etiquette experts say that only engraved stationery of the finest paper will be appropriate for a formal wedding. Others relax a bit and admit that invitations printed on good-quality stock are perfectly acceptable. Don't get caught up in what is considered proper. Since engraving is the most expensive means of getting your message across, you should think twice about investing in that process. If you want traditional stationery, feel comfortable using a printing method.

What's customary in many villages throughout the Motherland is even simpler. Our African traditions are based on oral history. We have *griots*, wise elders who share the lineage of our families and communities, rather than scribes. Instead of a fancy document, Africans often deliver their good news by word-of-mouth through a trusted family member. That person travels from home to home passing the word to loved ones and indicating the date of the big event. From that point on, folks get involved with the planning of festivities and the preparation of the two for marriage, making the actual ceremonial date a bit anticlimactic. In contemporary communities, even among Nigerians living in America, for instance, it is said that a call on the telephone would be a more likely way to deliver the good news than a formal invitation. That's not to say that Black folks do not or should not employ the written word. Because this country is so vast and our family and friends are often spread across many states (and countries), an invitation may even be necessary.

When the decision is to write it down, many of us do go the traditional route, at best with a little twist. When Elaine Ray, writer, and Darryl Alladice, actor and junior high school teacher, decided to get married in 1986, they knew they didn't want a standard, somewhat sterile notice to go to their loved ones. Somehow an image of a dove on white stock with engraving just didn't reflect the feelings these two shared (although they did use a live dove in their ceremony). During their search for the perfect wedding invitation, they decided that they wanted an invitation created by a Black artist. Through a friend they discovered blank note cards with Black images on them made by artist Varnette Honeywood. Two of her cards stood out—one called "The Wedding," the other "Courting." They selected "Courting," which had an illustration of a seated woman with her beau bringing her a cup of tea. They ordered enough boxes to accommodate their guest list. Separately, they ordered insert cards with the reception date and time printed on them (the ceremony itself was limited to immediate family) as well as return cards and envelopes. Margot Dashiell, a greeting card designer from Berkeley, California, incorporated a medley of cultural references for her African-inspired invitations when she and Alexander Ben got married in 1973. She found delicate off-white parchment paper that she had silk-screened with sepia-toned ink. To give the formally scripted message inside an Egyptian flavor, the invitations were rolled into scrolls and tied with raffia. Then each was hand-delivered by friends who served as couriers.

FINALIZING THE GUEST LIST

Herein lies one of the toughest and most expensive parts of planning a wedding. Even in the most amicable of relationships, you will probably have a few heated discussions with your parents—and each other—about whom to include and cut from your list. Take everyone's words to heart. The older folks who helped nurture you as a child should make their way onto your list. Relatives are a given, although for those of you with huge families, you may need to curtail the list to adults only. Your parents' dearest friends deserve consideration. Your and your fiancé's close friends shouldn't be excluded. When it comes to co-workers, be careful. There's no sure rule of thumb. Except this one: Never invite people to your wedding for purely political reasons. Your wedding is a sacred event. Your guests should be people who will support you "through thick and thin" in your new life together. If, even after great strides to cut it back, your list is still too long, remember that it is perfectly fitting to invite some people to the wedding and not to the reception (and vice versa).

You will need to decide about children at this point as well. The jury is still out on the most effective way to include children at a wedding celebration. Some couples have said that the sound of a crying baby just as they repeat their vows is not something they want to risk. Others either don't have the resources or the patience to have children at the wedding reception. These couples will normally send a "no children allowed" message through a verbal network to let folks know their policy. A big concern comes up for parents with children, though, especially when they are traveling to witness your wedding. One couple solved that problem quite creatively. Carol Hall and Cliff Holliday planned their 1990 wedding for Memorial Day weekend. Since most of their 185 guests were traveling from across the country, they sent a little packet in their invitations, complete with wedding invitation and response card, information on hotel accommodations, brochures from local tourist centers, including Disneyland, *and* a checklist of needs. On that list was a baby-sitting service for during the ceremony and the party scheduled for the evening after the wedding. Carol had arranged with teenagers at her church to care for any young children during each of those times. Everyone was invited to the reception.

SELECTING YOUR INVITATIONS

When it comes time to shop for wedding invitations, stay focused on what type of invitation you would like to have and how much money you have to spend. There are literally hundreds of choices in traditional wedding invitations, not to mention alternative choices that you will pore over before making your final selection. To make the activity a bit easier, here are some suggestions on how to shop for traditional and creative wedding invitations, as well as alternative suggestions that may be just what you need.

◆ **Begin your search at least four months in advance**—preferably earlier, making calls and visiting stationers. Ask for referrals from friends, your caterer, or your wedding consultant.

◆ **Look for traditional and contemporary stationery** at gift and card shops, department stores, bridal shops, and printers.

◆ **Do as Elaine and Darryl did and find an art card** that captures the essence of your relationship. You can still enclose the essential response card and inside envelopes by ordering them from a stationer. Black-owned bookstores, boutiques, and art stores often carry a sizable assortment. Also check at museum stores. Work with the store proprietor to make special orders. Better yet, read the back of the card for the company name and address, and write there asking to make

◆

THE GREAT DEBATE
ENGRAVING VS. THERMOGRAPHY

Wedding invitations can end up taking a meaty chunk out of your budget. Between the paper, the lettering style, and the means of lettering, you are talking about big dollars. Since colonial times, engraving has been the preferred method of sharing essential information. During the engraving process, according to John Black, president of Excelsior Process and Engraving Company, a piece of metal is cut with the selected lettering style to form a cavity to make a well that is filled with ink. The paper in turn picks up ink from the well. This process gives the lettering a raised appearance. Long ago, engraved invitations required a piece of tissue between the insert and the envelope, to allow the ink to dry. These days the tissue is not necessary, although many people still buy it.

Essentially, thermography is almost identical to regular offset or letter-press printing, except that a machine attaches to the back of the paper and applies a clear resin powder to the wet ink. What then happens is that a raised image appears, one that somewhat diffuses the print.

With both processes, a wide range of traditional lettering styles are available. The quality of the lettering is definitely different, with the engraving being more precise. The biggest difference overall is in price. Thermography costs roughly 40 percent less than engraving. Let your budget be your guide.

◆

direct orders. You may be able to negotiate a discount for large orders.

◆ **Select the actual paper for your invitations.** You can choose from a wide variety of papers that will either be some percentage of cotton or sulfite. Your decision should be based on what you like, how long you want it to last, and how much it costs. If you want your wedding invitation to be in great shape for your fiftieth wedding anniversary, you will need 100 percent cotton fiber, the most expensive and the most durable. Other grades of cotton paper are certainly available, as is sulfite paper, which is much more affordable.

◆ **Select ink color and typeface.** Determine whether they will be engraved or printed. Discuss the options offered.

◆ **Carefully review the samples available** and note prices for each item you will need.

◆ **Determine if stationer can print a map card to your reception,** if needed.

◆ **Find out if your stationer can imprint your engagement photo**—if you had one taken together—as the image on your invitation.

◆ **If your wedding is relatively small, make your invitations.** Gold-and-sepia–toned ink, cowrie shells, and raffia are a few materials that combine well to make cultural cards. Creative members of your bridal party may be interested in chipping in on the labor. You could arrange a party just for that purpose.

◆ **Enlist the help of a family member or friend and create a poem** or song that can be sung door to door and on the phone to spread the word in African fashion.

◆ **When time is tight and your wedding is informal, be contemporary and send a fax or a telegram.** Make it fun by using phrasing that joyfully expresses your commitment to get married and perhaps an illustration along with the details.

The words might say:

Delores and Mark just couldn't wait. So we're getting married on this date: July 4, 1993. Be there—at the San Diego Zoo, promptly at noon. Food will follow. Oh, and do R.S.V.P.! 555-7279

Wedding Stationery: What You Need

The types of stationery for a wedding seem to be endless. The basics include:

◆ outer envelope
◆ inner envelope (for formal weddings)
◆ reception response card with envelope
◆ map card (as needed)
◆ pew card (used to secure seating for invited guests only, either when your wedding is

large and is held at an attention-getting location or if you or your fiancé is a "celebrity")

♦ at-home cards (to let friends know when they can call you after your honeymoon, optional)

♦ announcements (to send to folks who weren't invited to the wedding who would like to know the great news, optional)

♦ place cards (for the reception; they should be blank to be filled in by a steady hand)

♦ wedding programs (can be printed separately by a different stationer, especially if you are having your wedding at your spiritual center, which may use its own printer. You definitely should have a program, though, so your guests can follow the script)

When It's Time to Order

Finalize your guest list at least three months in advance with both sets of parents and agree that no changes can be made. Once you have the final head count, determine the need for invitations by dividing your list into married couples, single adults, and families. If you are not inviting everyone to both the wedding and reception, divide your list again into who will be receiving which invitations. Be sure to include the members of your wedding party, your parents, and yourselves in your head count. All of you should receive a wedding invitation as a keepsake. When you have your final total, add a few extras to the list—just in case. Then review the list carefully, double-checking each other. Before you order, reverify the dates and times of your wedding and reception with your wedding officiate, reception hall, caterer, and all others.

Provide your stationer with a typed listing of all pertinent information in the wording you choose to ensure clarity. This may be included in your contract. Request a proof of your invitation for errors and carefully review it *before* you approve the printing. Also ask for a guarantee of replacement in case there are errors upon printing. Request envelopes even before invitations are completed, so that you can begin addressing them. They should be handwritten, traditionally in calligraphy, definitely in neat, legible script. Ask for a guaranteed delivery date for invitations, envelopes, insert cards, and all other stationery.

WORDING YOUR MESSAGE

Ensure that your guests receive the information about your wedding clearly and with the proper respect by providing some basic details, usually in the order that follows:

Names of those giving the wedding
Full names of bride and groom
Date and time of the ceremony
Location of ceremony
Location and time of reception (optional)
R.S.V.P. or "The favor of a reply is requested" (optional)

Customarily, the way that invitation basics are conveyed is treated with great rigidity, based on European standards. Below you will find examples of the most common formats for invitations, culled from many experts on the subject. Because this form of sharing information is not reflective of your ancestral culture, and, in some cases, is somewhat awkward, feel free to take liberties—just so long as you get the information across clearly.

Traditionally the parents of the bride give the wedding, and their names appear on the wedding invitation. More and more often couples are adding both sets of parents on their invitations, especially as families begin to share expenses more equally. Depending upon a couple's circumstances, a relative, close friend, or the couple themselves can issue the invitations. The guidelines for wording invitations are quite specific and can be followed to avoid confusion. They are as follows:

When the bride's family is hosting the wedding:

Mr. and Mrs. Martin Jones
request the honour of your presence
at the marriage of their daughter
Roxanna Joy
to
Mr. Jeffrey Attucks Smith
Saturday, the fifteenth of May
Nineteen hundred and ninety-three
Antioch Baptist Church
Atlanta, Georgia

Reception immediately following at The Hammond House
Please R.S.V.P.

(The reception information and response request can also appear on a separate reception card.)

When the bride's mother is widowed:

Mrs. Martin Jones
requests the honour of your presence
at the marriage of her daughter

When the father is widowed, it is appropriate to use his name and his daughter's.

When the bride's mother is divorced:

Mrs. Carrie Hayes Jones
requests the honour of your presence
at the marriage of her daughter

When the bride's mother is divorced and remarried, and she and her husband are hosting the wedding:

Mr. and Mrs. Alton Washington
request the honour of your presence
at the marriage of her daughter
Roxanna Joy Jones

When the bride's stepmother and father are the hosts:

Mr. and Mrs. Martin Jones
request the honour of your presence
at the marriage of Mrs. Jones's stepdaughter
Roxanna Joy

When both parents are divorced and remarried and are co-hosting the wedding, both names appear with the mother's first:

Mr. and Mrs. Alton Washington
and
Mr. and Mrs. Martin Jones
request the honour of your presence
at the marriage of
Roxanna Joy Jones

When the bride's parents are divorced but not remarried:

Mrs. Carrie Hayes Jones
and
Mr. Martin Jones

or:

Carrie Hayes Jones
and
Martin Jones
request the honour of your presence
at the marriage of their daughter
Roxanna Joy

When the groom's family sponsors the wedding:

Mr. and Mrs. Alexander Smith
request the honour of your presence
at the marriage of
Roxanna Joy Jones
to their son
Jeffrey Attucks Smith

When the couple are hosting their own wedding:

The honour of your presence
is requested at the marriage of
Roxanna Joy Jones
to
Jeffrey Attucks Smith

(Note that when the groom's family or the couple is hosting, the groom does not receive a prefix to his name. Rarely should a woman use a prefix on a wedding invitation, according to traditional practice, even, say, if she is a physician. The exception is for the military. Again, these are traditional rules that you can consider and then make your own decision.)

When it's a second wedding and the parents are the hosts:

Mr. and Mrs. Martin Jones
request the honour of your presence

at the marriage of their daughter
Roxanna Jones Preston
to
Mr. Jeffrey Attucks Smith

When it's a second wedding and the couple are the hosts:

The honour of your presence
is requested at the marriage of
Roxanna Jones Preston
to
Jeffrey Attucks Smith

(Note: The bride in a second wedding can drop her married name.)

When the hosts are siblings or other relatives, the form is as follows:

Mr. Matthew Jones
requests the honour of your presence
at the marriage of his sister
Roxanna Joy

When the groom, the father of the bride, the host of the wedding, or an invited guest is in the military, there are specific ways to address them. A member of the Army, the Navy, the Coast Guard, the Air Force, or the Marine Corps, or one who is on active duty in the reserve forces, uses his or her formal military title. It is proper for officers whose rank is captain in the Army or lieutenant, senior grade, or higher in the Navy to have their title on the same line as their names.

Captain Martin Jones, United States Army

An officer of a lower rank should have his name on one line with his title below. Those on active duty in the reserves would have their name on one line, with "Army of the United States" or "United States Naval Reserve" below it.

Etiquette soothsayers suggest that, out of respect, wedding invitations be worded with the bride's family first in nearly all cases—even if the bride and groom are actually hosting the event. Only in rare instances should the groom's family head the invitation, primarily if the bride's parents are deceased or unwilling to accept the marriage or if the bride's family lives in another country. You must make your own decision about the wording of your invitation and stick to it. Food for thought: Traditional African weddings support the union of both families to create a new, solid unit, so a joint invitation is most welcome.

Do's and Don'ts for the Couple

Wording for a religious ceremony on your invitation should read "the honour of your presence"; the reception card should read "the pleasure of your company." If the ceremony is held at home, it should read "the pleasure of your company."

When asking for a response to your wedding reception on your invitation, the wording can be: "R.S.V.P.," "The favor of a reply is requested," or "Please respond." Consider inserting a response card that formally requests an immediate reply. (Be aware that many of us tend to R.S.V.P. at the last minute, so you might want to keep a guest list with phone numbers that you check when it gets close to the date!)

Write out all names fully (first, middle, and surnames), including the title of the father of the bride. A title for the mother of the bride is generally considered inappropriate unless the couple are giving themselves away.

Spell out numbers in dates but not in very long addresses or in zip codes.

As briefly indicated earlier, include pew cards or admission cards only when you are having a wedding in a public place where you expect "crashers," if you are having a very large wedding in a limited space, or when you or your spouse is a celebrity and your privacy needs to be protected. (Historically in many African communities, it was a given that everyone was invited to a wedding to witness the growth of the community.)

If the date of your wedding changes after the invitations have been printed, obviously you must let your guests know as soon as possible. If you can, enclose a printed card in the invitations stating the change or neatly write in the new information in pen. If the invitations have already been mailed, either call each of your guests personally or mail a note stating the change.

THE MAILING

Formal wedding invitations consist of the invitation itself, an outer envelope, an inner envelope, a reception invitation card (optional), a response card and envelope (optional), a pew or admission card (optional), an at-home card (optional), a map (as needed). For even the simplest of informal weddings there are at least the invitation

◆

WHAT GUESTS SHOULD KNOW

When you receive your wedding invitation, respond immediately to let the couple know if you intend to come. If the couple has extended an invitation to you that includes the wedding reception, it is your duty to let them know your plans. They must inform the caterer of the head count for the feast. Let them know if your name should be on it or not.

Only the people whose names are written on the invitation are invited— period. If an invitation includes an inside envelope, additional names may be

written on the outside for children or, in the case of single people, "and guest." Don't assume, however, that your children are invited. Many couples simply can't afford to invite everyone's children to their reception and choose not to have them at their ceremony to preserve the sacredness and silence of the moment, to create more room for adult guests, or to make it more convenient for parents who will be traveling to the reception immediately following. Some couples do arrange for baby-sitting services at the ceremony site when children are invited to the reception. That message should be included in your invitation when it's applicable.

The only time that single people really should be offered an additional invitation is if they are engaged. If your fiancé did not receive an invitation or if the couple is not aware of your recent betrothal, you can let them know. Should they not be able to accommodate your partner, find a way to understand. A wedding is often an expensive venture, and the guest list simply cannot include everyone.

When it comes to weddings of co-workers, be considerate. Because most guest lists are limited, just because you received an invitation does not mean that your friend at work did as well. Don't spread the news to everyone at work that you will be attending the upcoming event. Your revelation could cause hurt feelings and discomfort for the couple who are doing their best to plan a joyous occasion for all.

◆

and an envelope. In all cases, the complete invitation must be stuffed, hand-addressed, and mailed by you. With that in mind, the most important advice to follow here is to start early.

Addressing Your Invitations

Enlist assistance from your fiancé, members of your bridal party, your mother, or a professional calligrapher, if you can afford it, to help address invitations. Make sure your volunteers have legible, attractive handwriting. Set aside a specific time each day to get the job done, or do it en masse on a weekend. The outer envelope must be handwritten in either black ink or the color of the type on the invitation. Return addresses should be engraved or printed on the upper-left-hand corner of the outside envelope. It is correct to write out all names fully as well as titles, and addresses including name of city and state and "street," "avenue," "boulevard," etc. Families should be addressed individually on one invitation, with parents being addressed on the outer envelope if there is an inner envelope; otherwise children should be listed separately, divided by boys and girls as "Misses" and "Messrs." or "Masters" followed by their names. Married couples who have different last names should be addressed on one invitation with their names listed in alphabetical order.

Stuffing Envelopes

Now here's where the real skill comes in! Putting all the pieces together for your invitations, in the right places, can be tedious. Take your time and make sure you work with clean, dry hands so that you keep your invitations crisp and fresh. The order for stuffing is like so:

Invitation goes into inner envelope (if used) or outer envelope with folded edge first and invitation front facing flap of envelope. All enclosures are inserted also facing the flap, on top of the invitation, with the reception invitation first, followed by the response card and envelope and others as used. When an inner envelope is used, the addressed side faces the flap of the outer envelope as it is inserted.

Purchase special stamps for your wedding invitations. Consider those with historical African-American leaders. No matter what, do not use an automatic stamping machine for your invitations. Send your fully stuffed invitations first class to ensure their prompt delivery. For formal weddings, mail invitations six to eight weeks in advance. For the most informal of ceremonies, allow guests at least ten days in advance to receive the invitation. Deliver your invitations to a post office to ensure their safe departure. Mail all invitations at the same time and keep a record of all responses.

VIA THE KOLA NUT

In historic African Islamic communities, the sharing of a kola nut, considered a symbol of fertility, represented an announcement of engagement. The young man's family delegation first comes to the young woman's family home and makes their intentions known. When the family has agreed to sanction the relationship, a kola nut is offered to the young woman who appears at that time, hopefully to accept the offer. The young man and his family also offer a small amount of money. Once the young woman accepts the nut, she breaks it open and the two eat a portion of it. It is subsequently shared with the family members in attendance, after which someone is assigned to go to the homes of loved ones in the community to announce the engagement. Each home visited is given a small portion of the kola nut and the offering.

A NOTE OF THANKS

Selecting your wedding invitations, whether they be traditional or some creative expression of you and your fiancé, is a tremendous responsibility. It requires that both of you—along with your parents, in many instances—have to explore your personal taste, learn how that fits into your budget, and make a "group" decision. The same goes for your thank-you notes, which should be ordered at the same time.

    If you are like most couples you will be showered with gifts at various preliminary parties, not to mention those that you will receive for your actual wedding. The best way to keep track of these gifts and to ensure that you thank everyone is to keep a log of the gifts you have received. This can be kept in your wedding journal or separately. You will need to sit down regularly and write a note of thanks. Many couples order note cards that are complementary to their wedding invitations to use for this purpose. The cards can have both of your names on the outside, blank on the inside. Traditionally they are written by hand by the bride, along with the assistance of enlisted family and friends. Of course you can change the rules and share the responsibility with your spouse so that you both are included.

For those gifts that are offered especially for the bride or for the groom, a personal thank-you note would be especially nice. This requires either that each of you has personalized stationery or that you have selected unprinted cards or stationery to use for this purpose. You don't *have* to order engraved or printed stationery. A wide assortment of note cards and specialty stationery are available these days, many with ethnic motifs. Select the cards that reflect your personality—and use them.

CHAPTER 7

YOUR WEDDING LOOK

Y ou've dreamed about it. You've even seen yourself walking down the aisle with that special someone with whom you plan to spend the rest of your life. But did you have a clear mental picture of what you had on? As you work to make your dream a reality, one of the toughest decisions you will make will be about your "look" on your wedding day. Of course you and your fiancé want to look your absolute best, to let your happiness and inner beauty shine through. This chapter will provide information on clothing options, suggestions for accessories, and pointers for hair and makeup.

WHAT WILL YOU WEAR?

Sit down together, with notebook in hand—the same notebook that should be the record for all of your important wedding details—and start talking. Most wedding planners will advise you to begin by agreeing on what time of day your wedding will be and how formal you intend to make it. Even more pivotal will be your decisions about style.

The Afrocentric Touch

As members of the diaspora, you have a wealth of cultures from which to choose. Don't be afraid of combining various elements to design a style that can be your signature statement. Learn as much as you can about African traditions so that you can understand the symbolism behind each element. Who knows, you may decide that you want a formal wedding, only formal doesn't translate into a long white gown with veil and train accompanied by white tie and tails. Instead, the two of you may choose formal West African as your theme, selecting Nigerian *asooke* or Ghanaian *kente* for your traditional four-piece *bubah* for both bride and groom.

At the top of your list, then, must be a decision on how cultural you intend your wedding to be and whether any of those cultural elements will make their way into your wardrobe. Don't feel pressured to follow any philosophy other than your own. Just make sure you've determined what your thinking is. The traditional

◆

HOW TO FIND THE RIGHT DESIGNER

Once you have a good idea of how you want to look, find someone to bring that look to life. Remember your community. The best people to ask for help are those right in your own backyard. These leads should prove fruitful:

◆ *your minister/spiritual officiant and other members of your place of worship*

◆ *the society editor at your local Black newspaper and other Black publications*

◆ *the owner of the local cultural boutique or gift shop*

◆ *the local Black museum and archives*

◆ *your hairdresser*

◆ *your cleaners (They know labels.)*

◆ *the friend whose wardrobe you admire the most (She will love offering you recommendations.)*

◆ *local Black media personalities*

◆ *Black theater, dance, and film groups (They may know costume designers whose work could be beautiful on you walking down the aisle.)*

◆ *the Yellow Pages (That's right. Let your fingers do the walking, and look for retailers who specialize in Afrocentric items.)*

◆

Western rules about wedding attire, which are listed in this chapter for your reference (with accompanying information on African traditions), are based on a European aesthetic dating back earlier than the eighteenth century. For this reason it is not essential that you adhere to them point for point, if at all. Couples today are seeking ways to incorporate elements of their family histories and of their individual styles into this special moment in their lives.

If you decide to go ethnic, you will most likely need a designer or dressmaker to create both your wedding gown and your groom's attire. (Many brides opt for a dressmaker even when they want traditional attire, so that they can get a great fit and design for what is often an affordable price.)

When you make the big decision to have a cultural dress made, first define

AN AFRICAN-AMERICAN WEDDING ALBUM

Your wedding day represents a blessed celebration that the two of you will remember for the rest of your lives. It is the moment when every aspect of planning your wedding comes into full bloom. During the magical hours when you pledge your love to each other and share your joy with loved ones you will want everything to be just right—from the way the ceremony and reception sites are decorated to the way you both look and feel. You may want to showcase unique treasures that reflect your own culture. As you work to give your wedding a signature statement, no doubt you will learn that it is the details that count the most in making your dreams come true. In this special insert you will see glimpses of those details, including wedding raiment and accessories specially made with you in mind, exquisite floral bouquets and boutonnieres, ethnic foods, and extraordinary gifts. Allow the images in this wedding album to inspire you to create nothing less than what you truly want on your own enchanted day!

LET SUBTLETY REIGN

Let your intuition be your guide. Do cultural symbols stir your soul? Perhaps use them in subtle ways. It may be that you want to wear an elegantly classic floral-lace gown with billowing train (*left*) at your outdoor wedding, and all that's decidedly ethnic is the designer who made it. A prize as tiny as a ring can exhibit cultural messages when it's cast with ancient Khamitic symbols. Link the old with the young by dressing your flower girl in a delicate lace dress complete with gold painting and cowrie shells (*below*).

SIGNATURE STYLE

Dare to be the bride and groom you've always dreamed of! Elegant and cultural, this couple appear regal with him in a rich *asooke* dinner jacket and black trousers and her in a sumptuous portrait-collar gown and African-inspired crown (*left*). You can go Ghanaian wearing authentic *kente* in traditional and Western silhouettes (*right*). (A Ghanian would normally wear a *bubah*.) Know that the headpiece can be a bride's crowning glory, especially when it's shaped like the spire of an Asian shrine and adorned with African cowrie shells and Western lace (*below*). When your energy is high and your legs are great, go for something short and sexy (*below left*).

ややややや

BOLD AND BEAUTIFUL

Everything from the way you wear your hair to the style of clothing you choose makes you unique on your wedding day. Goddess Queen N'zinga braids (*above*) create a headpiece of their own. Don't be afraid to wear something short and fitted (*left*). Just make sure you can sit comfortably! Pay close attention to your hosiery and shoes. For a Khamitic touch, wear a gilded *pedesa* (*top right*). Your second time around need not be restrictive— only respectful. When you are three, make your day special with the bride and daughter wearing complementary clothing (*near left*). The groom can add a cultural scarf to complete the circle. Be sophisticated and sure in silver and white, cowries, and lace while your groom remains conservatively Western (*far right*).

SOULFUL NOTES

Deep in our beings live the souls of our ancestors. What better time to reflect that powerful spirit than at your wedding? Adorned in icy blue-and-white traditional Yoruba *asooke* formal wear, this couple (*left*) proudly praises their forebears. Mixing Western and African messages (*top right*) is something you can do yourself. A bit of tulle, a treasure of *kente*, a dress and crown of lace, and tiny hair twists say together more than words ever could. Be more structured but no less cultural in Islamic-inspired raiment trimmed in cowrie shells (*bottom right*).

CROSSING THE THRESHOLD

Just think of it! You are about to get married, and everything has to be right. If your wedding is at home, consider lining the vestibule with African fabric to symbolize the sanctity of the day. You may even ask guests to remove their shoes before entering. African and Caribbean sculpture, food, and flowers can finish the setting magnificently. As a bride, don't feel you have to stop at the traditional. If you've got the figure, wear a body-skimming fishtail gown with Kenyan-inspired necklacing (*left*). When you have a fuller figure, allow simple necklines and delicate fabrics to enhance your natural assets (*above*).

HIS-STORY One of the best things a brother can do is buy wedding attire rather than rent it. You're guaranteed to get your money's worth down the road when you need the suit again and again for formal evenings out with your wife! Beyond the basic tuxedo, you can choose any number of cultural combinations, including wearing a traditional white jacket and black trousers with an *asooke*-print silver-and-black custom vest (*above*); all-the-way Nigerian with a Yoruba *asooke* jacket topping white pants and shirt (*near right*); or with just a touch of *kente* at the collar accenting a made-for-brothers full-leg double-breasted suit (*far right*).

COME ONE, COME ALL

Nothing brings us together better than a spread of good food. When it comes time for a wedding, Black folks are known to offer mouth-watering meals—especially when we are doing the cooking! The thought of potato salad, macaroni and cheese, and hickory-smoked turkey—not to mention hot peach cobbler—is enough to get everybody to the reception on time! Since cake cutting represents a ceremonial high point, why not give your cake a cultural design? You can ask a cake designer to make anything your heart desires, including the intricate West African *kente*-inspired motif shown here.

SO GIFTED

When you get married, you are gaining a partner for life as well as extended family and friends who promise to support and love you through thick and thin. Those offering their allegiance usually come bearing gifts—to help you launch your new life together. Western tradition calls for couples to register at a retail store to let their guests know specifically what they want. As you list those items that will most satisfy your family needs, spend time together talking about your taste preferences. Be sure to consider ethnic and contemporary treasures, such as those pictured here.

SEALED WITH
A KISS

As your guests shower
you with kernels of corn
(representing fertility)
and bid you best wishes,
steal a moment for a
kiss. Your bond is
beginning to blossom—
and you have everything
to be thankful for!

clearly what you mean by cultural. How ethnic do you intend to go? Which African (cowrie shells, mud cloth, *kente*, *asooke*), Caribbean (boldly printed cotton, embroidered lace) and Western (pearls, ribbon, tulle) materials do you like? African fabric is more likely to be a rich cotton or silk hand-loomed weave or brocade than alençon or chantilly lace—although a combination of those and many other textiles is growing in popularity. Are you interested in wearing traditional African garments or in incorporating more subtle uses of African motifs and fabrics in contemporary styles? Both are perfectly acceptable.

Only you can define your comfort zone. Study bridal and fashion magazines, bridal brochures, and cultural history books to glean ideas on how to put your look together. Look at the sketches, dresses, and suits shown throughout this book for ideas. (Each of the garments included in *Jumping the Broom* was designed with you in mind and is available through the designer by custom order. See the Resource Guide for details.) Collect fabric swatches, photographs, and any other references you can find before you sit down with a designer or dressmaker. Remember that the two of you need to agree on the style of clothing that you will wear, so it is at this early point that open discussion is most important.

Dressing Your Bridal Party

It's no secret that many couples moan when it comes time to get the wedding party dressed. Figuring out a color scheme that will be carried throughout the bridal party clothing, including the groom and his attendants' accessories, can be tough. Pastels, particularly peach and salmon, lead as favorite bridal party colors. (Our ancestors opted for brilliant reds, magentas, royal blues, and gold—which are also great choices.) The challenge, of course, is to find colors and garments that look good on more than one body type. No matter how tempting, no bride should determine who can be in her wedding based on how the person looks and what size dress she wears! At the same time, she doesn't want a group of women standing before the altar in clothes that they would never again wear, or that they feel uncomfortable wearing for those few hours. The men can simply rent tuxedos, though that's not always a shoe-in for brothers, either—often they need more room in the thighs and across the back. (See Chapter 13 for more on men's attire.) The challenge is even greater with mothers. They are supposed to wear colors and garments that are complementary to the bride and groom. Yet traditional soft pinks, fawns, powder blues, and dusty rose hues tend to age older women rather than show them elegantly vibrant and glowing with happiness. It's only for the junior bridesmaids and other children that

WEDDING WEAR

This chart is designed to show you both Western standards for wedding raiment as well as traditional attire in various African nations. The formality of traditional Western wedding wear is determined by time of day and the locations of the wedding ceremony and reception. Traditional African attire, however, follows different rules, with couples wearing specific clothing based largely on where they were born. Time of day has little to do with the decision making.

TYPE OF WEDDING	BRIDE	GROOM
FORMAL DAYTIME	White, ivory, or pale pastel floor-length dress with train. Train-length veil. Or ballroom gown with full skirt and/or full train. Matching shoes, bouquet, white gloves when gown has short sleeves.	VERY FORMAL: Cutaway coat, striped trousers, grey vest, wing-collar white shirt, striped ascot. FORMAL: Grey stroller, waistcoat, striped trousers, shirt, and tie. White or light color formal suit for summer.
FORMAL EVENING	Similar color as formal daytime, with floor- or ankle-length evening dress in rich fabrics: lace, brocade, velvet.	VERY FORMAL: Full-dress tailcoat, matching trousers, white waistcoat, bow tie, and wing-collar shirt. FORMAL: Dark dinner jacket, matching trousers or formal suit, dress shirt, bow tie, vest or cummerbund. White or ivory jacket, dark trousers for summer.
SEMIFORMAL DAYTIME	White, ivory, pastel, or floral floor- to above-the-knee length dress or suit in dressy fabric.	Formal suit or dinner jacket and trousers, dress shirt, tie or bow tie, vest or cummerbund.
SEMIFORMAL EVENING	Same as semiformal daytime with more elaborate fabric.	Same as semiformal daytime.
INFORMAL DAY OR EVENING	Dressy day suit or dress in any elegant fabric. Short veil or hat.	Same as semiformal daytime.
GHANAIAN	*D'Jallaba*; gown made of fine silk *Batakali*; *kente* with an equally intricate full top and headpiece to match (a wrap). Or *Kaba Set*: lace peplum top with straight *kente* skirt.	*Batakali* or *Buruba kente* wrap over trousers and top in white lace or velvet.
SENEGALESE	Dress and head-wrap of matching print, known as *Mameboye*; with much jewelry. Or *Tabas*: peplum top with leg-of-mutton sleeves and straight skirt. Or *Modiriere*: caftan over halter and *lappa* skirt.	Long embroidered tunic over pants, known as *Ngett Abdou* or *Grand Bubah*. Fabrics: *Asooke*, Guinea brocade, any royal fabrics.
IVORIAN (Ivory Coast)	Ivorian local *kente* cloth *bubah* in any colors made expressly for the bride; elaborate jewelry.	Similar to bride, with crown.
NIGERIAN	*Asooke Fugu*: *Lappa* skirt, top, tunic and head-wrap	*Agbada*: Four-piece garment with pants, tunic top, and soft hat.

choices become easier; they generally wear scaled-down versions of the adult attire.

Making the bridal party beautiful *can* happen. Your thinking may need to change a bit, though. There's no rule that says every female has to wear the exact same dress, that dresses must come from a bridal shop, or that everyone has to wear the same color (in fact, the maid or matron of honor usually wears a slightly different color from the rest). The only guideline you really should follow is that of keeping the group visually cohesive and attractive. Why not set up guidelines for bridesmaids' clothing and then have final approval on outfits before they are purchased or made? When Monique Greenwood got married, she had an individual designer assigned to each of her six bridesmaids. Because they were all different sizes with divergent personalities, the bridesmaids were given a welcome freedom. They could have the dress of their dreams, so long as it was teal and ankle-length with a drape incorporated into the design. One tall, small-breasted woman had her drape in the back, while another with a small waist and full hips had her drape across the hip to accentuate her best asset. In the end, everyone was happy.

Although you may not have the same resources as Monique, your imagination need be no less fertile. As you shop for bridesmaids' clothing, look in department stores and specialty shops, and look up dressmakers to see what insight they may bring to the project.

The Right Fit

Finding a dress that fits your body and your style is not the easiest pursuit, no matter what your size. If you are wrapping African fabric, your concerns lessen. In that case what you need most is the expertise to do the wrapping or an able assistant. Sybil Glover in Texas went so far as to consult with a Ghanaian priest to find out about the traditional clothing she wanted to wear. Then she enlisted the support of a parishioner of her church to dress her properly. Illona Rawlings of Baltimore, on the other hand, pored through magazines to see what cultural touches they suggested for bridal attire and adapted those ideas into her custom dress that also was wrapped by an astute African friend.

For those of you who are dressing in a more Western or constructed style, there are some guidelines that you can follow to help you make the right choices for your body *before* you make your purchases. Created by Atlanta-based fashion consultant Patrice McLeod, this chart will ensure that you accentuate the positive on your wedding day. The categories are based on a wide variety of concerns that we have when we are getting dressed.

Lower Body Fuller than Upper Body

You need to balance your figure by emphasizing the top half of your body and minimizing the bottom half.

◆ Do this by choosing design details that accentuate your upper body, such as elaborate bodices with lace, beads, jeweled appliqués, decorative flowers, embroidery, and off-the-shoulder silhouettes.

◆ Consider full-sleeve treatments such as padded shoulders that will extend the upper body.

◆ Go for elongated bodices with full skirts as well as peplums to camouflage hips and full derrieres.

◆ Flatter larger hips with soft pleats and minimal skirt interest.

◆ Look for stable fabrics such as taffeta, shantung, and heavy cottons that won't cling to your hips.

◆ Avoid horizontal lines, heavy gathers, and pleating at the hip area, and body hugging sheaths and large back bustles that add fullness.

Upper Body Wider than Lower Body

A full upper body indicates broad shoulders, a full bustline, a wide waistline or a combination of them all. What you want to do is proportion your figure with equal interest on the top and bottom of your dress.

◆ Look for stately, simple sleeves that will flatter your natural shoulder line or V-necklines to reduce upper body width.

◆ Balance your figure with the fullest of skirts or draped and wrapped sarong styles.

◆ Skirt interest and simple sleeves pull the eye downward and create proportional equilibrium.

◆ An elongated waist adds extra height.

◆ Avoid narrow skirts and severe necklines that draw the eye upward.

Full Figure

When you are already blessed with roundness, don't make the mistake of trying either to cover up your assets or overexpose them.

◆ Select necklines that show off your figure best, such as square, bateau, V-, or scoop.

◆ Look for a cultural sheath or caftan.

◆ Choose floating material such as chiffon or crepe that will camouflage extra pounds.

◆ Avoid gowns with too much fabric and detail near your face.

◆ If you need to wear an undergarment, avoid strapless or off-the-shoulder silhouettes.

◆ Avoid contrasting colors and clingy fabrics such as velvet and satin.

◆ Stay away from heavily beaded and overly ornate lace designs that add thickness.

Petite

If you are 5' 4" or under, rest assured that you don't have to look overly cute on your wedding day. Your figure can be enhanced with a minimum of frills, trims, and design details. Remember less is more.

◆ Look for small, delicate details.

◆ Well-proportioned leg-of-mutton and cap sleeves are good choices.

◆ Princess lines and other vertical details will lengthen your silhouette.

◆ Gowns with natural waistlines will balance your figure.

◆ Opt for delicate satins, taffetas, and lightweight laces.

◆ Avoid weighty and textured fabrics.

Tall

Height is definitely an asset if you use it to your advantage. Contrary to what you've been told, you can't wear *anything* and make it look good, though. Especially if your husband is not particularly tall, you should select a dress that balances your height.

◆ Horizontal details are perfect for you.

◆ Tiered or flounced skirts minimize height.

◆ Elaborate sleeves that extend the shoulder line; portrait and fichu collars and brimmed hats add width and deemphasize height.

Brooklyn designer Willie Mitchell reinterprets the Ghanaian *kaba set* with peplum portrait collar top and slim flare skirt on African printed cotton.

Thin

Feel comfortable by selecting from the wide array of dresses with lots of fabric.

- ◆ Fill out your figure with a full-skirted dress with pannes, bustles, or gathers.
- ◆ Create the illusion of curves by contrasting full skirts with wide and detailed collars or bateau necklines.
- ◆ Define the waist with princess styles that curve outward at the waistline.
- ◆ Select dimensional fabrics such as beaded and embroidered lace, Guinea brocade, george (a richly embroidered fabric), or velvet.
- ◆ Avoid sheaths and mermaid-style gowns or dresses with dropped waistlines and torsos.

Curvaceous

You should play up your figure by selecting styles that put your natural and best assets forward.

- ◆ An open neckline and off-the-shoulder sleeves flatter the shoulders and add width to the upper body.
- ◆ Deep or plunging necklines accentuate the bustline.
- ◆ Look for natural or slightly dropped waists.
- ◆ Choose a softly gathered skirt to balance a lightly embellished bodice.
- ◆ Select lace, organza, lightweight satin, or silks.
- ◆ Skip overly ornate fabrics on the bodice or skirt.
- ◆ Avoid extremes—high necklines, empire waists and elongated torsos—which can throw off your proportion.

Heavy Arms

Look for styles that deemphasize your shoulders and arms as they add vertical interest to your lower body.

A bride's second time around can be elegant and cultural when it's cocktail style, made from Guinea brocade or george, as designed by Willie Mitchell.

♦ Search for simple sleeves—elbow- or wrist-length—with natural shoulder lines and no padding.

♦ Sheath styles create a vertical silhouette and draw attention away from the sleeve area.

♦ Choose styles that feature peplums, bustles, gathers, or other horizontal details at the waistline or hip.

♦ Opt for interesting necklines that attract the eye upward.

♦ Stay away from horizontal detailing in the upper bodice.

♦ Avoid off-the-shoulder and strapless styles or full sleeves that are poufed or ballooned.

Your Bridal Trousseau

One woman from Mali told me how mothers in her neighborhood worked many hours making garments for their daughters in preparation for the wedding. It was a responsibility of honor that the family provided the basic lingerie and household necessities for the young woman. And they would go to great lengths to offer whatever bounty they could afford. That did not relieve the suitor of his duty, however. A young West African man intent on getting married is—to this day—required to give bolts of fabric for dresses and various other garments as part of his offering to his wife-to-be and her family. In the end, the bride is ideally to have enough undergarments, lingerie, and clothing for all of the anticipated activities of her first year of marriage.

Tradition in the United States has actually been quite similar. A bride's dowry came from her own family and often included her intimate wear as well as honeymoon clothing and other garments for life after the wedding. A bride was—and in many cases is—expected to have all of these items *before* the wedding. Even when brides have been established on their own for a while, they often choose to get new garments—especially intimate items—to start their life anew.

Today, a combination of shopping sprees yield the bride her necessities. Many a bridal shower has been hosted with a bride's measurements the hot list for guests' shopping. At these affairs, some brides have been known to receive many beautiful and fun lingerie pieces that they can use over the next year or more. Consider making a trip with your maid-of-honor or your mom expressly to pick out special pieces for your wedding night. You may want to do personal shopping for your honeymoon clothes as well.

Beautiful Budget Tips

The bridal gown is one of the most costly investments a bride will make. If you don't have the financing or the inclination to pay the going rates, consider a few options:

Wear your mother's dress. One of the oldest traditions in America, this sentimental sharing between generations can also prove quite cost-effective. Be sure you try your mother's dress on early in the process. A bit of alteration was necessary, for example, before Gina Gray of Baltimore was able to walk down the aisle in her mom's dress. She took the thirty-plus-year-old formal gown to a private seamstress and had the dress beautifully restored. If you take this route, be sure to ask about the strength of the fabric. Certain fabrics do break down over time, especially if the dress has not been properly stored. Get an estimate of cost for the restoration *before* you agree to the work. Compare prices to see if the work will be worth it.

Borrow a wedding dress from a family member or good friend. You'd be surprised at how honored most women would be to be able to share their treasured raiment with you on your special day. Do commit to taking care of the garment before you make your final handshake, including having it professionally dry-cleaned by a specialty bridal dress cleaning service.

Rent a gown from a formal wear rental company. More and more women are going this route. The prospective bride comes in usually six to eight months in advance, selects a gown, and is fitted for it. At Island Bridal Rental Gowns in Hicksville, New York, for example, once a bride gives her deposit, the dress is taken off the floor until after the wedding, so it temporarily becomes the bride's from that moment on. The difference in cost is anywhere from a few hundred dollars to thousands less than retail price. In some cases, bridesmaids' dresses are also available for rental.

Our folks have always had style. This silk jersey fitted gown with fishtail bottom, cultural fabric frontal panel, and jeweled headpiece is CD Greene's contemporary take on East African culture.

After the Wedding

Once you have walked down that aisle and joined your mate in matrimony, changed to go on your honeymoon, what happens to your dress? It's best to decide in advance. Here are some options:

Preserve your dress. Consider saving your wedding dress to pass down to your daughter for her wedding. This is a sweet tradition in America that encourages the building of generational links. (Do remember, however, that at the time of your daughter's wedding, she should be able to choose whether she wants to wear it or not.) To preserve your dress for future generations, find a reputable dry cleaning establishment that will clean and box your wedding dress for long-term keeping.

Wear it again. Depending upon the formality of your wedding and the type of dress you select, you may be able to wear it on special occasions.

Sell your dress. Your dress is a symbol of your union, yet you should not feel the need to be attached to it forever. If you need the money or the space in your closet, sell it. Bridal shops, consignment shops, secondhand stores, exclusive dry cleaners, and clothing-rental stores would be good sources to visit. Be sure to negotiate a fair price. If you work with a consignment shop, get your terms in writing.

THE RIGHT ACCESSORIES

The saying dictates that a bride should have something old, something new, something borrowed, and something blue in her possession in order to be safe and lucky on her wedding day. In honor of this superstition, many brides have used accessories to fill these slots—perhaps Grandma's pearl earrings, a dainty new handkerchief from the maid of honor, a sky-blue garter, and a best girlfriend's charm bracelet. On African shores, the requisite accessories were somewhat different—a bride's earring in the groom's ear, an elaborate necklace reserved for brides only, an embroidered ceremonial shawl.

Underneath It All

Whether you follow tradition or not, you will need to have a few basic accessories in order to be prepared for your wedding day. For the bride that starts with the right undergarments. Chances are your bridal dress will come with a slip. If you are having your gown made, request that a slip be made (and fitted) as well. If you need a special bra, remember to get it before your final fitting. Select hosiery that

◆

MANY HAPPY RETURNS

Before you purchase your dress from a bridal boutique, find out the store's return policy. (Just in case you or your honey gets cold feet, or you change your mind on the style of dress you want.) Some bridal shops will allow you to use the credit from one purchase toward another gown. Determine the time limit on exchanges, and be sure to request any changes before alterations have begun.

In the event that you cannot return your dress, you still have a couple of options. Some women store their bridal dresses "for a rainy day." If you do decide later to get married, be sure that you—and your fiancé—feel comfortable with your wearing the dress. Your fiancé is important in this decision primarily because you don't want to keep secrets from each other, especially one regarding the beginning of your life together. Another option is to sell your dress to a resale shop or a bridal gown rental company.

◆

complements your dress *and* your shoes—and have an extra pair on hand in case you get a run or a snag during the day. And then there's the garter. Whether you decide to have the whole garter ceremony at your reception doesn't matter. Having a sexy garter on after the wedding is over can be fun too! So many styles are on the market, but what can be extra special is one with cowrie shells sewn onto it or a crocheted version that incorporates pieces of African fabric.

For men, what's most important is that you wear an undershirt that complements your shirt and suit (white is fine), and that it's in good condition! Because you will probably be wearing dress shoes, your socks will be important too—the color, the texture, and the condition. One brother who got married twenty years ago loves to tell about how on his wedding day, to his surprise, his rental tux pants were about two inches too short. To his credit, his friends later commented that when he was standing at the altar repeating his vows all they could see were these incredible ribbed black silk socks!

Best Foot Forward

Getting married barefoot in the sand stirs up the most romantic images. But even couples with bare feet at the altar will need to put on shoes at some point during their wedding day. For those of you who will be wearing shoes for the duration, spend time selecting the right ones. The bride has several challenges facing her: color, style, and comfort. Your shoes will need to complement your wedding dress, especially when the dress rises above the floor. Choices abound, from dyeable *peau de soie* pumps to a wide assortment of designer wedding shoes that range in price from less than fifty dollars to more than five hundred dollars.

Be sure to purchase your bridal shoes at least two weeks in advance, and walk around in them indoors to break them in. If you think they may be uncomfortable as the day wears on, or that they may get soiled outdoors on a damp lawn (especially if they are expensive and can be worn again), bring another, more comfortable pair along. Ask your maid of honor or another trusted friend to be responsible for the extras.

Bejeweled

Brides from Brooklyn to Dakar bring out their best jewelry, including family heirlooms, on their wedding day. It's the time when folks like to wear "the real thing," when costume jewelry gets put back in the drawer. Or so it was. Today, women certainly do plan to look their best, but sometimes the perfect choker is a contemporary piece made of faux pearls. As you plan your wedding look, consider the jewelry that you own first to determine what goes best with your dress. Modesty reigns, particularly at a religious ceremony. Your jewelry should accentuate your natural beauty but not overpower you. Be sure to wear any keepsake jewelry that your fiancé has given you. The moment he notices will be one he will treasure for years to come! If you want to add a piece of family jewelry to your ensemble, gently ask the owner if you may borrow the ring, brooch, bracelet, or other item *for the day*. No matter how much you love the piece, return it to the owner on that same day, if you can.

And Don't Forget . . .

Apart from the basics, the bride should have these items with her on her wedding day:

A small bag, commonly called a money bag, to carry your lipstick and compact and to store gifts from your guests. A delicately woven fabric bag or other tiny purse with a string that doesn't call attention to itself works best.

A delicate handkerchief. Lace is considered traditional. Hand-batiked silk could make an exquisite ethnic alternative.

A little money. Even though it's your day, and everyone is ready to be at your disposal, having at least a quarter in case you need to make a call (or you need to instruct someone else to do so) is wise.

THAT ALL-IMPORTANT HAIRSTYLE

Pulling together your wedding-day look includes deciding what to do with your hair. The answer isn't always easy. Common from the North and East clear through to West African nations, both men and women have their hair finely braided and then often coated with a clay mixture of ocher and animal fat in honor of the impending celebration. Sisters in the Caribbean and in Brooklyn, Atlanta, D.C., and Oakland—as well as many points in between—go for braids as well. Braided hair with extensions is a popular style for Black women. When it comes to weddings it can make a dramatic statement—taking the place of the headpiece, if so desired, while being equally magnificent.

Relaxed, curled, and natural hair can also be beautifully styled for a wedding day look. What's most important is that you decide anywhere from a few months to a few weeks in advance of your wedding how you want to wear your hair—and then organize the details so that you can make it happen. Following are some of the most-asked questions concerning hair and your wedding day that should help you in your planning.

How far in advance should you get braiding consultation and make an appointment?

Anywhere between six months to six weeks is best, so you can get exactly the date and time you want as well as ideas on the style you would like to have.

What should you discuss during your consultation?

During an in-depth consultation you should tell

From the Samburu of Kenya to the Yoruba of Nigeria, African couples have braided their hair for their wedding day. Today brides often select braids in lieu of a separate headpiece, like these Goddess Queen N'zinga braids by Annu Prestonia of Khamit Kinks, NYC.

the braider what hairstyle you want to get, if you want it to be elaborate, if accessories will be included, as well as what type of lifestyle you live. An in-person consultation is essential, according to Annu Prestonia, co-owner of Khamit Kinks Salon in New York and Atlanta, so that your stylist can get a clear idea about the condition your hair is in—if it is strong enough or the right length for certain hairstyles. Be sure also to discuss if you will be wearing a headpiece, so that your stylist will design your hair accordingly.

How close to the wedding should you have the braiding done?

Just for the whole surprise of the event, do it the same day or the night before, so it can be as fresh as possible, and the whole mystique will be there for your husband and your guests. If you are getting single braids, which can take many hours to complete, consider having your hair braided the week before but the style you intend to wear put in place at the last possible moment.

What are the most popular braids women get, especially for a wedding?

It depends upon whether you are going to go on a honeymoon immediately following your wedding. If you will probably get your hair wet, Annu recommends tiny cornrows. Single braids hold up for a long time, especially when created with synthetic hair, because they will never come open. Human hair can creep open, allowing the weave to relax and hair to come out. With single braids, women have a wide variety of choices because the braids are as flexible—if not more—than your own hair. Some ornate styles can be created on single braids by weaving existing braids onto the cornrow base.

Some hairstyles will not allow for water, such as Goddess braids and corkscrews. In both cases, the hair may become too heavy and the braids may loosen up with the moisture. Annu adds, however, that many of her clients have not had any difficulty with these braids when they have gotten wet. Since Goddess braids can be pinned onto cornrows, it is possible for sisters to have it all. When they intend to swim, they can simply remove the Goddess piece.

Hair Basics

However you intend to wear your hair, you should heed the basic guidelines that follow to make your decision work best for you.

Secure a hairstylist two to three months in advance of your wedding. If you have a regular hairstylist, talk to him or her at your regularly scheduled appointments so that he or she can start thinking specifically about your wedding in advance. If you don't go to a stylist regularly, shop for one, and at least three months before the wedding have a trial run.

At your preliminary meeting be prepared to discuss the hairstyle you would like to have. The easiest way to determine how you want to wear your hair is to have your headpiece with you, or at least a picture of it. Check out bridal magazines that may have an example of one very close to yours. Nine times out of ten your headpiece will be key in your hairstyle. New York hairstylist Jeffrey Woodley explains, "Your headpiece will probably cover seventy-five percent of your head, so your hairstyle needs to be simple." Simplicity starts with making sure you get a good haircut. Your cut will make all the difference in how easily your style is maintained. A style that requires very little curl and will even look good without curl will be the best for you from your wedding through your honeymoon.

You must confirm your appointment time (and stick to it). Tell the stylist the date and time of the wedding, as well as when you plan to leave for the wedding site. Note that if the wedding is in the morning, before noon, clients usually want to have the prep work done the day before. Be clear when you decide on dates for preparations and styling.

Decide if you want personalized service at home. If you do, be prepared to pay for it. Fees range from hourly rates to a day rate, which you should negotiate at least a month in advance. If you decide not to have your hairstylist on site with you, you will have time to hire someone for the day or enlist the help of a family member or friend.

Decide in advance if any other people will be styled that day—and discuss this with your stylist. This has a lot to do with timing for the day. Everyone has to leave at the same time. If you expect the hairstylist to groom your mother and your bridesmaids, make sure that's discussed *in advance* of the wedding. It's unfair to the stylist to spring additional work on him or her at the last minute. A lot of times people will ask "Can you do my mother," which puts the stylist on the spot. In some cases it may not be a question of money, but instead one of time. The stylist could have prior commitments that are part of his or her business. If you do want the stylist to groom others, plan to pay for it. Discuss the cost in advance.

Help your bridal party to coordinate their hairstyling. Not everyone will need or want your assistance, but it's good to let your attendants know your plans. If anyone is coming from out of town, offer to set up an appointment for her at your salon. Let everyone know what your policy is on hair and makeup for the wedding day itself so that they will be fully aware of their responsibilities.

Selecting Your Headpiece

One of your greatest challenges may be finding the headpiece that best fits your head, reflects your personality, and complements your dress. Designers often present wedding ensembles, complete with headpieces that you may or may not like. Many milliners will and do design special headpieces. (See the Resource Guide for suggestions.) Whichever source you choose, know that all sorts of headgear are available, from traditional Western lace and tulle to African-inspired crowns and head wraps. To select yours, first decide on your dress. If you cannot find your topping at the same place where you get your garment, either bring the dress or a picture of it with you on your search. Take into consideration the color of your garment; the two should either match or be similar in color and tone. Think about how you want to wear your hair as well. Your hairstyle will directly affect what you will be able to fit. Many brides use their headpiece as the one Afrocentric element that they wear. Many a pillbox hat has been transformed into a regal crown. Wrapped fabric in complementary colors can be a beautiful accent for an otherwise Western look. Remember too that if this is not your first wedding, tradition says that you should eliminate the veil entirely.

Designers often make headpieces to match wedding dresses, such as this ensemble from Sesheni. Know that you can have a headpiece made, especially if you want to add a cultural touch to an otherwise Western look.

SKIN SO SOFT

Preparing for marriage includes many steps, including taking special care of your body. Throughout West and Central Africa, women traditionally immerse their bodies in cleansing baths to remove all existing impurities. Their focus is to prepare themselves for their new life. In Mali, for example, female elders are appointed to a bride-to-be and given the responsibility of washing her limbs and face with clear water. From Ghana to Mauritania, it is customary after the formal engagement for women to be hidden from view anywhere from a few days to up to several weeks. In their chamber they are covered with robes and fed rich meals to "fatten them up" for their husbands. The more round and voluptuous they become the more appealing they are in the eyes of their community. During this time, their skin is also cared for by several attendants whose responsibility it is to soften their entire bodies.

According to Georgiana Smith, owner of Skin and Body by Georgiana in New York City, her homeland of Cuba cherishes a soft, supple bride as well. She explains, "In my country, when the man calls for the girl, from there on everything has to be so special. Women start to brush their bodies, to have their bodies really nice and soft." For the past twenty-five years, Georgiana has been helping women either to do it themselves or with her assistance at her salon. Here, she offers suggestions for what you can do to prepare your body for your wedding day—and every special day.

To brush your body smooth, use a bristle brush or one used for fruit. Your goal is to take off all the dead skin, after which you massage your body with mud. Keep the mud on for a couple of hours, so it can tone your skin and your muscles.

Soften your body by massaging coconut or olive oil into your skin nightly.

Soften and purify your face by making chamomile tea and rubbing it into your face. For younger women or those with sensitive skin, boil a white rose and massage it into your skin. What's great about rose tea is that it vaporizes by itself. Women over forty should wash their skin with boiled patchouli herbs, found in health food stores. Essence of patchouli oil is good for older skin.

To keep calm, the day before you marry soak in a juniper bath, adding a few drops of juniper essence (found in health food stores) to your bath. Drinking chamomile tea will also relieve your tension.

Of course, many beauty products are available today that are designed to soften and purify all types of skin.

GETTING MADE UP

The way you feel is the most important thing on your wedding day. The way you look should be a reflection of your inner beauty, which means that you should appear natural, even if you are having a fancy evening affair. To make sure that your makeup turns out right, consider these points.

If you are doing your own makeup, a natural look is most appropriate. Your makeup shouldn't be overdone or severe. Remember you will be taking pictures. If your makeup is too heavy or unlike you, the photographs will only magnify the makeup more. When it comes to shades to choose, New York–based makeup artist Roxanna Floyd recommends earth tones for eyes, cheeks, and lips—soft pink shades, pink browns, and soft burgundies. Waterproof mascara and eyeliner are musts; they won't run if you cry! Matte or long-lasting lipstick won't be kissed off. Oil-controlling powder cuts down the shine.

To keep fresh all day, have your maid of honor or bridesmaid carry your lipstick and compact powder for quick touch-ups.

Choosing a Makeup Artist

When using a professional makeup artist's services for your wedding day, you should first know his or her work or at least have seen the work in person, on another bride, or in pictures.

Have a meeting in advance to discuss the look you would like to have. At that meeting, discuss in detail the number of people the makeup artist will be seeing. Just as in the hairstyling, don't spring any surprises on him or her. Do not change that number on the day of the wedding.

The price of a makeup artist varies depending upon the number of people or hours involved. Many makeup artists charge per person for weddings. The average rate in 1992 ran from twenty-five to seventy-five dollars per person. The rate can also change depending upon the reputation, popularity, and availability of the makeup artist you are considering.

If you are the only person being made up, the process normally takes about an hour—that is if you stay put during the entire period, which many brides do not! If you are asking your makeup artist to work with many people, find out exactly how long it will take. No matter what, start at least two to three hours ahead of time. Remember, time flies!

CHAPTER 8

CEREMONIAL NOTES

On a beautiful spring afternoon at the Pratt Mansion in Manhattan in 1992, Heather Bond and Samuel C. Bryant, Jr., joined hands in marriage. The very moment their guests entered the majestic old home, they experienced the warmest welcome. One of the most delightful aspects of their wedding was the variety of music that marked each step of their big day. It began with the sweet sounds of a duet—guitarist and flutist—who were soon accompanied by a pianist. The processional music was not Wagner's traditional "Bridal Chorus" from Lohengrin, but instead an original composition by Heather's father, designed to illustrate their love. A male soloist serenaded the two during the ceremony, with both contemporary and original music. By reception time a five-piece band had quietly taken its place and begun to play soft jazz, the perfect backdrop for comfortable dinner conversation. After dessert a pair of drummers challenged each other to an African beat that led to a booming crescendo. As the finale, the groom's mother garlanded Heather and Sam with one vibrant strip of *kente* cloth, and they jumped together over a ribbon-draped broom.

Records dating back to slavery indicate the importance of music and dance at our wedding celebrations. Whether the beat was one of drums with participants honoring the couple, of fiddles with group square dances, or, as one account mentions, "The Virginia Reel," we have long enjoyed good entertainment during this sacred rite of passage.

How will *you* celebrate your union? Make sure that you plan every aspect of the event carefully. Take comfort in knowing that there is no *one* proper wedding ceremony. Among Christians there are innumerable variations on the way that couples marry, primarily because there is no specific agenda for the ritual in the Bible. In the Christian community alone, there are Catholics, Presbyterians, United Methodist, African Methodist Episcopal, Baptist, Jehovah's Witnesses, and many more faiths, each having variations on marriage rites. In the Black community, there are several other religious paths that are common, including Muslim, Judaism, Yoruba, and Khamitic. Also growing in popularity are Eastern paths, including Buddhism and

Siddha Yoga. Your religious or spiritual background will usually determine the basis for your service, although you may incorporate your own unique additions to highlight your love and devotion to one another.

Take a moment and reminisce about weddings that you have attended or in which you participated that were especially moving. What was it about the ceremony that was so special? Was it the intimacy of the environment? The background and solo music? The words of the officiate? The exchange of vows? The decor? Quite often it's the combination of everything that brings a wedding to life and envelopes the entire congregation with joy.

Now try to imagine your own wedding and what you feel is essential to the ceremony—an event that can be as short as fifteen minutes or longer than an hour. Remember to consider where you intend to marry, who will stand up with you, and what time of day you expect your wedding to be. Envision your ideal at first, and then work back from that. Characteristically it is the reception that eats up a tremendous amount of money and planning, yet the wedding itself can run up costs as well. The many elements that go into making a grand and elegant affair may include flowers and other decorations, an organist, a soloist, a choir, as well as all of the attire for the wedding party.

TYPES OF SERVICES

Whether you get married in a spiritual home, in a hall, or at home, it is important to check with your wedding officiate to learn about what basic service he or she normally follows. (If you haven't already found a minister or other member of the clergy to marry you, do so right away. Ask family members and friends for referrals. Make sure the person you choose is licensed by your state, because it will be his or her signature on your license, along with your witness—usually the best man—that legalizes your marriage.) The examples here will give you a good idea of the order of service for several types of ceremonies.

Protestant

Prelude
Solo (or special selection)
Processional
Call to worship
Hymn (or special selection)

Charge (minister's words describing the nature of a Christian marriage)

Declaration of Intent (the bride and groom respond to minister's questions about their commitment. When applicable, the bride is given away.)

Reading of Scriptures

Homily

Exchange of vows

Exchange of rings

Unity (Christ) candle

Pronouncement of marriage

Prayer for the couple

The Lord's Prayer

Benediction

Recessional

Postlude

Roman Catholic

The preparation rites (informal welcome of the congregation and any directions regarding the liturgy)

Welcome of bride and groom by presiding priest

Processional

Opening prayer for liturgy

The first reading

Silence

Hallelujah chorus

The Gospel reading

The rite of marriage

Questions and answers

Exchange of vows

Exchange of rings

Prayer

The intercessory prayer of the faithful

Preparation of the table

Solo (optional)

Prayer

Liturgy of the Eucharist

The communion

The conclusion
Solo (optional)
Recessional

◆

FOR CATHOLICS ONLY

There are a few additional details you should know for a Catholic wedding:

◆ *When both of you are Catholic, marriage banns must be announced three times. This can happen during Mass on Sundays or holy days or in writing in the calendar of each of the couple's parishes.*

◆ *When yours is an interfaith marriage, check with your priest to determine if an interfaith ceremony will be allowed.*

◆ *If either of you has been divorced, you will need to get a church-sanctioned annulment in order to remarry.*

◆ *To have the most traditional of Catholic ceremonies, plan a Nuptial Mass, which occurs at high noon.*

◆ *Take note that the father of the bride does* not *give the bride away. Instead there is a joining of families. (Many non-Catholic families today take offense at the notion of the father of the bride or anyone else actually "giving the bride away," because, they say, the practice describes her as property. They find greater comfort in either having both parents say that they stand up with the bride, support her, and so forth. In some cases, couples eliminate this element of the service completely.)*

◆ *Traditional vows are required with only slight variations, which must be approved by your priest.*

◆ *It is best not to have a wedding on Sundays or holy days or after six o'clock in the evening on Saturday.*

◆

Ausar Auset

(based on ancestral African Khamitic tradition)

Purification of the grounds
Procession of the Shekhem Ur Shekhem and the priesthood
Procession of the wedding couple escorted by priestesses

Libation (traditional African rite, paying homage to ancestors)

Opening comments by Shekhem Ur Shekhem

Invocation

Summoning of the divine aspects of the Supreme Being (deities) for purifying, energizing, and counseling of the couple

Deity (e.g., Sebek, deity who opens the way)

Deity (e.g., Auset, deity of nurturing and devotion)

Mantra (e.g., Gouri, of enduring and unselfish love)

Address to the couple (by married members of the society)

Exchange of vows

Exchange of rings

Dedication and counsel (from family and friends)

Recessional

Military Ceremony

A growing number of African Americans are enlisting in the U.S. military. If you or your intended is enlisted or is in the Reserves, there are special provisions of the wedding ceremony designed to pay tribute to your position and service.

◆ Traditionally, military services are held at military chapels, although this is not a requirement. For couples overseas, this makes getting married easier and more like home!

◆ Appropriate military attire for the groom and any military attendants is expected. A bride in the military can wear a traditional wedding gown or her military dress uniform.

◆ Boutonnieres are not considered appropriate.

◆ Guests who are not in the military can wear appropriate formal attire.

Civil Ceremony

We've all heard of couples who stood in line at City Hall and were married a couple of hours later. A civil ceremony is not just a wedding held at City Hall or a judge's chambers. Basically it is any nonreligious ceremony that is held outside of a spiritual center. The signing of the marriage certificate in the presence of a witness is the only legal requirement; the couple and/or the officiate can design the ceremony to their preference. Many couples choose a civil service if they want to marry right away and cannot afford a full-blown wedding and reception. Others don't have a spiritual home or choose not to get married in a religious context. Still others are marrying for the second or third time and find this means of marrying easier to manage. If you decide on a civil ceremony, you can still have a reception, large or small.

A Double Wedding

On occasion couples still do marry two at a time. Most often the double ceremony occurs when family members get engaged close to one another. Because a wedding can be a big expense, this provides a more economical solution. If you choose to marry in union with a family member or close friend, take great care in mapping out all of the details, including the wording on your invitation, and put the entire plan in writing. For the ceremony itself, decide who will enter the site first and what the order of the program will be. When in doubt about order, defer to the more senior bride.

Once you determine exactly what your program will entail, you will need to fill in all of the particulars. Use one of the samples just described as a base, unless you already have your own. Your wedding consultant or coordinator can be helpful here, too.

◆

TRADITIONAL YORUBA COURTING AND CEREMONY

Among the Yoruba of Nigeria, the wedding ceremony represents a unique sharing of gifts and love. The union begins at odudo, *when the suitor's family comes to state their son's interest in "picking the rose," or marrying the young woman, and ends in a joyous day. That day is organized by an older woman who offers proper counseling and oversees planning for all of the festivities.*

Before the actual wedding ceremony two young women are sent to the groom instead of his fiancée (much like Eddie Murphy showed in his comedy, Coming to America). *The groom-to-be shakes his head as they approach, sending them away. When the third woman arrives—his true bride, who is dressed in hand-loomed* asooke *fabric and anklets called* odoodo—*the music changes. The oldest woman in the gathering blesses the couple with gin. The husband is introduced and he prostrates himself. Everyone then starts to hit him, telling him that he must take great care of the bride. The bride then accepts her gifts, kisses her husband, and chooses the white Bible above all other keepsakes. Her choice places the Bible in the highest place, showing that she values her spiritual life above material goods. Family members offer encouragement, and there is much fanfare that can make a wedding celebration last as long as five hours or into the night.*

◆

THE ROLES OF YOUR BRIDAL PARTY MEMBERS

Key members of your bridal party will have specific responsibilities that will help to keep your wedding running smoothly. If you are having a moderate to large-size wedding (anywhere from one hundred to four hundred guests), you should have ample assistance right in your wedding party. Their responsibilities at typical Western weddings are as follows:

The maid of honor helps to keep all logistical details and personal needs organized for the bride from the beginning of the planning through to the end of the wedding day. This includes keeping in touch with the best man to coordinate arrival at the church, making sure that the limousine or other means of transportation is waiting for the bride and her attendants when it's time to leave for the ceremony site, *and* that the getaway transportation is waiting after the reception. She must also make sure that all attendants have their bouquets and boutonnieres, and that mothers have their corsages. At the ceremony she will be in charge of holding the bride's bouquet before the sharing of the rings—and returning it before their exit as husband and wife. In some cases she may be responsible for holding the wedding rings before the ceremony.

The bridesmaids are mainly responsible for being present on time to prepare for the wedding. They should also mingle with guests at the reception.

The best man assists the groom in getting dressed and delivers him to the ceremony site on time. He should reconfirm transportation for all of the male members of the wedding party. Serving as primary witness to the great union, he also sometimes is the guardian of the rings prior to the ceremony. He makes sure that the clergy member and the ceremony site receive proper fees. The best man makes the first toast at a traditional reception. He signs the marriage certificate, thus making the union legal.

The groomsmen serve double duty at the ceremony site, escorting guests to their seats while also standing up for the groom during the program. At the reception, they should mingle with guests.

Ushers are usually men who are asked to assist in showing guests to their seats. They may also be asked to unroll the white carpet on which the bride, her father, and the flower girl walk during the processional. After the recessional they assist in leading guests to the next center of activity, usually the receiving line or departure for the reception site. You should have one usher for every fifty guests. (Sometimes groomsmen are referred to as ushers as well.)

Others can be asked to handle additional needs. For instance an aunt, cousin, or close family friend may be assigned to the guest book, making sure that everyone signs it as he or she exits the ceremony or reception area.

Teenage family members can help you with reception seating by informing guests of their table assignments and handing out place cards if they are not already on the tables.

A family friend, your family housekeeper, or a hired guard should be asked to stay at each of your family homes on your wedding day. Although no one wants to think about vandalism, if many of the wedding gifts are being temporarily stored at one of your homes, it becomes a prime target. There is probably someone who would feel honored to take on this role. If not, hire a professional. This goes even for couples who marry away from home. If you or your parents are going to be away for a weekend or longer and folks know why, stepped up security at your home or through your neighborhood watch is advisable.

Order of Procession

Again, if you are having a religious ceremony, you must check with your officiate regarding all aspects of the service, including order. A basic rule of thumb in the Christian tradition is: Beginning with the tallest bridesmaid, each female should enter the wedding site individually and walk to the altar, filling in the space from the outside in. The maid of honor should come right before the ring bearer. After the ring bearer, the ushers roll out the white carpet. The flower girl comes right before the bride and her father or chosen escort, covering the carpet with flower petals. The groom, his best man, and the ushers should be in place before the processional begins.

THE WORDS TO SAY IT: YOUR VOWS

Every minister interviewed for this book spoke of the exchange of vows as the single most significant moment in a wedding. It is then, they explained, that a couple should be speaking from their hearts the most profound truth about their commitment one to the other—whether they speak the particular words of their spiritual center or they use their own.

To write your own vows can be a joy of exploration in and of itself. If you want to craft your own pledge, again go to your book and begin to write out key words and phrases that capture your feelings for each other. Think back on your relationship, on moments when your partner's commitment to you was most clear. How did it make you feel? What qualities do you feel are necessary to make your marriage last?

Poet and director of the Afro-American Studies Resource Center at Howard University E. Ethelbert Miller and his wife, Denise King Miller, an administrator for the American Psychological Association, wrote their own vows, which were actually modifications of traditional Christian vows. At their wedding in Washington, D.C., in 1982, the sequence went as follows:

MINISTER: Do you, Ethelbert, take Denise to be the wife of your days, to love and to cherish, to honor and to comfort, in sorrow or in joy, in hardship or in ease, to have and to hold from this day forth?

ETHELBERT: I do.

MINISTER: What pledge do you offer in token of these vows?

ETHELBERT: This ring.

MINISTER: Ethelbert, as you place this ring, symbol of your commitment in marriage, on the third finger of Denise's left hand, repeat after me: *With this ring I wed you and pledge my faithful love. I take you as my wife and pledge to share my life openly with you, to speak the truth to you in love. I promise to honor and tenderly care for you, to cherish and encourage your fulfillment as an individual through all the changes of our lives.*

The same was then repeated by Denise.

As you search for the right words to express your love, you may also want to refer to spiritual prose to help you along. Select passages from the Bible, especially from Psalms, for guidance. Look in the Holy Koran and even in Kahlil Gibran's, *The Prophet.* One sister, Barbara Eklof, wrote a book, *With These Words . . . I Thee Wed,* that includes many suggestions, from the religious to the secular. Here's a great choice:

I come to you freely, clear of thought, willingly.
Before, my strength was the strength of one—
today, my strength is of much more than two.

You have captured my mind and soul, and I here
commit them to our union. From this hour, may we

surrender to one another completely—rejoicing
in the power of our new partnership, secure in
our own identities, and certain in our bond.

We will search for the stars as we walk together
on the earth. Drawing on the strength that comes
with true love, we will content ourselves with
both the horizons ahead of us and the pathways at
our feet. This I, (name), pledge to you,
(partner's name), from this day forward.

◆

OTHER SPECIAL TOUCHES

In a nonsecular ceremony as well as within many religious services, you do have the freedom to bring in a number of your own personal touches to personalize your wedding ceremony. Among the popular choices are:
◆ write poetry for each other and read it during the ceremony or simply include it in the program
◆ sing a duet or to each other
◆ surprise your guests and hire a popular singer to serenade the two of you
◆ organize a reading from a sensitive Black leader or poet's work, such as Dr. Martin Luther King, Jr., Sonia Sanchez, Nikki Giovanni, Haki Madhubuti, E. Ethelbert Miller

◆

THE PERFECT ACCOMPANIMENT

When it comes to your wedding music, the choices may seem endless. Since you have to make some musical decisions, start with the basics. Ask yourselves what kind of music you both like. What about your parents? Your older and younger relatives and friends? Even though this is your big day, it's important to consider the entire group when making music decisions. Consider it a matter of respect.

As you plan the music for your wedding, think about the whole event: processional, recessional, and reception. Review the traditional types of wedding music and

determine your taste. If you are having a religious ceremony, be sure to check with your wedding officiate to
determine whether your choices are appropriate. Couples
often have an organist or pianist as well as a soloist perform at the ceremony, before the processional, and at key
junctures during the ceremony. One of the sweetest ways
to share your love with your guests is to select heartfelt
instrumentals and lyrics that celebrate your union.

A great way of ensuring everyone's ease at your
reception is to pace the music. During the dinner hour
have soft background music playing. After dessert, dance
music can begin. Include a few oldies for senior family
members to enjoy.

Before the Ceremony

The music you select for this segment depends
largely on where your wedding is held. If it's in a spiritual
center, you're likely to have certain restrictions regarding
music. Many Christian churches, for instance, ask that
music be either spiritual or instrumental. Within the spiritual category, there is a wide selection of hymns from
which to choose, varying from standards to gospel and spiritual favorites. In the A.M.E. (African Methodist Episcopal) and Baptist churches, the music is often infused with
deep soulfulness that could be a perfect entree into a
solemn but joyous event. Organ prelude ideas include:

"Jesu, Joy of Man's Desiring" by J. S. Bach;

"Adagio (sonata #2)" by Felix Mendelssohn;

"Now Thank We All Our God" by Sigfrid Karg-
Elert; and

"Saviour, Like a Shepherd Lead Us," by William
Bradbury.

Processional Music

Co-workers and friends alike may have been hum-
ming the classic processional march to you for weeks.

**I NOW PRONOUNCE
YOU. . .**
What marks a couple
actually married varies
widely. We know that
African slaves and their
descendants considered
their union tied after they
jumped over a broom.
Among the Asante in
Ghana the turning point
comes with the acceptance
of gifts from the groom's
family by the bride's
family. The final act that
declared a couple married
among the Kgatla of South
Africa back in the early
1900s was quite dramatic.
Sacred cattle, called
bogadi, were slaughtered
especially for wedding
ceremonies. Only after the
peritoneum (a membrane
found in the cavity of the
abdomen) of the cow was
cut in two and hung around
the necks of the couple
were they considered
married. As the Kgatla
began to feel the influence
of Western trends, the
bogadi continued to be
slaughtered but the
peritoneum was offered
symbolically rather than
draped across their
shoulders.

Even so, you don't have to walk to "The Wedding March" by Richard Wagner, that is, "Here Comes the Bride." If you want to, that's another story! What's most important about processional music is that the bride and her attendants (in their full wedding raiment) can comfortably walk to its beat. Music that is too fast-paced or loud can prove disruptive as the bride—even with the help of her father—makes her way toward her groom. Perhaps that's why one sister enlisted the classical violin of a close friend for her long walk down more than a dozen winding steps at her outdoor wedding in 1992. That's not to say that only harps, violins, or soft organ music is appropriate. The constant beat of the *kalimba* brought dancer Sheryl Pollard to her husband, dancer Dwayne Thomas in 1992, and she had absolutely no trouble taking each step in her Ghanaian-inspired wrap gown. Two traditional classics: "The Trumpet Voluntary" arranged by Henry Purcell; and "Jesu, Joy of Man's Desiring" by Bach.

During the Ceremony

Music can fill a wedding ceremony with joy and fond memories. To make that happen throughout your ceremony takes careful planning *and* screening of potential soloists and musicians. If you are marrying in a church, and you are familiar with and like the choir, find out if the choir will be available to sing at your wedding. A smaller, select group of choir members might be even more fitting for the occasion. Even if you marry away from your church home, you may be able to have them come to you. If you go this route, provide them with sheet music of the selections you would like to have performed and listen to their rendering well in advance of your big day. Be sure to discuss fees with them, and be prepared to pay on the day of your wedding. For those of you from other faiths, check with your spiritual officiate regarding available musicians.

Another musical option is to hire outside musicians and singers. Start looking for them at least four months in advance of your wedding if you can. Ask for referrals from family, friends, and business associates first. You can also contact local Black organizations who often organize big events. Your local Black newspaper society editor is bound to have ideas. Whomever you choose, be sure to listen to the musicians perform and approve the way that they perform your selections. Although Black folks love heart-filled, improvised music, you need to agree with your artists on exactly how they intend to perform on your day—reminding them of where the attention must be—on the two of you! Some traditional ideas:

"A Wedding Song" by William Stookey

"Ave Maria" by Bach, Charles-François Gounod, or Franz Schubert

"Because" by Schubert

"Be Thou With Me" by Bach

"Eternal Life" (words of St. Francis of Assisi) by Dungan

"I Love You Truly" by Carrie Bond

"Oh Perfect Love" by Barney

"Oh Promise Me" by Reginald De Koven, Opus 50

"The Lord's Prayer" by Malotte

"The Bridal Chorus" by Richard Wagner

Recessional Music

Make it upbeat! Check with your officiate to see if particular music is recommended. If you have no limitations, just search for the most joyous instrumental that you and your fiancé like. Suggestions: "Psalm 118" ("The Lord is my lofty crag, my fortress, my champion, my God, my rock in whom I find shelter") by Benedetto Marcello; "The Wedding March" by Mendelssohn from *A Midsummer Night's Dream*.

For secular music recommendations that may work for your wedding ceremony as well as your reception, see Chapter 9.

◆

FEES FOR CEREMONIAL MUSIC

Any couple getting married in a spiritual home should consult with the officiate or minister about the music before making a final selection. The following are general guidelines, based on 1992 figures, for payment for participants in your service. Keep them in mind even when your money gets tight. As one church music director explained, even when couples spend upwards of ten thousand dollars on a wedding, they sometimes offer no compensation or a terribly low amount, primarily because there is no set rate. The fee is often considered a contribution or gift.

◆ *Soloists should be paid fifty dollars or more, depending upon experience. Some professionals get as much as five hundred dollars for a wedding.*

◆ *Offer an organist at least one hundred dollars. A highly qualified musician should be given more. At some churches fee schedules are written into the contracts already. That amount includes one rehearsal and the wedding itself. Additional rehearsals can, of course, be arranged if needed. Even if the organist is paid through a contractual agreement with the church, the couple should offer to pay the organist a separate fee.*

◆

CHAPTER 9

THE PERFECT SETTING

Where a couple was going to get married rarely entered into the minds of our ancestors in the Motherland or even in the Old South. The ceremony and reception occurred at home, on family land. In certain African countries, the community square became the site for festivities. Tales from slave narratives describe exuberant celebrations on plantations, either near the slave quarters or on the master's property. Because the wedding marked a time of great celebration and sharing, it was only natural for all of the family members and friends nearby to pay tribute to the union by joining in the festivities.

Today weddings occur just about anywhere and in any way. A couple's limitations are literally based on their imaginations—and the family wallet! Because the capacity of the location represents a finite number while the expense can seem to be endless, your decision about choosing the perfect setting for your wedding ceremony and reception needs to happen early on. You now have a good sense of the logistics of a wedding ceremony, wherever it may be held. In addition to actually settling on your wedding and reception location, you will need to finalize the flowers and decorations, table arrangements and other logistical details, entertainment, and transportation in order to complete your wedding day in impeccable style.

CHOOSING A LOCATION

Some brides can think of no better place to marry than their spiritual home. It's possible to have a reception there as well if there is an adjoining facility that can accommodate you and your guests. As you secure your agreement, go over all of the details, including whether or not alcohol and dancing are allowed. Also, determine if there are enough chairs, tables, linens, and flatware for your needs.

Whether you are having a reception for several hundred or an intimate group of fifty or so, a catering facility can serve your needs. They range from grand establishments with many halls in one location to individual buildings in remote areas with breathtaking landscapes. As you shop, look for a facility that specializes in weddings.

Ask for references from friends and family, and also check your local newspaper's wedding supplement for advertisements describing appealing sites. Any business that specializes in weddings will most likely be busiest on Saturdays from May to October. If your wedding is scheduled during that period, do your best to secure a location at least a year in advance.

Especially when couples have invited many guests from out-of-town they consider booking a hotel for their wedding reception. The benefits are that all services are available at the one facility—from food and beverages to lodging. Package deals can be organized for use of a grand hall for the wedding and/or reception as well as smaller rooms for special meals that you may want to host for your guests during their stay. The down side is that many hotels will not allow you to reserve space more than six months in advance. Of course, a hotel can also be used simply as a base, with your reception elsewhere.

Wedding Site Alternatives

Consider these alternatives, which can double as reception sites:

Go alfresco at a public facility, such as a botanical garden, a beach, a campground, a park, or a fountain. Be sure to check with the proper officials at least two months in advance to secure permits and to rent chairs. If the location and the time

◆

TRIMMING THE PRICE

Throwing a big party for your wedding doesn't have to be prohibitive if you think creatively. You can host your affair at your favorite establishment if you plan it properly, according to Jim Fornaro, vice president of sales for Martin's, Inc., a catering facility in Maryland. Here are a few tips on how to cut costs:

◆ *Get married on any day other than Saturday. Friday nights, Sundays, the weekday before a major holiday (such as the Monday before fourth of July, the Wednesday before Thanksgiving, Memorial Day Monday, Labor Day Monday) are likely to be discounted.*

◆ *Opt to marry during the off months of January, February, July, or August.*

◆ *Book your location within two months of the date. Although not recommended by rental facilities because you run the risk of finding no free space, last-minute reservations can gain you a discount from 10 to 20 percent off the base price.*

◆

are prime, check further in advance. The fee is usually nominal. If your event is out-of-doors, check for a gazebo or other enclosure that might be accessible in case of rain. If none is available, find out if you can bring a rented tent, tables, and chairs onto the property.

All sorts of boats can be hired, either for sailing (which can be quite costly due to insurance and staffing requirements) or at dock.

Don't forget your own backyard (or that of your parents!). The price is right, plus it's traditional, as mentioned earlier, in many African communities for the wedding to be held at home in the company of those who nurtured you.

Consider a foreign land with an opulent backdrop in the Caribbean or on African shores.

Double-checking Details

Once you have a good idea of where you want your event to be, you will need to follow a few basic steps to put your plan into place. Wherever you decide to marry, you must fine-tune all the details with the catering director or other person in charge. The number of people you are hosting and the way in which your meal will be presented (buffet, sit-down, and so forth) will determine your needs.

Make an appointment to meet with a representative in person.

Take a tour of the facility to see what types of accommodations they have to offer. Be sure to check the appearance and suitability of the bridal suite, if there is one, and the rest of the rooms to make sure that they are clean.

Discuss your specific needs.

This includes the date, time, and location of the wedding, the preferred time of the reception, the number of guests, the type of food you would like to serve, and the amount of money you would like to spend.

Review any dietary needs early on.

This ensures that appropriate food will be available on your wedding day. (See Chapter 10 for details.) Most facilities can prepare extra meals for people with special diets, such as vegetarian, diabetic, or salt free.

Find out if the facility can accommodate you and your guests.

Do they have enough chairs and tables? Where will they be placed? Create a seating chart for all of your guests, including the bridal party. Check off where everyone will be placed if you are having a sit-down affair, so that place cards can be written for each person. Make sure that a table is earmarked for place cards. Hostesses can be appointed to hand them out as guests arrive.

Your bridal party can be seated together at a long, rectangular table that faces your guests, or at a round table in the center of the room. On either side can be tables for parents and honored guests. Throughout the space can be seating for the rest of your guests. In the case of an informal affair, do make sure that there are tables and chairs for any elders who are in attendance. You will make these detailed plans after you secure your location, but it's good to ask about the possibilities and review the space in advance.

Check to see how the location works with the entertainment.

Find out if you can bring your own live or recorded music. Double-check to determine where your entertainment can be set up. If you are having live musicians or a D.J., you will need seating as well as microphones. Determine if proper wiring is available for any electrical equipment. If your affair is outside, make sure your entertainment knows that, so that they can bring the requisite equipment.

Ask about who handles the decorations.

In many instances, your reception facility will be able to provide basic decorations, including tablecloths in white or other colors. Any place cards, flowers, centerpieces, or other specialized items that you want to use to adorn your reception space will need to be put in place *in advance* of your guests' arrivals. Find out if you can have someone do the actual placement or if a member of the staff there will handle it. If the establishment handles the placement, appoint someone you trust to come to the site *before* you and your guests arrive to make sure everything is in order.

If you like the location, request that a hold be placed on your chosen date.

Then go home and think about it. Don't feel pressured to give a deposit at that initial meeting.

Verify the logistics.

Make sure that your guests can comfortably reach your reception site from the wedding at the agreed-upon time.

Find out what the terms of payment are.

Many facilities these days allow couples to pay in several ways, either with a deposit followed by two payments, or installments over time that are more comfortable for your budget.

Once you are sure about your reception location, secure the date with the full deposit.

LET THERE BE FLOWERS!

Beginning with the floral adornment of the wedding party and the ceremony site on to the reception, celebratory flowers are key to a festive wedding ceremony. They are also expensive and must be figured into your initial wedding budget, so that you can keep a handle on your costs. You have several options when it comes to incorporating flowers into your wedding, from hiring a florist to design bouquets for the entire wedding party, the ceremony site, and the reception site, to doing some or all of it yourself. To determine just how you want to use flowers in your wedding, Saundra Parks, owner of The Daily Blossom in New York City, offers the following guidelines

What Kinds and How Many?

Most couples today *do* incorporate flowers into their wedding ceremony and reception. If you are planning to use them during your celebration, take time to consider what you like, what you need, and how much it all costs. It's easiest to select the bridal bouquet first, which should be a collection of your favorite flowers, designed to reflect the style and proportion of your gown. Especially if you are wearing traditional African clothing, you should consider carefully the flowers that will best complement the colors and style of your outfit. There are several bouquet styles you may select from, from the absolutely lavish to the most simple and elegant. The basics are as follows:

◆ **Arm bouquet.** Long-stemmed flowers that are hand-tied or French-braided with ribbon. They are carried cradled in the arm.

◆ **Cascade.** Flowers, ivy, and other greenery that flow vertically and drape downward from the bouquet and extend outward from the center.

◆ **Nosegay or Posy.** Tightly designed, compact collections of flowers that are often tied with a decorative ribbon and carried in the hand.

The types of flowers that brides choose vary depending upon taste. Yet there are a few longtime favorites. Many brides are still selecting roses as their first choice because they offer such a romantic, traditional appeal as well as a refreshing aroma.

Other flowers such as gardenias, stephanotis, georgiana orchid, and lily of the valley are popular thanks to their enchanting fragrances.

For the groom.

Normally the bride is responsible for selecting all of the flowers, although the groom and his family are customarily asked to absorb part of the bill. Brides normally select one flower out of their bouquet and have it made into a boutonniere. Wouldn't it be better if you both sat down to discuss your floral selections? If that doesn't happen, at least the bride should double-check with the groom on his preferences for his own boutonniere. When it comes to your man, be just as thoughtful about his boutonniere as you were about your bouquet. The best complement would be a sleek miniature replica of the bridal bouquet that appears to be almost "plucked" out of it, finished off with a touch of ivy.

For the bridesmaids.

A simplified version of the bride's bouquet is appropriate, although some brides choose to add color to their bridesmaids' bouquets, leaving their own white. The arrangement can be much simpler, based on just one flower from the bride's bouquet when budgets are tight.

For the groomsmen, ushers, and fathers.

A miniature replica of the bridesmaids' bouquet will suit them just fine, as will a single flower chosen from the bridal bouquet or a simple carnation.

For the mothers.

An elegant corsage is appropriate for both mothers, one that complements the bride's and bridesmaids' with a bit more sophistication. A simpler corsage would be perfect for a grandmother.

For honored guests.

A simple corsage for the women and boutonniere for the men (especially the ushers) that complement the wedding party colors.

For the flower girl.

A basket of flowers or flower petals used to be the standard for flower girls, who would scatter them along the white carpet leading to the altar in anticipation of the bride. (That's what I did when my cousin Patricia Johnson married George Branch back in 1968.) Today the flower girl often carries a beautiful basket with a floral display in it (not meant to be scattered) or a small bouquet of her own. Make sure your florist knows the size of your flower girl, so that the basket isn't overwhelming or too heavy.

Choosing Colors

When it comes to color, white is still the most popular, and is considered the most traditional, formal, and classic flower of all. What's great about white bouquets is that many white wedding favorites are available year-round. All-white bouquets can be accessorized with tiny strands of pearls, woven in and out of the flowers or dangling softly from the arrangement. Also beautifully complementary are touches of gilded leaves and branches.

Many brides prefer to offset their all-white gowns with shades of pastels. Soft and romantic with a garden effect, they are created with mixed palettes of champagne, peach, salmon, and lavender with tucks of ivy lacing the arrangement.

Brides also request flowers with bursts of color, particularly rich jewel tones and vibrant brights. From hot reds to yellows, oranges to purples and magentas, dramatic bouquets can be designed to make bold, exciting, yet sophisticated color statements. This approach also lends itself to an Afrocentric feeling. When you're wearing a bold African or Caribbean print or a traditional West African *bubah*, you need something other than a delicate white bouquet to finish off your look. Tropicals from the Caribbean—anthuriums, calla lilies, birds of paradise, tropical green foliage accented with *kente* cloth, mud cloth, braided raffia, tufted African beads, lotus pods gilded with gold or braided ribbon in brilliant colors—are the perfect solution for an African-American ceremony.

Selecting a Florist

How much time you have, how big your budget is, and how creative you and your bridal party are will determine how you go about choosing flowers for your wedding. If you decide to use a florist, be sure to select a reputable one who can create the arrangements that you want. Consult friends, relatives, and co-workers for recommendations, and interview two or more florists before settling on the best one for *your* wedding and *your* budget. Ask to see the florist's work by reviewing wedding albums of prior weddings, or ask to take a peek at arrangements for upcoming weddings.

Have a formal consultation with the florist you select, during which you discuss your personal flowers, bridal party flowers, reception and church arrangements. Bring a photo or detailed sketch of your wedding dress and fabric swatches for the bridesmaids to match flowers with your clothing. Order a sample arrangement to see if you like the interpretive style that the florist uses. You may order samples from your two or three favorite florists, and let the best work be the deciding factor on whom you will choose.

Discuss your budget with the florist at the outset. Request a detailed proposal confirming all floral themes, colors, and costs as agreed. Secure your florist as far in advance as possible, preferably six months to a year, particularly if you have selected a popular company.

Delightfully Affordable Floral Ideas

◆ Select seasonal flowers. They will be in abundance and will cost less.

◆ Tie bunches of flowers, such as carnations and baby's breath, together in one "mass," and wrap with gorgeous French ribbon or raffia to make an impressive and bold statement. Accessorize with tulle or cultural fabric for added elegance.

◆ Tie or French braid one or two stems of flowers with ivy or vine for a slender bouquet.

◆ Put your flowers on double duty, using those that were in the church or at your ceremony site at your reception.

◆ Opt for more affordable—and equally opulent—flowering plants for the reception area.

◆ Branches in season provide dramatic impact for a small percentage of the cost of cut flowers. In the springtime cherry blossoms, dogwood, and lilac are beautiful when displayed in a huge glass vase for both the ceremony and the reception.

◆ Hold your wedding during the off-season to defray costs. Keep in mind that flowers are more costly during holidays such as Christmas, Valentine's Day, and Mother's Day.

◆ Especially if you have an evening wedding, provide your bridesmaids with candles instead of flowers to carry down the aisle.

◆ Use fresh or silk bouquets for your bridesmaids that can be recycled as reception-table arrangements. Make sure that there are containers in which they can stand comfortably. If the flowers are fresh, have them collected and delivered to the reception site immediately following the wedding so that they don't get crushed.

CREATING THE IDEAL AMBIENCE

Less emphasis was placed on decorating the environment for a wedding than on ornamenting the actual couple in traditional African communities. Depending upon where

◆

KEEPING FLOWERS FRESH

You must take great care when handling flowers. By following a few basic precautions, whether you are working with a florist or on your own, your floral bouquets and table arrangements will stay beautiful the whole day through!

◆ *Have flowers delivered to your home and ceremony site two hours before your wedding.*

◆ *Request that they be delivered in a cellophane-wrapped box, well-misted for freshness.*

◆ *Be sure to keep flowers away from extreme heat or cold.*

◆ *No matter how beautiful flowers may look, don't handle the flowers at all—especially the blooms—as they bruise easily.*

◆ *Keep all loose flowers and bouquets in water until use.*

◆ *Offer table arrangements to your guests after the reception, so that they can enjoy them while they last!*

◆

couples lived, flowers might have been in abundance or their backdrop might have been the sparse landscape of the desert plain. The intricacy of the couple's costumes, from their elaborate dress to their ornate jewelry, didn't call for any greater punctuation than the natural glow of the couple themselves.

Borrowing from European and Christian customs, most Americans have incorporated quite detailed external decoration into wedding day events. They extend from flowers to religious symbols, family emblems, table decorations, and more. What's exciting about decorations today, especially for couples seeking to include Afrocentric touches, is that they can be added to the wedding environment with great care and subtlety to make a vibrant and unique statement without seeming too fussy.

Beautifying Your Wedding Site

No matter where you hold your wedding, you will want to embellish it with special adornments on your wedding day. The choices are as vast as your pocketbook—which means that you should think carefully about each item you include. What you will need to decide right away is what style your wedding will take. As was mentioned in Chapter 7, you do need to pay attention to what clothing and colors the wedding party will wear as well as the style of dress. When you know these details, it will be easier for you to determine what color flowers should be in your bouquet, at the wedding, and at the reception site. For instance, for winter weddings many brides choose to have their bridesmaids wear burgundy or teal velvet—the colors look rich in the cold weather, and the velvet keeps them warm and elegant. With either of those colors deep tones of crimson would be more compatible than bright pinks or yellows for flowers or hall decorations.

Seasonless items that make great decorations are candles, ribbon, and African art for those who are looking to add ethnic inspiration. Some ideas below offer a sprinkling of decorating suggestions that may spark an idea of your own.

If your wedding is being held in a church or other spiritual center, it is appropriate to offer flowers for the altar. The flowers can be reflective of your bridal bouquet or can simply be large flowering plants.

You will want to reserve the first few aisles on both sides of the hall for family and special guests. This can be done with garlands of fresh or silk flowers, streamers, ribbon, or other fabric. A great idea would be streamers of authentic *kente* strips or other festive African fabric.

Before your guests enter the wedding site, and even during the ceremony, you may want to borrow an African—and Catholic—custom and burn incense, frankincense, and myrrh to purify the air.

Especially if your ceremony is in the evening or if your sanctuary allows only minimal light, line the space with candles that are lit before your guests arrive. Upon their arrival, offer your guests a unity candle that will be lit later at an appointed moment in your ceremony.

If your ceremony is at home or in a private space, incorporate African art pieces such as ankhs and fertility dolls with Christian crosses or other religious symbols into your altar as Sheryl Pollard and Dwayne Thomas did in 1991 at their wedding in their dance studio. You can create your own altar by covering furniture with decorative cloth and your chosen relics.

Instead of a white carpet, make a *kente* carpet from cotton-printed *kente*. (It would be difficult to find an authentic runner long enough to fill the expanse of the average church aisle. Plus the cost might be prohibitive.) Know that *kente* is not usually walked on, but during a sacred ceremony it would be acceptable.

Beautifying Your Reception Site

Depending upon where you hold your reception, the decorations may already be in place. If you are working with a hotel or a catering facility, you can negotiate with them on the particulars, such as the colors of tablecloths and runners, and floral arrangements. Our heritage points to a wide range of colors, from earth tones to royal blues, reds, and greens. When it comes to table decorations and party favors, you should specify your wishes. Often these are items you will order from your stationer or other private vendor.

In addition to matchbooks, napkins, and cake boxes printed with the names of the newlyweds on them, consider following Benilde Little and Clifford Virgin's lead. They had decided not to jump the broom during their wedding ceremony, but they wanted some ethnic touch to remind guests of their heritage. So the couple put a miniature straw broom wrapped in ribbon printed with their names and marriage date at each place setting. At Monique Greenwood's wedding reception, each table had a runner made of *kente*-printed cotton. That theme was carried out in the wedding attire. Each of the groomsmen wore a *kente* bow tie and cummerbund. The groom, Glenn Pogue, wore a *kente* vest and tie with his formal tuxedo.

THE SOUNDS OF CELEBRATION: MUSIC

The music for your wedding reception can be more lively than that of your wedding ceremony. Your choices can range from spiritual music for a religious reception to all manner of popular and classical music in more relaxed environs. A point worthy of reiterating now is that your guests should take top priority as you make your selections. Once you've decided on the type of music you want to have at your reception, it's time to go shopping, either for a live band, a D.J., or both. Some couples choose to combine the two so that they have continuous music throughout their reception. Depending upon how well the musicians or D.J. are known or how many pieces are in the group will determine how high their fees are, but generally the two can be close in price. Also, you should know that you can get just about any musician or performer to appear at your wedding—if the price is right. Consider the following pointers during your search.

Where to Shop

◆ Ask other couples who have recently married about their music.

◆ Check with your reception site for suggestions.

◆ Contact your local radio D.J. for ideas.

◆ Call a band agency who can show you videos of their bands during performances.

◆ Check newspaper ads for listings of bands that play weddings. Call those whose names you recognize or who seem legitimate.

What to Ask

◆ Discuss fees, including overtime. Most groups play for four-hour periods with breaks.

◆ Ask for a video of a recent performance or access to seeing the group perform in the near future.

◆ Determine the band's composition, including vocalist. If it's a D.J., find out how many people are employed.

◆ Find out if the leader of the group will make announcements during your reception.

◆ Request references. (Be sure to contact each of them once you've decided on the group you like.)

◆

HIRING DRUMMERS

Add a powerful element of African-American culture to your wedding by hiring traditional drummers to perform. You can hire drummers to play for a specified segment of your wedding or reception; some couples appreciate drumming accompaniment during a jumping the broom ceremony. Drummers can perform throughout your day, usually with other percussion instruments such as the shekere (shake-a-ray), a gourd that is covered with beads and cowrie shells, and cowbells as well as singing. Montego Joe, a master drummer for more than thirty-five years, says that a few drummers, himself included, can accompany more traditional American standards to add a bit of spice to an affair. There are different styles of drumming for each geographical region in Africa, but you don't have to be a drumming connoisseur to provide quality music at your wedding or reception. Through contacts, your local Black newspaper, or a music school you can find a drummer who will be able to offer you a wide range of drumming selections. New York–based Jaffa Productions offers a service for locating drummers throughout the country. (See the Resource Guide for further information.) As with other musicians, be sure to hear a sample of the artist's work and draw up a contract before hiring. Rates in 1992 were normally one hundred dollars per hour.

◆

Before Signing an Agreement

◆ Meet with the leader and determine the group's repertoire—and if they can learn songs if necessary. (Be ready to supply music if you have specific requests.)

◆ Be sure that the band knows your theme song or that it's available on a recording for your D.J.

◆ Define the number and length of breaks when considering a live band. If you want continuous music, discuss playing tapes during breaks.

◆ Agree on attire for band members or D.J.

◆ Determine if the group accepts special requests.

◆ Before you sign, put *all* of the terms of your agreement in writing and have the group leader sign. Make a down payment at signing; pay the balance at the end of the reception. (Either the groom, the best man, a trusted family member, or your wedding consultant should handle the back end of the payment.)

Some Wedding Favorites

Our African-American heritage is brimming with songs that speak to a newly married couple's love. Below is a partial listing of songs performed by Black artists that you may want to play at your reception or have sung at your wedding. To find oldies, check your local library. Most have music sections from which you can either borrow or listen.

JAZZ STANDARDS

Louis Armstrong	"Let's Do It, Let's Fall in Love" (Verve)
Lavern Baker	"My Happiness Forever" (Atlantic)
Nat "King" Cole	"Get Me to the Church on Time" (Capitol)
	"Love" (Capitol)
	"The Very Thought of You" (Capitol)
John Coltrane	"Say It Over and Over Again" (Impulse)
John Coltrane and Johnny Hartman	"My One and Only Love" (Impulse)
Miles Davis	"Someday My Prince Will Come" (Columbia)
	"There Is No Greater Love" (Columbia)
Duke Ellington and Count Basie	"Until I Met You" (Columbia)
Duke Ellington and Mahalia Jackson	"Come Sunday" (Columbia)

◆

MUSICAL COST-CUTTERS

When you are using live music, find out if you can get a "package" deal, having musicians do double duty at the wedding and the reception at a discounted rate.

Ask a friend or family member who sings or plays a musical instrument to perform at your reception (and wedding too). The invitation could be considered a tremendous honor. Be sure to offer an honorarium even when someone volunteers.

Contact music schools or music departments in local colleges to ask about discounted rates for musicians who might play at your reception. Be sure to listen to them perform before you sign an agreement—no matter how great the price.

Make your own tapes of your favorite musical selections, taking care to make the transitions between each recording smooth. Label tapes separately for each part of your reception: predinner conversation hour(s), dinner music, dancing, exit time.

◆

Ella Fitzgerald	"Night and Day" (Verve)
	"Let's Fall in Love" (Verve)
Billie Holiday	"Easy to Love" (Verve)
	"Life Begins When You're in Love" (Columbia)
Milt Jackson	"What Are You Doing the Rest of Your Life?" (CTI)
Al Jarreau	"We're in This Love Together" (Warner Bros.)
	"After All" (Warner Bros.)
Abbey Lincoln	"What Are You Doing the Rest of Your Life?" (Enja)
Nina Simone	"My Baby Just Cares for Me" (RCA)

R & B

Patti Austin and James Ingram	"Come to Me" (Warner Bros.)
Anita Baker	"You Bring Me Joy" (Elektra)
Regina Belle	"After the Love Has Lost Its Shine" (Columbia)
Jerry Butler and Brenda Lee Eager	"As the Seasons Change" (Mercury)
Mariah Carey	"So Blessed" (Columbia)
	"Vision of Love" (Columbia)

The Commodores	"Three Times a Lady" (Motown)
Sam Cooke	"You Send Me" (RCA)
DeBarge	"Time Will Reveal" (Motown)
The Deele	"Two Occasions" (Solar)
Roberta Flack	"The First Time Ever I Saw Your Face" (Atlantic)
	"Just When I Needed You" (1981)
Roberta Flack and Peabo Bryson	"Tonight I Celebrate My Love for You" (Atlantic)
Roberta Flack and Donny Hathaway	"The Closer I Get to You" (Atlantic)
	"You Are My Heaven" (Atlantic)
The Four Tops	"I Believe in You and Me" (Polygram)
Marvin Gaye and Tammi Terrell	"Ain't Nothing Like the Real Thing, Baby" (Tamla)
	"You're All I Need to Get By" (Tamla)
Larry Graham	"When We Get Married" (Warner Bros.)
	"One in a Million" (Warner Bros.)
Tom Grant and Sharon Bryant	"I've Just Begun to Love You" (Verve)
Al Green	"Let's Stay Together" (Motown)
	"Let's Get Married" (Motown)
Guy	"Let's Chill" (MCA)
Richie Havens	"Dreamin' as One" (A&M)
Edwin Hawkins	"How I Love You" (FIXIT Records)
Heatwave	"Always and Forever" (Epic)
Bill Henderson	"At Long Last" (Verve)
Howard Hewitt	"I Do" (Elektra)
Whitney Houston and Jermaine Jackson	"Nobody Loves Me Like You Do" (Arista)
Impressions	"I'm So Proud" (ABC)
Isley Brothers	"For the Love of You" (T/Neck)
Michael Jackson	"One Day I Will Marry You" (Motown)
	"The Lady in My Life" (Epic)
Gladys Knight and the Pips	"Best Thing That Ever Happened to Me" (Buddah)
Patti Labelle and The Blue Bells	"Down the Aisle" (Atlantic)

Johnny Mathis	"We've Only Just Begun" (Columbia)
Stephanie Mills and Teddy Pendergrass	"Two Hearts" (20th Century Fox /Polygram)
Modern Jazz Quartet	"For Someone I Love" (Atlantic)
Melba Moore	"Lean on Me" (Mercury)
O'Jays	"Forever Mine" (Philadelphia International)
Jeffrey Osborne	"We're Going All the Way" (A&M)
Charlie Parker	"April in Paris" (Verve)
Prince	"Forever in My Life" (Paisley Park)
	"Adore" (Paisley Park)
Ray, Goodman and Brown	"Celebrate Our Love" (EMI)
Otis Redding	"Home in Your Heart" (Atlantic)
Lionel Richie	"Truly" (Motown)
Minnie Ripperton	"Lovin' You" (Epic)
Smokey Robinson	"The Wedding Song" (Motown)
Smokey Robinson and the Miracles	"You Can Depend on Me" (Tamla)
Diana Ross and Marvin Gaye	"You Are Everything" (Motown)
Diana Ross and Lionel Richie	"Endless Love" (Motown)
Sade	"Nothing Can Come Between Us" (Epic)
Shalimar	"For the Lover in You" (Solar)
Percy Sledge	"When a Man Loves a Woman" (Atlantic)
Spinners	"Just as Long as We Have Love" (Atlantic)
Billy Stewart	"I Do Love You" (MCA)
The Stylistics	"You Are Everything" (Avco)
	"You Make Me Feel Brand New " (Avco)
	"Betcha By Golly Wow" (Avco)
Surface	"Shower Me with Your Love" (Columbia)
The Temptations	"You're My Everything" (Motown)
Luther Vandross	"Forever, For Always, For Love" (Epic)
Grover Washington, Jr., and Bill Withers	"Just the Two of Us" (Elektra)
Ben Webster	"Someone to Watch Over Me" (Impulse)
Denise Williams and Johnny Mathis	"So Deep in Love" (Columbia)
BeBe and CeCe Winans	"Lost Without You" (Capitol)

	"Wanna Be More" (Capitol)
	"For Always" (Capitol)
	"I Will Be Here" (Capitol)
Witness	"Would Not Change a Thing" (FIXIT Records)
	"You Haven't Lived" (FIXIT Records)
Stevie Wonder	"You and I" (Tamla)
	"Ribbon in the Sky" (Tamla)
	"You Are the Sunshine of My Life" (Motown)

REGGAE

Bob Marley	"Is This Love?" (Island Records)
Yellowman	"I'm Getting Married" (J & J Records)

GETTING AROUND IN STYLE

Transportation for you, your wedding party, and your out-of-town guests is your responsibility. What's most important is that you get everybody "to the church on time"—or wherever you are getting married. You must also remember to arrange for getting them—and the two of you—to the reception and back to where they are staying after the event is over. The actual logistics of organizing transportation is not difficult. What you must do is get an accurate head count, which can be determined by going down a checklist of your wedding party and out-of-town guests. (That list should be in your trusty book with all other vital information.)

Getting to the Wedding

◆ The bride and her bridesmaids often travel together in a limousine to the site of the ceremony, usually with the mother of the bride. When there are more people than will comfortably fit into the limousine, two should be provided. The bride does not normally travel with the groom nor does she even allow the groom or others to see her on that day until the wedding.

◆ The groom and his attendants travel separately either in a limousine, in rented cars, or in sparkling clean cars provided by members of the wedding party.

◆ The parents of both the bride and the groom provide their own transportation, except for the mother of the bride, who usually rides in the limousine with her daughter. Sometimes the bride travels with her father, who stays by her side until he "gives" her away during the ceremony.

◆ Out-of-town guests go directly to the ceremony site via pre-arranged transportation. Often relatives and family friends will be happy to help out with this responsibility. Be sure that everyone you ask to drive is known to be a punctual, safe driver, has a valid driver's license and a clean car.

Getting to the Reception

Once the wedding has ended and photographs have been taken, it will be time to dash to the reception site, unless, of course, you are already there! Two factors will ensure that everybody gets to the location with ease—clear, easy-to-follow directions and a ride! Ask your wedding coordinator or a responsible friend to double-check that everyone leaves the wedding site comfortably. If written directions are needed, they should be provided in the invitation on a separate map card. Guests should be reminded that they can honk horns and be merry on their way to the reception, but they *cannot* drive through red lights. It is illegal!

Getting Home or . . .

Even if you have hired a limousine, drop-off service after the reception is not usually included, so you may need to organize another way home. Your maid of honor or best man can be assigned the responsibility of following up on this detail on your wedding day, but you must arrange the transportation in advance. Of course, you must account for your out-of-town guests; it's easiest for them to travel the same way that they came. Additionally, you should ask several friends and family members to serve as designated drivers in case any of your guests gets intoxicated at your reception. Contact a cab company who can be on alert for anyone without a ride or unable to drive.

Hiring a Limousine Service

If you find that you need or want a limousine to transport the bridal party on the wedding day, you must handle the necessary plans to make it happen. Chauffeured transportation is a welcome luxury that you have to book in advance. Arthur Grier, manager of Paramount Limousine Service in Baltimore, Maryland, and president of the Maryland Limousine Commission, explains that using a limousine service can offer you the ease and comfort that you need most on your wedding day. Here he answers some of your most-asked questions on how to do it.

What services does a limousine company provide for a wedding?

The norm for any wedding rental is three hours. Rental time includes the bride and her attendants being picked up from where the bride is being dressed, allowing time for taking pictures outside with the vehicle before leaving for the wedding, travel time to the actual place of the ceremony, waiting until the bride comes out, kicking out the red carpet from the car to the entrance, toasting the bride and groom, and driving the couple to the reception site.

Who rides in the limousine from the wedding to the reception?

Normally just the bride and groom travel in the limousine. This just might be the first time that the two get to be alone since they've been married. It's a wonderfully intimate moment for them to share before the festivities begin. Sometimes the maid of honor and best man travel with them as well.

What is the average price of a limousine rental?

Nationwide in 1992 the average is forty-five dollars to seventy-five dollars per hour.

What should I do *before* hiring a limousine company?

1. Make sure the company you are dealing with is properly insured or is part of a public utility company that provides insurance for it. There are a lot of gypsy services out there (companies or individual cars without credentials) who may take your deposit and not show up on your wedding day.

2. Make sure you see the vehicle *before* you sign a contract. The car shouldn't have rust in it or be torn inside. Find out if you can confirm a particular car and driver. If you live in another city, ask someone living there to come out to see the vehicle and review the contract.

3. Book your car at least six months in advance, particularly if you are getting married during "high season."

4. Find out if the limousine company has any other service to offer, tuxedos, florists, etc. Many are tied into other operations, and you may be able to get a discount.

Historically, the wedding feast sealed a couple's new union. It was during this time that loved ones gathered to share in the fullness of the moment and wish the newlyweds well. These celebrations stay fresh in our memories thanks to priceless photographs such as this one, Brownstone Wedding, taken by legendary African-American photographer James Van Der Zee in 1926.

CHAPTER 10

The Wedding Feast

O ne of the primary links among African, Caribbean, and African-American weddings is a tremendous feast. From engagement to the final sealing of the union, food and merriment are central to the celebration, and expectations run high. In some West African communities it is not until the breaking of bread that a couple is actually considered married. Among the Akan of Ghana, Mali, and the Ivory Coast, for example, there are several huge feasts brimming with food, drink, and entertainment to which the entire village is often invited to celebrate each step of the marriage process. Preparing a West African feast typically represents a time of unity, because family members and friends alike join forces to create what appears to be an endless spread of delicious food for all.

Here in the United States, wedding feasts are prepared by many different hands—sometimes a caterer's, sometimes your own. No matter who is doing the cooking, the food must look stunning and sumptuous and taste scrumptious. Serving foods rich in our Southern, Caribbean, or African cultures will further heighten the festive atmosphere and add to the sense of values and continuity that mark the glorious day.

No matter what the style of your celebration—whether intimate or a big bash, a do-it-yourselfer or professionally catered—in addition to your food budget, you should keep several points in mind as you plan your menu:

◆ **Healthfulness.** Feature fresh vegetables and fruits and whole grains; avoid dishes with excess fat, salt, and sugar.

◆ **Food preferences of guests.** Don't go gourmet; choose family favorites instead, the ones they hanker for and enjoy. Include nonmeat selections for vegetarians and natural fruit desserts for diabetics and others avoiding refined sugar.

◆ **Available preparation time.** If preparing the feast yourself, don't take on more than you can chew; keep it simple.

◆ **Seasonality.** Take advantage of the high quality and low-to-moderate cost of fresh produce in season, especially those foods popular in your area.

◆ **Tradition.** Scour Black heritage cookbooks and the food section of African-American magazines for recipes of dishes that epitomize good eating and great times. (See the Selected Bibliography for assistance.)

GREAT MENU IDEAS

As you plan the many events leading up to your wedding, take great care in putting your menus together. On the following pages are five different menus with selected recipes, all created by food expert Jonell Nash, that should give you ideas for your own key events, including your reception and rehearsal dinner.

Make It Breakfast or Brunch

Following a sunrise wedding or other morning nuptial, a breakfast reception is an ideal way to celebrate. In years past, breakfast was a major repast in the South; as the first meal of the day, it was rib-sticking and substantial—hearty food served in abundance.

In recent years there has been a revival of the simple pleasures of a good breakfast. Brunch is now, nationwide, one of the most popular and heartwarming ways to entertain. With fat and calories streamlined, egg dishes such as huevos rancheros and vegetable-filled omelets and frittatas take center stage. Sausage links and patties are more likely to be made from turkey or beef. Bread baskets overflow with whole-grain and fruit-studded muffins, cinnamon buns, nut breads, and ever popular biscuits.

SOUTHERN BRUNCH MENU

Spinach-Mushroom Quiche or
Scrambled Eggs with Mushrooms

Breakfast Sausage Links and Patties

Homestyle Potatoes

Baked Cheese Grits*

Fried Apple Rings

Fresh Citrus Cup: Orange and
grapefruit sections and kumquats

Banana-Nut Bread · Buttermilk Biscuits

Peach Preserves · Blackberry Jam · Honey

Mimosas with Fresh Strawberries

Coffee with Crème de Cacao · Hot Herbal Tea

Wedding Cake

Featuring some of the humblest of ingredients, early-morning meals can be the least expensive of wedding feasts. Because of the time of day, a breakfast reception does not require an open bar or hard liquor, which cuts costs even further. (Note that items with asterisks are accompanied by recipes.)

An Outdoor Summer Wedding Buffet

Whether on the lawn of a country estate, in the natural splendor of a municipal botanical garden, or in the comfort of a loved one's backyard, the outdoors can provide an ideal setting for a wedding reception. Perhaps the fresh air and the sense of boundlessness of the outdoors are what seem so in keeping with newlyweds embarking on their new life.

In planning your warm weather buffet, feature light, health-conscious fare—fish, poultry, or lean meat and lots of vegetables. Select from the stunning profusion of summer's bounty. Think salads—tossed and other. When selecting salad greens don't stop with iceberg; consider arugula, watercress, red oakleaf, spinach, dandelion, chicory, and romaine. There's an almost endless variety of raw and cooked vegetables and other foods that can be added to lettuce or lettuce beds to make salads. For many folks, a summer buffet is incomplete without a scooped-out watermelon loaded with fresh berries and fruit pieces. When it comes to summer cooking, go with the number one technique—grilling (smoker cooking is also hot!). Grilling works well for fish and vegetables as well as poultry and the usual meats. Even a whole turkey, which is an economical and tasty way to feed a crowd, can be cooked on a covered grill or in a smoker. Marinating and using naturally flavored wood such as hickory, maple, or mesquite further enhance grilled flavors. The most tantalizing and characteristic barbecue flavor and aroma come, of course, from the fiery basting sauces we have ritually mopped on foods since the earliest cookouts in the Motherland.

BAKED CHEESE GRITS

4 qts. water

2 tsps. salt (optional)

4 cups regular hominy grits (not quick grits)

1 cup (2 sticks) butter or margarine

6 large eggs, at room temperature

3 cups shredded cheddar cheese

1/4 cup chopped parsley

2 large cloves garlic, minced (optional)

1 tsp. cayenne pepper or hot pepper sauce (amount according to taste)

In kettle or stockpot, bring water and salt to boil. Using wooden spoon, gradually stir in grits; cook until mixture begins to thicken. Cover pot; reduce heat to low. Cook 25 minutes, stirring occasionally. Meanwhile, heat oven to 350° F. Grease 12" x 20" x 2" full counter pan or aluminum foil 12" x 16" x 2" roaster pan; set aside. Remove cooked grits from heat. Stir in butter. In medium-size bowl, beat eggs; stir in cheese, parsley, garlic, and pepper. Stir cheese mixture into grits, mixing well. Spoon into prepared baking dish. Bake 40 to 50 minutes. Makes 25 servings.

DEVILED EGGS

50 eggs, at room temperature
Water
1/4 cup milk
1 1/2 cups mayonnaise or whipped-
   style salad dressing
1 tab. salt (optional)
2 tsps. dry mustard
1/4 cup cider vinegar

Optional garnishes: pimento
strips, parsley leaves, paprika
In large kettle about 2/3 filled with
water, bring water to boil. Place
eggs in wire basket; lower into
boiling water. Simmer 15 minutes.
Immerse eggs in cold water (to
stop further cooking and to
prevent forming of dark circle
around yolk). Peel eggs. Cut
lengthwise or crosswise into
halves. Carefully remove yolks and
place in large mixing bowl.
Arrange whites on trays. Mash
yolks; stir in milk until blended.
Add mayonnaise, salt (if desired),
mustard, and vinegar. Mix on low
speed until blended. With a plain
or rose tip inserted, fill pastry bag
with yolk mixture. Pipe filling into
whites. Garnish with pimento
strip and parsley leaf, or as
desired. Makes 50 servings (two
per portion).
Variations: Cooked shrimp, flaked
tuna, crabmeat, capers, pickle
relish, or chopped olives are
among the ingredients you can stir
into the egg yolk mixture.

SUMMER MENU

HORS D'OEUVRES

(passed by server)

Maryland Crab Cakes with Mustard Sauce

Deviled Eggs*

BUFFET

Hickory-Smoked Whole Turkey

Confetti Rice
(with green peas and diced carrots)

Sautéed Okra and Tomatoes

Corn Pudding

Potato Salad with Olives

Sweet Potato Biscuits

Fresh Summer Fruit Platter
(watermelon, papaya, pineapple)

Champagne Punch · Lemonade

DESSERT

Fresh Peach Cobbler with Rum Whipped Cream

Chocolate-Dipped Strawberries

Wedding Cake

Coffee · Tea

Do-It-Yourself Rehearsal Dinner

The eve of a wedding is usually the day of
the run-through of the actual wedding ceremony.
Traditionally, a sit-down dinner, hosted by the
groom's parents, follows the rehearsal. This is an
opportunity for the groom's side to pay tribute to

WINTER MENU

FIRST COURSE

Seafood Gumbo

French Bread

MAIN COURSE

Roasted Rock Cornish Hens
Stuffed with Southern Dressing
or
Burgundy Short Ribs of Beef

Orange-Glazed Sweet Potatoes*

Sautéed Kale and Leeks
or
Green Cabbage Au Gratin

Cornsticks

DESSERT

Pecan Pie

Champagne · Sparkling Apple Juice

Coffee · Tea

ORANGE-GLAZED SWEET POTATOES

16 lbs. yams or sweet potatoes
1 lb. box brown sugar
2 cups water
8 oz. (2 sticks) margarine or
    butter
1/4 cup grated orange peel
2 tsps. ground cinnamon
1 tsp. ground nutmeg
1 tsp. salt (optional)
4 oranges, sliced, seeded

In large kettle or stock pot 2/3 filled with water, bring water to boil. Meanwhile, scrub potatoes well; do not peel. Cook potatoes in two batches for even cooking. Add potatoes to boiling water; when water returns to boiling point, partially cover and begin timing. Cook 30 to 40 minutes. Meanwhile, to prepare syrup, combine sugar, water, margarine, orange peel, spices, and salt (if desired) in large saucepan; bring to boil, stirring to melt sugar. When yams are cooked and cool enough to handle, peel and cut crosswise into slices. In two large aluminum foil roasting pans or other large shallow pans, arrange yam and orange slices; drizzle with syrup. Bake until potatoes are glazed, about 20 to 30 minutes. Makes 50 servings.

the couple and provide an enjoyable occasion for the two families, members of the wedding party, officiating clergy and spouse, and special out-of-town guests to become acquainted.

Even when there is no wedding rehearsal, as in the event of a small or very simple ceremony, a special meal the evening before the wedding is a way to bring all parties together. If not the parents of the groom, friends or relatives of the bride or groom or the couple themselves can host this occasion.

A Cocktail-Party Reception

A cocktail-party format is ideal for late-afternoon receptions that fall between the usual hours for lunch and dinner. Though more casual in style, finger foods offer the luxury and indulgence of a variety of exciting tastes, colors, and shapes.

APPETIZER MENU

Transport your guests to the sunny shores of the Caribbean with this island-inspired menu of flashy finger foods.

HOT HORS D'OEUVRES

Codfish Cakes

Barbecued Chicken Drumettes
(meaty portion of wing)

Fried Sweet Plantain

Coconut Shrimp

Marinated Lamb or Goat Kabobs*

Jamaican Vegetable or Beef Patties

Mango Chutney

COLD HORS D'OEUVRES

Curried Egg Salad Tea Sandwiches

Bean or Avocado Dip

Basket of Vegetables for Dipping
(Christophene [chayote]; carrot and zucchini sticks; string beans and broccoli florets)

Bananas Baked with Rum

BEVERAGES

Ginger Beer · Tamarind Punch

DESSERT

Black Cake (Wedding Cake)

Choose from hors d'oeuvres—hot and cold finger foods that feature fresh vegetables and fruits, pickles, olives, cheese, fish, sausages, or combinations; dips—hot or cold, creamy or chunky mixtures for dunking fruits, vegetables, crackers, or chips with which they are served; canapés—bite-sized bits of savory food spread on edible bases such as cutout bread slices, crackers, tiny biscuits, or puff-pastry shells, then garnished or decorated. For cocktails, see section on beverages.

How many appetizers should you order? According to Los Angeles caterer Yvonne E. White, "Allow a *minimum* of eight items per person; ten is closer to average, and twelve makes an ideal party with ample food for all appetites." As a cost-cutter, White suggests having the hors d'oeuvres passed by servers to save the expense and bother of renting buffet tables, chafing dishes, and so on. (She also suggests that a cocktail-party format is a good way to avoid the wedding reception politics of who-sits-where-and-with-whom!)

An African-Style Dinner

It is not surprising that rice, which symbolizes fertility and bounty in African and Western cultures, would be customarily served at West African ceremonial feasts. But not plain rice, which is a staple eaten almost daily. Weddings call for Jollof Rice—a festive dish made especially rich by adding meat, seafood, vegetables, and spices. This meal-in-itself dish is similar to a Louisiana Creole jambalaya or a Caribbean *peleau*. Completely adaptive to your taste

---

HOMELAND MENU

HORS D'OEUVRES

(passed by server)

Bean Fritters with Peanut Sauce

Spicy Beef Kabobs

Kelewele (fried plantain)

FIRST COURSE

Curried Fish Stew

MAIN COURSE

Jollof Rice*

Steamed Spinach

Ghana Homestyle Tossed Salad
(lettuce, tomatoes, onions, chopped eggs)

DESSERT

Coconut Wedding Cake

Twisted Cakes
(small fried cakes)

Fresh Fruit Basket

Palm wine · Sparkling Wine or Cider

MARINATED LAMB KABOBS

4 ½ lbs. boneless leg of lamb
5 large bell peppers (use assorted colors—red, green, yellow, orange), seeded, cut into 1-inch pieces
Marinade:
2 cups vegetable oil
1 cup sodium-reduced soy sauce
1 cup fresh lemon juice
½ cup prepared mustard
1 tab. coarsely cracked pepper
4 medium-size cloves garlic, minced
50 to 60 7-inch wooden skewers

To cut lamb into cubes, cut meat into ¾- 1-inch thick slices; then cut slices ¾- 1-inch lengthwise and crosswise. In large mixing bowl, combine marinade ingredients; using a whisk or rotary beater, beat ingredients until blended. Add lamb cubes to bowl. Cover and marinate, stirring and turning occasionally, in refrigerator 24 hours. Soak skewers in water about 1 hour to prevent them from burning. Prepare grill or broiler; adjust grid to about 5 inches from heat source. Skewer cubes alternately with bell peppers. Arrange kabobs in single layer on grill on broiler rack; baste with leftover marinade. Grill until lamb is cooked through to medium, about 3 minutes on each side. Makes approximately 50 to 60 kabobs.

CEREMONIAL MEAT

Meat of any kind is a luxury in much of Africa. To symbolize prosperity and abundance, livestock are slaughtered for feasting. Depending on the region, killing a cow or ox can bring the most prestige and acclaim. Goats, sheep, wild game, and chickens are also killed—by the men—for these special occasions. The meat is grilled, simmered in soups and stews, eaten with a variety of grains, or made into flavorful sauces.

and choosing, ingredients can be added or omitted from Jollof Rice as desired.

Spicy stews, soups, and fritters made with peanuts, yams, cassavas, eggplants, dried peas and beans, okra, ripe plantains, and hot peppers as well as beef, goat, chicken, and seafood characterize West African cookery. *Aboloo* (dumplings), *kelewele* (fried plantains), twisted cakes (small fried breads), *garri foto* (milled-cassava stew), and lentil *wat* (lentil stew) contribute to wedding merrymaking that lasts until dawn.

JOLLOF RICE

This traditional dish of many African nations can be prepared in near infinite variations—add cooked black-eyed peas, shrimp, or meat or omit meat altogether for a savory vegetarian main dish.

3 3-lb. broiler-fryer chickens

½ cup vegetable oil

4 large onions, chopped

4 large cloves garlic, minced

¼ cup grated fresh gingerroot

6 cups converted long-grain rice

1 3-oz. can tomato paste

2 tabs. curry powder, or to taste

1 tab. cayenne pepper, or to taste

2 tsps. salt (optional)

2 lbs. carrots, peeled, diced small

1 lb. string beans, ends trimmed, cut into 1- to 1½-inch pieces

10 cups chicken broth, water, or combination

Rinse poultry thoroughly with cold running water; pat dry with paper towels. Cut chickens into standard pieces, then cut meat from bones into about 2-inch pieces. In Dutch oven or iron kettle, heat oil. Brown chicken (in batches, if needed) on all sides, about 8 minutes. Using slotted spoon, remove chicken to pan; set aside. Heat oven to 350° F. Add onion, garlic, and gingerroot to pot; sauté until wilted. Add rice; stir to completely coat. Add tomato paste, curry powder, cayenne, and salt (if desired). Spoon rice mixture evenly into 12" x 20" x 4" baking pan or 2 aluminum-foil large roaster pans. Stir in chicken, carrots, green beans, and broth, mixing well. Cover pan well with foil; bake 40 minutes. Stir before serving. Makes 25 main dish servings; 50 side-dish servings.

YOUR WEDDING CAKE

When it comes to the flavor and design of your cake, your choices are as wide as your imaginings. The adopted tradition of a round, three-tier, bland white cake with white icing, topped with a plastic figurine of a bride and groom is boring. Today's wedding reception guests are treated to types of cakes that include: banana, coconut, carrot, chocolate, nut, spice, and the increasingly popular, Caribbean black cake (see page 158). If you cannot decide on one flavor, consider selecting a different flavor for each tier!

Tiers can be square, rectangular, oval, diamond-shaped, or hexagonal. Sandwich layers with rich flavor fillings such as vanilla custard, praline, mocha, butterscotch, or rum, or fruit flavors such as pineapple, lemon, orange, apricot, and raspberry.

The "icing on the cake" can be a fanciful frosting of butter cream, royal icing (ornamental frosting), cream cheese, whipped cream, or rolled fondant. Then embellish your grand confection with a cascade of edible real flowers, spun sugar, or marzipan flowers, fresh fruit and berries, or encrust it with grated fresh coconut, chopped nuts, dragées, or the favorite of cake designer, Charmaine Jones—edible gold!

◆

TIPS FOR WORKING WITH A BAKER

◆ *Look through cake and dessert cookbooks, bridal magazines, and books for ideas for your cake's design and display; have these pictures or sketches with you when you meet with the baker.*

◆ *Ask to see photographs of wedding cakes the baker has created; most have portfolios of their work.*

◆ *Request a tasting of cake samples.*

◆ *Get all details of the cake you are ordering in writing—flavor of cake layers, filling, and icing; number of tiers, their shape and size; description of colors, design, and decoration; delivery date, time, and place; setup; and, of course, price.*

◆

The Groom's Cake

This Southern tradition of a dark chocolate or nutty flavored cake (often laced with liquor) is becoming popular in all regions of the country. Usually a sheetcake, it's often presented in a whimsical shape of a sporting activity (football, sailboat, etc.)

CARIBBEAN BLACK CAKE

Throughout the Caribbean, but particularly among the southern islands such as Grenada, Barbados, and St. Lucia, not only is black cake an expected part of wedding celebrations, but it is also joyfully anticipated. And justifiably so. This dark, rich, intensely flavored cake, made with dried fruits and rum, can take months to prepare. Making a black cake represents a commitment of time and money to heritage. Recipes are from generations past— handed down from mother to daughter, aunt to niece—each adding her own touch here and there. The basic formula is that of a "pound" cake—a pound each of raisins, prunes, currants, glacé cherries, butter, dark brown sugar, and flour, plus a dozen eggs and flavorings.

This master cake-making technique begins with mixing the dried fruits and rum in a heavy crock to soak for at least two weeks and for up to six months!

or other interest of the couple. This cake can be served at the rehearsal dinner or other prenuptial celebration or cut after the bridal cake and boxed for guests to carry home.

Cutting and Serving

The cake-cutting ceremony is a fun, light-hearted ritual and one of the high points of the reception. With both holding the cake-cutter, the bride and groom cut (from the bottom layer) the first slice. The bride feeds the first bite to the groom; he reciprocates by offering her the second bite. The cake is then cut by a designated member of the catering staff. Parents, then guests, are served. The top layer is removed and saved by the bride and groom to enjoy on their first anniversary. Cake baker Joanne Baylor of Creative Cakes in the Bronx, New York, confirms that the top layer can taste moist and flavorful up to a year later if wrapped thoroughly, solidly frozen, and thawed in the refrigerator a day before serving.

WHAT'S TO DRINK?

To make your celebration the toast of the town, don't run out of great drinks. It's important to have on hand a range of refreshing choices. With today's focus on health and fitness and the awareness that drinking and driving do not mix, many adults are drinking fewer alcoholic beverages or opting for alcohol-free drinks.

In the West Indies, fruit juices regularly accompany meals and festive occasions. Tropical juices and nectars such as banana, guava, passion fruit, mango, or papaya are now widely available either fresh, canned, or bottled in the United States. Serve them straight or mixed with other juices, sparkling water, or the spirited drink of the Caribbean— rum! Ginger beer, sorrel punch, and tamarind juice are also pleasures of the islands and sub-Saharan Africa. Piña Coladas and daiquiris actually originated in the Caribbean.

If you are having only one wine, select a dry white; these are versatile wines that can complement spicy as well as delicately seasoned foods. Chenin blanc is a good choice. If serving red wine also, go for cabernet sauvignon.

How much to buy? Allow one drink per person per hour, or an average of three drinks per person. Here's the rule of thumb in stocking up on spirits, wine, and other beverages.

Liquor bottles are now metric. What was formerly termed a fifth ($\frac{1}{5}$ gallon) is now 750 milliliters; this is the standard size for wine and liquor bottles and the size referred to in the chart.

SPARKLING APRICOT–PINEAPPLE PUNCH

3 qts. apricot nectar
3 qts. pineapple juice
1 16-oz. container
   frozen lemonade
2 qts. cold water
2 qts. ginger ale,
   flavored seltzer, or
   sparkling water

In punch bowl, combine apricot nectar, pineapple juice, frozen lemonade, and water; stir until blended. Right before serving, stir in ginger ale. Makes 2 $\frac{1}{2}$ gallons; 80 4-ounce servings.

QUANTITY	NUMBER OF DRINKS
1 bottle of wine	6 drinks
1 bottle fortified wine (sherry, port, madeira)	8 drinks
1 bottle hard liquor	17 1-jigger (1 $\frac{1}{2}$-ounce) drinks 12 2-ounce drinks
1 bottle champagne	8 servings
1 case of 12 bottles	approximately 100 guests to have one drink
$\frac{1}{2}$ keg beer	260 8-ounce glasses

Also have on hand to serve as beverages and mixers: sparkling apple or grape juice; flavored and plain sparkling water; diet and regular soft drinks, fruit juices, and regular and decaffeinated coffees and teas.

Ice—you can't have too much. Allow a minimum of one half pound per person; double the amount in hot weather.

WORKING WITH A CATERER

ICE RING
An ice-ring mold made
with lemonade is an
ideal way to keep punch
cold without diluting the
taste with plain ice
cubes. To make the ring
even more decorative,
place pineapple rings
and fresh mint sprigs in
bottom of mold; fill 3/4
full with lemonade.
Freeze until time to add
to punch. Unmold the
ring; float upside down
in punch bowl.

Before dawn in Ghana on the day of the wedding (*Yokpeemor*), the women of the bride's family gather with other women of their village, to prepare the feast. With the sound of drumbeats in the distance, on the night before, the men slaughtered the chickens, goats, and possibly a cow, which on the wedding day, in a spirit of sisterhood and celebration, the women make ready.

In the United States, a communal wedding reception, where family and friends all pitch in to do the cooking or arrive with potluck dishes in hand, remains an option that has a special warmth and charm. In a similar homespun fashion, a member of the church or community who is known as a superb cook is often asked to prepare the celebration meal. You may prefer, as do more and more of today's brides, to turn this job, which is of such magnitude, over to trained professionals.

If you decide to go with a pro you still have a range of choices. Standard caterers provide the basics of menu planning and preparing as well as presenting food; they will also arrange for needed serving equipment and personnel. Many caterers over the years (and over many receptions) expand their services and become party and event planners. Their area of specialty can cover the planning of the entire wedding reception—but not the ceremony and etiquette that are the domain of the wedding consultant. Party planners can assist with decor, flowers, and music, as well as design and prepare your menu. Most of the major banquet halls have in-house catering; arrangements for the room, food, and drink are all made with their banquet manager. Another option is having an ethnic restaurant or bakery specializing in Southern, Caribbean, or African cooking cater your event.

Whatever your choice, start working with the caterer right away; this gives you the best chance of getting all the details right. Weigh their suggestions carefully, in order to get the

most benefit from their skill and experience; yet don't feel that you have to settle for a preset menu and presentation. With an early start you have enough time to hire someone else if things are not working out.

The starting point of planning your menu is your budget. How much you have to spend determines the type and amount of food, service people, and equipment. The caterer will determine the food charges on a cost-per-person basis.

After creating your menu, tasting samples of the food, and working out the specifics of service, the next vitally important step in working with a caterer, according to Norma Jean Darden of the popular Spoonbread, Inc., in New York City, is to get all of the details in writing. A contract helps ensure that you will receive the services you anticipate. Having it in writing is the best way to avoid miscommunication and nightmarish situations. In the event that you do not get items requested and paid for, the contract also offers recourse. Your catering contract should include the following:

Date and location of event
Time of setup and time of event
Menu: all courses detailed
Beverages
Labor: including the number of managers, captains, bartenders, waitpersons, and
    kitchen helpers
Supplies and equipment provided by the caterer

Supplies and equipment to be rented

The rate per person for food; the rate per person for the bar

Number of people to be served

Total contract price

Be sure you understand every part of the contract; if something is not clear, ask questions. Any agreed-upon changes should be added to or removed from the contract. Discuss possible additional fees such as gratuities and overtime. Determine when you have to provide a final guest count. (Don't forget to include photographers and musicians.) Be aware of the cancellation fees. Make sure the caterer signs the contract. Consider making arrangements for leftover food to be donated to a homeless shelter or food bank.

CULINARY COST-CUTTERS

There are ways to economize on your wedding feast without sacrificing quality or style. The key is to look for the best value rather than the lowest price.

Food

The time of day and the time of year of your reception have a major influence on costs—the earlier the meal the less expensive it tends to be. A morning wedding can be festively followed by a coffee, breakfast, or brunch; all of which can provide a major savings over luncheons and dinners. A coffee can simply consist of one or more warm breads, a fruit tray attractively arranged with sliced or bite-size pieces of fresh fruit, and an ample amount of fresh regular and decaffeinated coffees, teas, and fruit juices.

A self-service buffet is generally less expensive than a sit-down meal where guests are served. A cocktail party is less expensive than a buffet. A cocktail party menu of all cold appetizers is less expensive than one with hot and cold finger foods.

Moving down the food chain also lowers costs. Menus that feature fresh vegetables, dried peas and beans, and grains in main dishes, and use meat only as a seasoning or as a garnish are less expensive. Stews, casseroles, and other dishes such as curries, which cook meat, poultry, or fish with vegetables and are ladled over rice, bulgur, or couscous can be cost-effective as well as flavorful.

Shrimp is less expensive than lobster, crab is less expensive than shrimp, and canned tuna is cheaper yet!

The season of year also affects costs. Summer menus that feature fresh produce in season are less expensive (and sometimes more flavorful) than winter receptions that rely more on higher priced canned and frozen fruits and vegetables or include produce purchased at a premium.

Culinary schools or cooking/baking programs within vocational schools can be a source of well-prepared party food without labor costs.

Drinks

Serve lesser-known or generic brands, which are less expensive than name brands.

If using a banquet facility or caterer, request to provide the liquor, which you can purchase at a more economical price from a discount liquor store.

Buy liter-size bottles.

Instead of French champagne, serve California, Spanish, or Italian sparkling wine.

CHAPTER 11

CAPTURING THE MOMENT

ou know how the saying goes, "A picture's worth a thousand words." This is undeniably true when it comes to your wedding. You and your guests will cherish rich memories from that *one* day for many years. Sure enough, some pictures will be painted verbally—at family gatherings, on the back porch with neighbors, over a cup of coffee with elders—in the tradition of our predecessors who shared stories of family and community with one another and with their children to preserve our ancestral memory. Others will be artfully recorded on film, with still images, video, or both. If you plan these pictures right, it will take only a moment for the full story of your wedding day to spin out before your very eyes—twenty years from now!

Needless to say, organizing photography requires careful consideration and decision making. There's rarely a wedding where an aunt or an uncle doesn't pull out an automatic 35mm or a video camera to record the action. Yet only in rare instances do those pictures turn out better than the work of a hired professional. If your budget allows, you should not rely solely on amateurs to record your wedding. They may not be agile or quiet enough to cover the ground you need covered—without disturbing the guests. They may not have mastered lighting, which could yield you dark, blurry pictures. And there may be too many people recording your wedding, which could turn it into a spectacle rather than a sacred moment. The record of your wedding is just as important as all of the other components that go into making it happen. So don't skimp on this important aspect of your day. Think twice about asking a good friend, even if the person is a photographer, to shoot your wedding. That person will not be able to enjoy the festivities without compromising the images he or she gets on film. Whomever you choose to record the events of your wedding day should be briefed on your needs in advance. Others should be discouraged from constant shooting, particularly during the ceremony, when their flashes and general activity could prove unsettling.

To get good shots requires clarity on your part—in your selection of an able photographer (preferably a professional), in your discussions about your specific

◆

THE SOUTHERN WAY

Dating back to the earliest days of America, it was common for women to sit for their portraits in full wedding attire. The tradition lives on in Black communities in the South. One African-American bride who married in 1988 in Richmond, Virginia, greeted her guests at the entrance to her wedding reception with a full-length oil painting of herself on an easel. Although her portrait was of her alone in traditional Western wedding raiment, couples who are having more ethnic weddings could modify this idea to suit their own tastes. A portrait of the two of you wearing cultural accents could be a wonderful start to your art collection—one that will conjure up pleasant memories for many years to come.

If you decide to get a wedding portrait either painted or photographed, make sure that you prepare yourself the way you will appear on your wedding day. You should have your actual wedding clothing and accessories, the same hairstyle and makeup. Grooms should wear the same clothing as well—even if it has to be rented. If possible, you should have replicas of your flowers too. This portrait can be used as a family treasure as well as a picture for your announcement in the local newspaper.

◆

needs, and in your attention to detail. Many couples forget to consider when and for how long their formal shots will be taken, for instance, and end up spending more than an hour of their day away from their guests. To ensure that everything goes well with your pictures also means that you have to make your selection anywhere from six months to a year in advance. As with all individuals or businesses hired to provide service at your wedding, make sure that you draw up and sign a contract outlining the photographer or videographer's commitment.

SELECTING A PHOTOGRAPHER

A good way to find a reputable photographer is by word-of-mouth. Friends who've recently married, members of your place of worship, even associates on your job may provide great leads. When looking further, consult any of the professionals already part of your wedding (for example, florist, caterer, etc.), the local chapter of the National Association of Black Journalists, who should have a roster of Black photographers who may offer their services for weddings, or the Professional Photographers of America (708) 299-8161.

To make an informed selection, interview a number of recommended photographers and review their portfolios. Make sure that you feel comfortable with the photographer. Since you will spend an entire day with this person, you also want to get a feel for how quickly and easily he or she understands your needs and complements your personality. Before you make your final decision, answer the following questions.

Are the photographer's images crisp and clear? Did he or she capture the spirit of the day, on many faces?

Our grandparents' photos are likely to reveal long faces, with few smiles. Somber visages used to be the only acceptable expression. Today we enjoy much more flexibility and ease as we get photographed. Your photographer should be able to shoot people candidly as well as in posed settings, capturing the subtlety that lives behind the eyes.

Are the photographs composed well, with interesting background elements that you can see? Do you feel comfortable with the photographer and his or her work?

When you are satisfied with a photographer's work, find out a few particulars before making a final agreement:

What kind of film will the photographer be using?

The jury is still out on which film is the absolute best for a wedding. The two most popular formats are 35-mm and $2\frac{1}{4}$" film. The latter offers a larger image that is often more crisp and vibrant. It is also more costly. The former is great for moving images, because it is a faster film. Rarely is a couple doing so much quick activity that the $2\frac{1}{4}$" film would miss, however. Let your taste be your guide.

What is the standard length of time that the photographer will be with the couple?

In addition to the wedding ceremony and the entire reception, you should request that your photographer attend the rehearsal. It is there that he or she will see the sequence of your ceremony, meet the bridal party, and learn of any restrictions from the wedding officiant. Often lights are not allowed in the sanctuary in religious centers; photographers are discouraged from moving around during the service; and they may be forbidden from shooting at the altar. Be clear on how long the photographer will stay at the reception and what, if any, overtime fees may be applicable.

How many pictures will the photographer take?

You need to get a feeling for how much time and expense your photographer will need in order to complete the job. Get a sense of how long you will be spending with him or her for specific shots, especially any posed images that will take you away from your guests. Although not common, if you will be paying for film processing, be clear on the number of rolls of film the photographer will take. Processing can be quite costly.

Does the photographer keep negatives? For how long? How are they stored?

Many photographers do keep the negatives and charge additional fees when you want to order more prints. If you search hard enough, you may find a photographer who will give you the negatives back. Washington, D.C.–based free-lancer Tvon Brown, for example, believes in giving them back so that the couple can have access to their wedding for years to come—without needing him as a go-between. If your photographer will be keeping your negatives, make sure that they are stored in a fireproof safe.

Does the photographer offer package deals?

Photographers who specialize in weddings often have created packages where the couple gets a specified number of images for a set price. Additional pictures are available for a fee, which you should determine in advance. Your needs will determine what package works best for you. A good example includes: all proofs (which you use to select the prints); several eight-by-ten-inch prints; parent albums; your own wedding album.

If you think you want to have wallet-size photographs made for yourself or a group of shots for your thank-you notes or even holiday cards, build those into your package if you can.

What is the basic fee for the work you need? What additional fees, if any, does the photographer anticipate?

Fee schedules range dramatically from city to city and from package to package. Minimum charges usually start at eight hundred dollars for covering a wedding and a four-hour reception; the prices can rise to several thousand. Let your photographer know your budget. If your first-choice plan is too expensive, he or she may be able to tailor a plan that will better satisfy you. To avoid surprises down the road, go over the details carefully and inquire specifically about other fees, for instance, for overtime, processing, film type, five-by-seven-inch prints, and so on. This information should be written into your contract.

Find out the payment schedule. Expect to pay anywhere from one-third to one-half of the total to secure the date. The balance is either paid in two payments—at the wedding and upon delivery—or in full at the wedding. It's a good idea to pay in full before the wedding, Tvon Brown has learned, so that you can get your pictures right after your honeymoon, and you won't have to worry about having to set aside the money or raise it when you return.

What should be included in the photographer's contract?

Every detail listed above should be included in your contract. Be sure to make special notice of:

♦ whether the photographer will attend the rehearsal

♦ what time he or she should arrive at the wedding site and what time he or she should be with the bride prior to the wedding if desired

♦ what time period the photographer is scheduled to be with the wedding party, from start to finish

♦ a listing of what's included in your package

♦ delivery date for proofs and prints

♦ liability in the event that originals are lost

♦ terms for engagement and/or bridal portrait

♦ terms of payment

♦ terms of cancellation

Although not usually included in your contract, a written list of pictures you want the photographer to take should be provided in advance of the wedding. It's best to appoint a hostess or other trusted friend or family member who knows most or all of your guests to help the photographer identify the people on the list. See the checklist at the end of this chapter for ideas on the main shots you may want.

SELECTING A VIDEOGRAPHER

The wonders of technology have made video images of our lives commonplace. Lots of folks have home video cameras these days. Rest assured that an uncle, an adventurous friend, or some other guest will whip out a video camera to capture your wedding memories. It's unlikely, however, that any of these people can document your wedding as well as a professional videographer. If you have room in your budget, consider hiring a pro to record your wedding. A world of possibilities awaits you, from simple recording of the day's activities, to a mini–music video complete with dubbing.

Start in your community to find a videographer. Follow the same basic steps as you used for finding a photographer. Once you have identified likely prospects, interview them carefully to select the best candidate for your wedding. Here are pointers for your interview:

Ask to view sample wedding tapes.

Is the sound clear, the lighting bright enough without being too harsh, transitions from scene to scene smooth? Do you like the videographer's style? The way he or she captured the couple, family, and friends on tape? Would you like to have him or her create your wedding video?

If the answer is yes, continue your interview with these guidelines:

Determine how many cameras will be necessary and how they will be used.

One camera works well when you will be using raw footage or film with very little editing. It's best, however, to have two cameras at your wedding, so that there are two sets of images from which the videographer can create perfect edits for the final film. One camera will normally be used as the main camera, according to New York videographer Kerwin Devonish, while the other is reserved for panning the room, recording guests interacting, and taping interviews. The camera(s) used should either be compatible with your home VCR or converted to your format for your final version.

What can be included in the editing process?

Great wedding videos include all sorts of images, many that are combined through editing after the shooting is long over. Check with your videographer on what, if any, editing is standard in your fee. Often the basic editing of the wedding and reception film to make the product smooth is included, although some videographers will actually turn the film over to you after the reception if you so choose. Beyond the standards are such special effects as dubbed music (that you can select and sometimes provide), titles (graphics on the page such as name, date, etc.), incorporation of baby pictures and interviews interspersed throughout the film. Some companies even include stills within their videotape, thereby adding even greater dimension to the visual display.

Discuss length of wedding and reception with regard to price.

Be sure that your videographer will be shooting for an agreed-upon time period—normally including the entire wedding ceremony, the entrance of the wedding party at your reception, and all other activities there, including the toast, the garter and bouquet ceremonies, the cutting of the cake, dancing, and other moments. Find out in advance after what time you will be charged overtime fees. Decide how long final edited tape will be.

Describe what you want to capture on video.

Find out if your plan can be executed and how much editing will be required. Normally the greater the editing time, the greater the cost.

Determine what the cost will be for the services you want.

Prices for videographers can begin as low as four hundred dollars for the day. Once you add on editing fees, which often are accrued hourly, and other special effects, the fee can rise into the thousands. You will need to discuss all details of your plan to secure a rate that you find acceptable.

Find out when the edited video be delivered to you and how many copies you will get.

Because most videos do require some editing work, you won't receive yours immediately. Negotiate your delivery date and include that in your contract (which should resemble that of your photographer's). One copy of your video is standard, but you may be able to secure up to four for your parents if you make your request in advance. Some videographers will be willing to comply, providing you with original copies (rather than you making copies at home) so that their work remains of a consistent quality.

Discuss protocol with your videographer.

Avoid having your wedding look like a movie production by requiring that your videographer stay in the background. It's never appropriate to block your guests' view of the couple or the festivities. If your wedding site does not allow for your videographer to film during the ceremony, find out if a camera can be placed on a tripod at the altar so that the proceedings can be captured.

SHOTS TO REMEMBER

The only way you can avoid missing important details is to write things down. When it comes to your shot list, be sure to keep a copy, give one to each photo professional, and another to the guardian you appoint to the photo/videographers. Here is a standard listing of wedding images. You can tailor your shot list to your own needs.

Before Your Wedding

At the bride's home or hotel

Bride getting dressed

Bride and bridesmaids

Each attendant individually

Group shot of female attendants (with flower girl and any junior bridesmaids)

Bride and maid or matron of honor

Bride and her parents together and individually

Bride and her siblings

Bride's grandparents

Bride's parents with her grandparents

Make sure you take your bridal portraits early on, so that everyone looks fresh.

At the groom's home or hotel or at wedding site

Groom alone

Groom and groomsmen

Group shot of male attendants (with ring bearer)

Groom and best man

Groom and his parents together and individually

Groom's grandparents

Groom and his grandparents

Groom's parents and his grandparents

Wedding book attendants

During the Wedding Ceremony

Groom's grandmother and usher as they walk to her seat

Bride's grandmother being ushered to her seat
Groom's mother being ushered to her seat
Bride's mother being ushered to her seat
Each bridesmaid walking to altar
Maid or matron of honor walking to altar
Flower girl
Ring bearer
Bride and her father walking down the aisle
The couple exchanging vows
The newlyweds' first kiss
Other moments as they can be discreetly captured
Bride and groom leading the recessional

After the Ceremony

If you decide to have posed shots in your wedding album, the time to take them is right after the ceremony, before the reception. Ask your photographer to allow your friends and relatives about fifteen minutes for their own shots. Then he can graciously move in, asking others to refrain from shooting while he records images for your wedding album. Guests can use what shouldn't be more than forty minutes to mingle before heading to the reception site.

The happy couple
The bride alone, full-length and up close
The groom alone, full-length and up close
The bride's bouquet (before it gets crushed!)
The couple's rings close up
The bridal party
Bride and groom with the little ones: ring bearer and flower girl
Bride with flower girl
Groom with ring bearer
Bride and groom with maid or matron of honor and best man
The couple with bridesmaids
The couple with groomsmen
The couple with the bride's parents
The couple with the groom's parents
The couple with the bride's grandparents
The couple with the groom's grandparents

The couple with the bride's immediate family
The couple with the groom's immediate family
The couple with the bride's extended family
The couple with the groom's extended family
The couple with the wedding officiant(s)
The receiving line
Candids of guests

During the Reception

Each of the activities that occurs during your reception should be documented. At the same time, you want your photographer to look for unique moments. Ask him or her to spend time photographing candids of the two of you and of your guests that will make wonderful supplementary shots. (Know that some couples eliminate all of the posed shots and go for professional candids, because they love the spontaneity in the pictures.)

The newlyweds' entrance
The entrance of the bride's parents
The entrance of the groom's parents
The entrance of the bridal party
The display of food (early before it's touched!)
The cake
The cutting of the cake
The entertainment
Throwing the bouquet
Throwing the garter
Best man's toast
Bridal party table
Other tables
The first dance
Bride and her father dancing
Groom and his mother dancing
The couple visiting with guests
The grand exit

Any preorganized shots with the couple and special guests. (This should be listed for the photographer in advance. To be included are your boss, co-workers, members of your clubs or associations, and others.)

CHAPTER 12

FOR GROOMS ONLY

Okay, brothers, this one's for you. Countless women can attest to the fact that their men did *not* participate in the planning of their wedding. The stories go like this, "He just stopped talking to me," or "He said he really didn't care what we did—he just wanted to get married," or "He kept giving me the constant refrain, 'Whatever you say, dear.'" Now, to be fair, in some instances, this is what sisters want. It gives them the opportunity to explore their wedding fantasies without restrictions, from you at least. When the tug-of-war begins between your future wife and her mother, it may seem easier for a groom to check out than to jump into an already boiling debate.

But, is this really the best way to enter into your marriage? In many African societies, brothers are involved from childhood. Among the Samburu of Kenya, for instance, the road to marriage, including roles for all the males, is mapped out in intricate detail. There are rites of passage beginning at a young age through which all boys must pass before they are even allowed to marry. As mentioned earlier, they must become *moran*, of the warrior age-set, first, before they are eligible for marriage. Once they are given permission to marry, usually between ages twenty-five and thirty-five, they must seek out a wife in a neighboring village and follow a precise series of steps, including providing the requisite "bride price," a gift of an ewe to the bride's mother, and the slaughtering of the wedding ox, *rikoret*. Because the rituals are ancient and basically unyielding, these young men simply and reverently follow them.

BE INVOLVED—IN YOUR OWN WAY

Here in America there's much greater flexibility for a groom's involvement in the marriage rites, which shouldn't, however, lead to abdication from the process. It's especially important for men to participate when they are seeking a culturally inspired union. Married since 1979 to attorney Illona Sheffey Rawlings, Dallas-based internist M. Keith Rawlings contends that both partners have to remember that you're not only joining two individuals, but also two families. "That sometimes gets lost in the process of planning for this specific ceremony, particularly from the man's perspective. A lot of times the decisions about what color this or that should be, whether this garment style is better than that one, or in what order individuals should come down the aisle makes you lose the essence of what you are attempting to do." Rather than defer entirely to the bride, her mother, or the wedding coordinator, Rawlings says that brothers should interact and learn to communicate with their betrothed. Communication is key to the success of a marriage, and most likely the first big high-stress situation the two of you will face will be your wedding.

For the Glovers, also Dallas-based, whom we met earlier, the scenario was similar. The Reverend Clarence Glover, originally from Shreveport, Louisiana, had spent many years studying the Black family and researching African culture. When it came time for him and Sybil Pruitt, of Athens, Texas, to marry in 1992—both for the second time—each of them wanted to consider the ramifications of their union carefully. They did what Sybil calls "untraditional" dating (though it's actually embracing an old, very traditional notion!), in that they spent a fair amount of time together truly *just getting to know each other*. That process helped them, as Clarence says, to "move beyond merely romanticizing each other. We look at each other as two human beings who are not simply attracted to each other, but who have faults, attractiveness, and weaknesses."

As a spiritual adviser, Clarence believes that what brothers need to understand the most is how to consider women in a deeply spiritual way. That means paying close attention to them—from the beginning. "Men tend to distort the concept of love," he says. "Particularly regarding sex, men need to see the act of intercourse as a culmination of physical union that grows out of a loving attitude, something that is treasured by both people."

As an "old married man," Rawlings adds, "Being in love with somebody, the passion, the infatuation, is important and is not to be trivialized. But the thing that will keep the fire going ten, fifteen, twenty, even thirty-five years later is not that. You had better like that person, meaning the person you are marrying as opposed to the person you think she will become."

Unsolicited Advice

Lots of issues come up in the planning of your wedding. Keep a level head and turn to your partner for help when you need it. Beyond that, consider these tidbits from brothers who have already gotten married:

Rely on your best man to be a tremendous support. He should be there for you from the moment that he accepts this role, but you will need to let him know how to work with you. Be specific about what needs to be done, and enlist his support in making it happen.

If your best man lives in another town or is very busy, ask one or more of your other attendants to take up the slack.

Don't invite any ex-girlfriends who may stir up bad feelings for you, your wife, or your guests. Your guest list should be limited to neutral and supportive family and friends.

Avoid one of the easiest faux pas around—getting drunk the night before your wedding. Let your best man know that you would like your bachelor party to be a week or so ahead of your ceremony. If the party has to be on your wedding eve, be moderate in your alcohol intake. It's no fun, nor is it respectful, having a hangover when you say, "I do."

Be in Sync

Instead of getting cold feet, participate in the process of your marriage *and* have fun! Follow the recommendations offered to *both* of you throughout this book.

The first step is to get a blank book, preferably one with a handsome cover, to record your plans and your thoughts. Use this as or in addition to the book in which you and your fiancée will keep all wedding details. Writing down your thoughts is a good practice to begin anyway. When times get tight and you can't seem to find the words to tell your wife what you're feeling, you may be able to record them with a clear head first and then communicate them to her later—either by verbal or written word.

Be sure to participate in the informative quiz that appears at the end of Chapter 2. It will help you and your fiancée to discover important aspects of your personalities and iron out any differences that you may have.

Contemplate your own ideas about your wedding. Have you ever thought about how it might be organized? What details would you like to include? Share those ideas with your bride early on. Discuss her ideas as well. Make sure that you both understand what is important to each of you. Decide together what the theme and style of your wedding and reception will be. And then inquire about important details as they unfold. Let your fiancée know that you really are interested in your wedding, and be there for her—and with her—throughout the process, even if her parents are footing the entire bill.

When you are contributing to the cost, be clear about what expenses you are incurring and honest about your ability to meet your obligations on time. Especially when times get tense, continue to talk to your fiancée about the upcoming events.

The Question of Rings

When it comes to buying your fiancée an engagement ring, think long and hard on how you want to handle things. There's the traditional way of doing it—spring it on her in the most romantic setting you can find at the same time that you ask her to marry you. You can also talk to her about what she likes to ensure that you spend your money on something both of you will appreciate. Stockbroker Clifford Virgin III, whom we met earlier, did a little of both. With the intention of surprising his fiancée with a beautiful diamond ring, he went shopping first for diamonds, then for settings. After a rather exhaustive search, he made his selection and left a deposit. He and his fiancée, Benilde Little, had already agreed to marry each other, and as they discussed their upcoming wedding and life together, Benilde mentioned that she would love to have an emerald-cut diamond. Meanwhile, Cliff's choice was a healthy round cut. So, unbeknownst to Benilde, he quickly called his jeweler and asked for another stone, more to her taste. (Because he was buying from the same source, and the jeweler was a business associate, he was able to make the trade without losing his deposit.) When Benilde discovered her ring at the bottom of her kahlua and cream glass, she was thrilled—and so was he. Cliff says, "I wanted to pick out the ring myself. I was glad, though, to know what she liked, because I really thought that she had said she liked round stones." It pays to check!

The ring question took a unique twist for Khephra Burns. Having rings made or otherwise investing in jewelry wasn't terribly important to him or his fiancée, Susan Taylor. What was vital was the link that they shared with their families. As they contemplated how to include their families into their marriage, rings they already had took on new meaning. When Susan's mother was hospitalized, she had taken a band of diamonds that she wore and which had belonged to her mother. She had placed it on Susan's hand for safekeeping and asked that she keep it in the family and eventually pass it on to Susan's daughter, Nequai. Khephra hadn't removed an interlocking ring from his finger since his parents had given it to him several years earlier, so it was a perfect ring to offer to their union. In the end, they used those family treasures as symbols of their union.

YOUR WEDDING ATTIRE

One of your basic responsibilities is selecting and securing the clothes for you, your groomsmen, and your ushers. So, don't let your fiancée decide everything for you. Traditionally in America and throughout Africa, the bride isn't even viewed by the groom for a certain period before the wedding. During that time she is busy readying her body, her mind, and her clothing for her new life. The man doesn't just sit around waiting, either. Among the Maasai and Samburu of Kenya, a groom also has preparatory rituals that he must perform. His hair is braided and coated with red ochre as he also paints his face in the same color, using elaborate designs. Getting dressed for the Samburu includes adorning the groom's head, face, and neck with beads and placing *urauri*, copper earrings worn by married women, in his ears. He also wears garters made of lion skins along with vivid red-and-white draped fabric.

You probably won't be sporting lion skins, but you should seriously consider what you will wear on your big day. Start out by thinking about how you want to look and feel; talk to your fiancée about your ideas. Chances are she already has specific ideas on the style of clothing she would like to wear—the two of you should complement each other. Even if she wants to keep her actual dress a secret (a long-lived tradition dating back to eighteenth-century Europe and precolonial West Africa), she should be able to tell you some basics.

Be creative. As long as you remain tasteful in your attire, you can take certain liberties. African Americans have the wonderful opportunity to borrow ideas from our many cultures and meld them together to make an individual statement. So, for example, if your wife wants to wear a traditional Ghanaian wedding dress—a long *kente* wrap skirt and white blouse, you don't have to wear the traditional complement, a *kente* wrap that resembles a toga. You could opt for *kente* in a more Western variation, such as a sports coat with black evening pants as shown in the African-American Wedding Album in this book.

Men's wedding style varies in different African nations, but traditional attire is normally made from a delicately woven fabric from the man's home region that is draped across his body. It is sometimes accompanied by a hat, called a *gelee*, a shawl, and sandals. Designer Sesheni has reinterpreted and updated an ancient Nubian or Khamitic design of evening wear for men that is both comfortable and cultural. Called a *heb-sa*, which means protective clothing in Mtu Ntr or ancient hieroglyphic language, Sesheni says, "It is basically a tunic that you pull on that has deep pleats on the shoulders, three inches wide, meant to accentuate the broad squareness of an African man's physique—without shoulder pads. Generally it has no buttons or buttonholes and does have a slit neckline and Nehru collar." With the tunic come pants that have no buttons or zippers, but instead a closure that laps over itself; or sometimes the garment is kilted, which is not like the Scottish kilt but more like the pants worn by rap singer M.C. Hammer. (See the women's complement, called *pede-sa,* also meaning protective covering.) For bride and groom, these garments are generally made in natural fabrics, such as silk, linen, cotton, or with a blend of rayon. Sometimes embroidered as many West African fabrics are made now, they can incorporate wings—pleats symbolizing the wings of the falcon, or strength and power.

Whereas men's clothing in the African tradition is known for its comfort and ease of design, the European style of dressing the groom that is predominant in America is more confining. Draped hand-loomed fabric and slippers, for example, are replaced here by starched white shirts, tails, tailored trousers, and patent-leather shoes. But who's to say that you can't mix it up for your big day?

If you decide to wear a classic tuxedo, which is appropriate for nearly any style wedding, consider either buying the tuxedo or having it made. Your wedding is just the first of many formal affairs that you can expect to attend with your wife. Lucky for men, you don't have to create a different look each time you go black-tie. So, why not invest in your future and end up with a form-fitting tuxedo for your wedding day at the same time!

Dressing Your Attendants

When the time comes to select your attendants' attire, go with your best man—or, better yet, your fiancée—to the rental shop to make choices. Although this shouldn't determine the final count for your bridal party, you should know that rental businesses often offer discounts for parties of six or more. Your best man, groomsmen, and ushers are responsible for paying for their own clothes, so take price into careful consideration. Also, make everyone aware that they should wear clothing that is complementary to yours. If you are wearing traditional African dress, and you either can't arrange for the same for them or the cost becomes prohibitive, feel free to have them wear tuxedos or dinner jackets and trousers accented with African print bow ties and cummerbunds to keep the ethnic theme alive. (See the Resource Guide for businesses that can help.)

You can expect to order suits, along with shirts, accessories, and shoes at a rental shop. If your group does not order everything, make sure that you see your

◆

HOW TO BUY AND KEEP A TUXEDO

To find a tuxedo (or any other suit) that fits well and is made of high-quality, long-lasting material, follow these simple steps, offered by my father, Judge Harry A. Cole, a man who has been having his suits tailor-made for more than forty years:

1. Look at someone who is well dressed and ask him where he gets his clothes. Then go there. Ask the salesperson to show you different suits and to explain the differences among them. Pay particular attention to fabric content, style, and price.

2. Black men sometimes experience fit problems with ready-made suits. If you are hard to fit, consider having a tuxedo made. Find a reputable tailor and examine his work closely before you order. You will need to select the style and fabric and verify delivery for at least two weeks before your big day.

3. Alteration can be almost as important as having a suit made from scratch. Ultimately you want to have a suit that fits you, that makes you look good, and that will last. A good tailor should be able to alter ready-made clothes to fit your body like a glove.

4. Consider going to a fabric store where you can learn the difference in quality of material. The salespeople will tell you about the weaves of various fabrics, the kinds of thread you should use to strengthen buttons and hems, and how suiting fabric should be cleaned and cared for.

5. If you find a ready-made tuxedo that meets your needs, purchase it at least two months in advance and arrange to have it altered to fit.

6. Look at the care labels on your new tuxedo and on clothes that you already own to learn how to clean them properly.

7. Learn that you don't have to press clothes as frequently as people tend to. Your suits will actually last longer if you steam them. This can be done with an actual steamer that can be purchased in the housewares department. Hang your suit and wave the steamer's wand up and down the garment, holding it about six inches away from the fabric; wrinkles will gently fall out. If you don't have a steamer you can hang your suit in the bathroom and let the steam from the shower loosen up wrinkles.

8. Hang up your clothes after you wear them to keep them wrinkle-free.

◆

attendants' shoes and other accessories, especially if they intend to wear their own. No matter how much you trust them, you want to ensure that the group is represented as one unit. It doesn't hurt any to have all shoes in good repair, either!

Don't feel that you are required to follow hard-and-fast fashion rules, though. In 1990 when Charmaine Williams, a cake designer, got married, her husband, television producer Jay Jones decided to let his "boys" be comfortable. One big concern Jay had was with shoes. Since guys normally end up renting shoes that ache by evening's end, he didn't want to chance discomfort. That meant that the whole male half of the bridal party wore high-top basketball sneakers—with their tuxedos, in black and white so that they would be color-coordinated. (Jay, who was dressed in white tie and tails, wore all-white Converses.) One brother even wore his signature fedora. As Charmaine explains it, "He never goes anywhere without his hat, and my husband didn't want to force him to do something that would make him uncomfortable. He wanted everybody to have a great time."

THE HONEYMOON

Although this book doesn't spend much time talking about the honeymoon (it could be a book in itself!), I thought it appropriate to mention a few points here. Western custom says that the groom is responsible for footing the bill and making the necessary arrangements for the honeymoon. Sometimes that means that the destination becomes a surprise for both the bride and the family. Of course, the suggestion here is that the two of you discuss honeymoon options together—early on.

First on the agenda should be whether you will actually go on a honeymoon. I know that in 1957, when my parents got married, the farthest away they went was into their new house. The same was true for two of my friends in North Carolina who married more than thirty years later, in 1991. Although passing on a getaway may seem odd and disappointing, it actually is common in many African communities. In fact, none of my research shows that African couples take vacations after they marry. Instead, they often spend time with their families, settling into married life!

If a trip with your honey is your intention, begin shopping *together* for a location at least four months in advance—if not earlier. You will need to decide how much money you can afford to spend—and include that figure into your budget. Be careful not to overspend on your trip. Time away can be the most romantic, but you don't want the bill to sour the experience. Check newspaper ads for special deals, and contact a travel agent who can help you in your search. If you use a travel agent, find

◆

HONEYMOON ON A BUDGET

When your money is tight but you really want to take a vacation, brainstorm with your fiancée, and think creatively. These suggestions may help:

◆ *Get married during the off-season for wherever you plan to go. Most of the islands in the Caribbean, for instance, enjoy high season in the winter when tourists want to leave their cold-weather homes for more sunny shores. So plan your trip for the more affordable summer months.*

◆ *Select a location that is near your home where you can drive instead of flying. Along the eastern seaboard, as well as the Pacific rim, delightful bed-and-breakfasts provide intimate settings for romantic getaways.*

◆ *Charge your trip to American Express Sign & Travel. Your payments will be spaced out over a specified number of months, so that you can pay them easily. Be aware, though, that the interest rate is high. If you go this route, pay more than the minimum so you don't end up paying twice the price you thought your trip cost!*

◆ *Have your honeymoon at home, where it's just the two of you. You can even tell your family that you will be going away so that no one will call. Why not order in takeout every night? Or better yet, plan meals where you cook together and for each other.*

◆ *Postpone your honeymoon until you are better able to afford it, maybe even for your first anniversary.*

◆

out the cutoff date for when you must give a down payment or actually pay for your tickets, so that you will be able to hold the rate that you were quoted. Make sure if you are going out of the country that you find out what travel documents are required; usually you need at least a valid passport. Some Caribbean islands will allow you to use your birth certificate, though.

CHAPTER 13

TOUCHY SUBJECTS

As much as we relish the idea of it, getting married is not a continually smooth-sailing process. Usually a few glitches present themselves along the way, sometimes creating a couple's first real challenge. For your upcoming wedding, be prepared to manage what comes along. Know that your families will not always agree with your ideas, nor will the two of you be of one mind on all matters. You are bound to discover the intricacies of the art of compromise along the way. This chapter should help you with some of the toughest, most common concerns.

THE ART OF ELOPING

What a romantic prospect: to jet away with your honey to a remote location and get married. Whether the setting is in the mountains or on the shore, the mood can be tranquil and serene, a perfect start for your life together. For New York publicist Carl McCaskill and architect Betty Dubuisson, a trip to Martha's Vineyard in the quiet of winter was the perfect antidote to the hustle and bustle of the Big Apple. Because the two didn't have the resources or the time to put together a big wedding when they were ready to make their formal commitment, they just stole away, not telling anyone the news until many months later. Yet knowing that Betty's mom, a devout Haitian Catholic, and both of their families really wanted to share in the communion of a wedding, they did end up having a proper Catholic ceremony a year later!

Therein lies one of the big dilemmas with eloping. As exhilarating as it may seem to you, your family may not share your enthusiasm—especially if they aren't informed or invited. Historically, couples eloped because their parents disapproved of their union, and they decided to get married anyway. Naturally when the couple returned it wasn't usually to open arms. Today the reasons aren't always as severe. Some couples who know that their immediate relatives or closest friends will be devastated *do* invite a select few to join them at their wedding site, provided they know when to get lost! Others at least inform their families of their plans, giving them the opportunity to be in the know before the news becomes public.

How you handle your elopement is your decision. The pros are several: You can get married when *you* choose—exclusive of your parents and friends. You may be able to spend a lot less money, because you will only have each other to entertain, not 150 or so loved ones. Your fringe benefit will be a built-in vacation.

Couples eloping must be aware of any rules and regulations regarding the marriage license. In other words, as much as you want to pick up and just do it, you still have to do some prep work. In foreign countries especially you will need to find out the requirements in advance. Make sure that you follow it precisely, so that you can avoid hassles when you arrive. In many places you have to wait about a week before your papers can be processed. Wherever you go, call ahead to arrange for a licensed officiate for that area who will validate your marriage. If you've been married previously, make sure that your officiate will agree to marry you. (Some couples have experienced difficulty even with a divorce decree in hand.) Remember that you will need a witness.

For those of you who dash off to get married, consider your loved ones—if only briefly!—while you are away, and do something special for them. You will probably be taking lots of pictures anyway. Why not create a special photo album or home movie and plan a small gathering to share your good times when you return? Some couples host a big party, where their friends get to mingle and share in their happiness—even if it's after the ceremony.

THE SECOND TIME AROUND

Let's face it. For more reasons than people can name, many couples don't fulfill the forever part of their wedding vows. In America the numbers rise yearly, for couples who have been married from one or two years all the way up to thirty years and beyond. Still, divorce doesn't mean that life is over. People who have lived through one, however, know that it can be a whole lot easier to tie the knot than to untie it. They also can attest that there is no pain quite as devastating as being rejected by someone you've promised to love and honor for the rest of his or her life and vice versa. And the mending process is slow.

If you are fortunate enough to have found "the right one" on your second or third attempt, rejoice. *And* do some serious contemplation about why your previous marriage(s) didn't work out, what you really want in a marriage, and if, realistically, in this new union you believe you can be a fully committed and fulfilled partner. Spiritual advisers suggest that all engaged couples need to be realistic about the relationship ahead. Marriage cannot be defined by ideals. Instead, when a marriage works, it does so because it is crafted by two individuals into a mutually loving, respectful bond of friendship, trust, and commitment for the long haul. Especially if you are planning to marry someone who has not been married before, talk openly about your expectations for marriage as well as your thoughts on the realities of what is called by some, "the oldest institution known to man." Be sure to listen to your partner's ideas as well. (Just because you have been married before doesn't mean you are an authority.)

When you decide to get married you should know the basic guidelines that are considered proper for second weddings, although you should feel free to have the wedding of your choice. Second-time brides were historically considered insensitive when they wore white or a veil, both being symbols of virginity. The train has been considered inappropriate as well. Traditionally, a bride who has been married previously should wear either an elegant dress or a suit that is as formal as the time requires. She may wear a hat and gloves, but no modest covering over her face. (Many first-time brides these days opt to lose the veil anyway, especially when they are mature women.)

Colors from antique white and ivory to pale peach, bone, and blue are considered fitting. If you look back to African and European culture, however, the notion of white being the most revered wedding dress color, regardless of whether it was a first or second marriage, loses its strength. On both continents, vibrantly colored fabrics and designs were commonplace. In England the switch to white came rather abruptly in 1840 when Queen Victoria married Prince Albert and effectively began the romantic period still revered today, known as Victorian. In Ghana, in particular, African clothing is still worn for some contemporary weddings, regardless of the number of marriages. Throughout the Motherland, though, Western fashion trends have spread, and white dresses predominate.

Nowadays white dresses of all lengths are marching down the aisles of second-time brides too. One woman who remarried in 1982 says that she felt no shame whatsoever in wearing a formal white gown to her outdoor evening wedding. She says she had waited too long for the right man to come along to limit her celebration in any way.

When it's the bride's first marriage and the groom's second no such strict rules apply. Tradition says that in such cases a couple can have a big wedding with all the trimmings. And of course, the bride can wear white. If either of the betrothed is widowed, the same basic rules apply: no veils, but white is acceptable. Again, it's up to you.

In the Muslim faith and tradition, when a man or a woman has been widowed or divorced and wants to remarry, he or she must find a mate who is also divorced.

You may be surprised to learn that if you've been previously married you are not supposed to accept any gifts. That's right. On the first go-round loved ones may have showered you with best wishes and beautiful presents. Since you have been on your own, and many of the same people may have given you gifts before, you are traditionally not supposed to register, have bridal showers, or accept wedding presents. Rest assured that countless couples do not follow this tradition. For practical reasons and otherwise, many do welcome gifts and do register. Divorced couples do not always divide their belongings equally, thereby often leaving one partner without a basic stock of household needs. Further, couples who are starting a new life together may want to start anew with a home and belongings that are common only to them.

INTERFAITH MARRIAGES

A 1992 PBS documentary explored a most frustrating situation that contemporary families now face—that of interfaith marriage. The program looked into the lives of people from various traditions, especially Greek Orthodox, Catholic, and Jewish. When the program briefly considered the role of religion in the African-American community, information blurred considerably. An assertion was made that in the Black community there is much less divisiveness regarding religious background, that there is much more homogeneity within marriage. That assertion is only partially true. It is a fact that more Blacks marry each other in America than they marry people of other racial backgrounds. But with regard to religious practice, the situation changes. African Americans follow a wide assortment of paths to God, such as Catholicism, Protestantism (including Baptist, United Methodist, African Methodist Episcopal, Seventh Day Adventist, Jehovah's Witnesses, Pentecostal, and many more), Judaism, Buddhism, Siddha Yoga, Islam, Yoruba. What happens when individuals in the Black community who worship in different ways come together to marry?

The Reverend Wendell Phillips of Baltimore says that it can all work out well—if the couple contemplate their differences seriously *before* they get married. He recommends that couples receive special premarital counseling when they are of different faiths, so that they can discuss their feelings about religion and spirituality and come to terms with how they intend to lead their lives as a married couple. One couple in Oakland had an experience that's common today—they were both Baptists but from different churches. In their case, the husband-to-be happily agreed to join his wife's church so that they could worship together. Unfortunately, some couples who married without really hashing out their thoughts on this fundamental issue say they have spent years either working overtime trying to strong-arm their partners their way or feeling rejected. If you find that you and your fiancé cannot come to terms on your religious beliefs, talk to your spiritual adviser about it. It may be that there's hope for your marriage anyway. For instance, although you may not worship in the same manner or in the same place, you can develop a common prayer or spiritual practice at home that the two of you share to keep your relationship strong.

You have several choices regarding your wedding ceremony. What's most important is that neither of you should be forced to choose between religious officiates. Your spiritual home may welcome the option of including your fiancé's officiate in your ceremony. Executing a service efficiently where officiates co-preside often is a happy medium that requires careful coordination and clear communication to ensure that the ceremony runs smoothly. Some interfaith couples decide to marry away from their spiritual home—with their officiates—so that their wedding can be held on neutral ground. Still others opt for a civil ceremony, which has no religious affiliation.

Make sure that you sit down with your parents, at the point of your engagement and at some point during the wedding planning, to let them know of your unique circumstances. Should you run into opposition from your parents or your future in-laws, work to iron out your differences in advance. One way to ease their concern is to let them know that you are both walking in God's path, albeit in different ways.

IT'S A FAMILY AFFAIR

Marriage from the Motherland to the Caribbean and the United States has at least one common denominator—it is supposed to be a union of two families. Reflecting communal values and promoting the growth of the family, it also serves as a welcome turning point in the evolution of a given community. In the midst of so much goodwill, tensions do flare as this rite of passage nears.

When You Already Have Kids

It's no secret that the numbers are high for how many Black women and men are heads of single-parent households. What happens when people with children get married? It used to be that when adults with children decided to marry, it was considered in poor taste for the children to be included in the wedding activities at all. That belief is less common now, although children shouldn't be included unless

both parents agree to their involvement. Conflicts arise today when children sometimes feel threatened by the partner who appears to them to be an intruder. If you
find yourself in this predicament, think long and hard about your child, remembering
that you are making the effort to expand your family, not exclude your child from
your life. Take care in getting that point across well in advance of your wedding.
Actively include your child in your plans.

Many couples have developed strategies to ease their children into a marriage.
When Michele Miles and David Watson got married in the summer of 1992, they
had a great idea for Michele's nineteen-year-old son. The couple staged what
amounted to a wedding for African-American royalty—in a park in New Jersey.
Michele was delivered to David via an ornamented box, à la Cleopatra, that was
designed and crafted by her son. Once her box was set down (by her five brothers and
one nephew who carried her), he took her arm and escorted her to her future husband.
(For more information on sharing the news with your children, see Chapter 3.)

When One's on the Way

Times have changed a bit since Dad came running after that so-and-so who
got his daughter pregnant, and forced the couple into a "shotgun" wedding. That's
not to say, however, that parents are any more comfortable with the notion of their

children having sex *before* marriage. It's true,
fifties values live on. (Some mothers from New
York to Nigeria are known even today to hold
bloodied wedding sheets in the highest esteem.)
What should you do if you find yourself pregnant
and in a relationship that promises to be lasting?

First, stop feeling guilty. It's a blessing
that you are accepting your responsibility to be a
parent, *and* that you are in the wonderful position
of marrying your child's father. Bearing children
is considered the world over as one of the most
highly revered acts that a couple can consum-
mate. Children are our legacy. That the two of
you plan to forge a formal union to embrace your new family should be commended.

If the two of you were not originally planning to marry, talk about your
relationship with a spiritual or psychological adviser. Explore your needs and desires
and your plans for the future of your relationship and that of your growing family.

In order to make a marriage last you will need to be open and honest about your expectations. (See Chapter 2 for a quiz that can help you sort through your thoughts.)

Logistically, you will have to make some quick decisions. If you intend to keep the news between you and your fiancé or within the family, you will need to get married right away. Many women begin to show after the first trimester. One couple in Atlanta who had planned on marrying within a year chose another route. When they discovered that they were pregnant, the two simply changed their plans and took a long weekend in Jamaica, where they got married. It wasn't until three months later that their friends learned of their news. If you would like to get married in your spiritual home, consult your officiate to see if he or she will still agree to perform the ceremony. In many cases, you will have no problem, but it is important to ask.

You may find it interesting that some African regional groups historically placed the highest honor on a young couple who were fertile at marriage. For the Kgatla people of South Africa, for example, it was the pre-Christian tradition that young people didn't actually marry *until* they successfully consummated. In fact, the couple were encouraged to cohabitate. Only after the young woman was found to be pregnant was it customary for the formal marriage discussions to be conducted, the food preparations to take place, and the festivities to occur. The young woman meantime was placed in seclusion for a brief period of time, "in order to grow fat and beautiful," which doesn't necessarily refer to pregnancy but rather to voluptuousness, explains I. Schapera in his book, *Married Life in an African Tribe.* They did go through specific engagement ceremonies, beginning with the young man's family asking the young woman's family for permission to let him "enter her hut."

Family Squabbles

The scene is tense. Everybody is at the wedding: the couple, both families, the guests. At first glance it looks like all is well. A second glance tells a different story. Your folks are not getting along. Why? They haven't for years. But up until now, they haven't had to spend much time in each other's company. Unfortunately, if one of your greatest fears for your wedding day is that your divorced parents will have a standoff, you are not alone. Soaring divorce rates mean that parents are often uncoupled or recoupled at the time of their children's weddings. In order to smooth out what could be periodic moments of disaster, take action now.

Here is a partial listing of the questions that you may need to answer before your wedding. Some are based on scenarios common to a traditional Western wedding.

When you know that your parents don't get along, is there anything you can say before the wedding to comfort everyone involved?

Of course. First, make some attempts to create space to think seriously about your family problem. Find a place in your heart for forgiveness of whatever troubles you have experienced in the past. Then sit down with your parents individually and have a heart-to-heart. Let them know that you are embarking on a new journey and that you want them to join you on it. Present it to them as a time for healing old wounds and regaining respect and love in your family. If you sense tremendous discomfort, encourage them to enter into counseling separately or with you, as you prepare for your married life. Even if neither of them takes you up on your offer fully, both should be able to see the love that you are offering them and may, in turn, work on being supportive during your big day.

Beyond your plea for reconciliation, you can help by mapping out your wedding and reception seating to accommodate their differences.

If your father hasn't been around, and you want your stepfather to "give you away," what should you do?

Don't feel that you have to offer this position of honor to your father if he has not been there for you while your stepfather has. You can offer the role to your stepfather, but if your father is living, you should be sure to invite him to the wedding and seat him in one of the first few reserved rows. You do not have to be "given away" at all or by only a father figure, though. Many parents today are standing up together to offer their daughter to her new life.

If your parents are divorced and one or both of your parents is remarried, where do they sit at the wedding itself?

If everyone gets along, both parents and the new spouse(s) can sit in the front row—on the left for the bride's family, on the right for the groom's. Sometimes the two parents will sit next to each other in the first row with the new spouse seated one or two rows behind. If relations aren't so smooth, it's best to have either the parent who cared for you for most of your life sit in the first row with his or her new spouse as applicable, with the other parent and spouse seated behind, or your mother to sit in the first seat of honor, with your father behind. Consult your wedding officiate when you're in doubt.

When your parents don't get along, how should you organize them on the receiving line?

Again, it is important for the married couple to greet all of their guests individually to thank them for being witnesses to their blessed union. It is not a requirement that this be handled in line formation. Should you want the simplicity of having a receiving line and greeting guests early on, especially if they are not all invited to the reception, you can do what most couples do anyway—not have the fathers be on the line, instead asking them to mingle with the guests. Normally both mothers, the wedding couple, and the female members of the bridal party stand in the receiving line, which should be set up near refreshments so that your guests will be comfortable as they extend their best wishes. Although there is a traditional line up, you don't have to follow it. Listen to your instincts instead, and focus on making everyone at your wedding feel at ease—especially your parents.

At the reception, taking care of your parents is a little easier to manage. If you have someone introducing the bridal party upon your entrance, have each parent introduced individually, with the bride's mother coming first. When it comes to seating, don't put your parents at the same table. Often the bridal party sits together, and the families are seated at tables of honor nearby. Flag an additional table as one of honor to accommodate all three groups of parents.

Changing Your Name

Customarily, the way people are known to one another in patrilineal societies throughout Africa is by their family name. In the Caribbean this is also common. Sometimes people are identified solely by using that family name. What happens to that appellation when folks get married? Historically, in many countries, including throughout eastern Africa, when young women moved away from home to their husband's region this was not an issue, because they simply took on the identification of their husband's family. In marriages where the couple lived nearby, the woman was still called by her maiden name as well as her new surname.

In the United States women have customarily dropped their family name and adopted their husband's upon marriage. When they received formal correspondence, they used their husband's name, becoming, for instance, in the case of my grandmother, Carrie Alsup, who married Harvey Freeland in the early 1900s, Mrs. Harvey Freeland. With the advent of the women's rights movement, which gained momentum in the 1960s, many women began to challenge what appeared to some to be a loss of self-identity on the one hand and unwelcome ownership on the other. Women have heatedly argued against accepting the unwritten requirement that they take on their husband's name at marriage. What has happened is that a number of choices have become available. They include the traditional, accepting his name at marriage; a unified compromise, hyphenating the two names, with his coming last or adding his name, making hers a middle name; using his name socially and hers professionally; not changing her name at all; or in some cases, having both partners hyphenate their names, making a new last name.

     If you decide that you or you and your spouse will change your name, there are several steps you must take.

◆ Most important is that if you change your name legally, you must adopt a new signature that you use consistently on all legal documents. This applies specifically for legal papers even if you use your maiden name professionally.

◆ You will need to change your name on your Social Security card, your credit cards, and any other forms of identification that you have. You should contact each of these companies by mail.

◆ Note that in the worst case of a divorce down the road or perhaps of your husband having poor credit, you may want to keep a credit card in your own name. The credit that you have developed over the years—or will build—may fare you, and your spouse, well during tough times.

THE PRENUPTIAL AGREEMENT

One of the touchiest topics of all is that of personal property protection and marriage. The very foundation of marriage is that two individuals are joining as one, "til death do us part." Their pledge to each other and to God, before selected witnesses, ensures that they will remain together, fortifying their bond of love and commitment *forever*. So why a prenuptial agreement? To many intended spouses, the request for one seems like a self-fulfilling prophecy of defeat before the marriage even begins. Many say that asking them to sign such a document means that their partners don't trust them. Without trust, they ask, why should they get married? Legitimate gripes? Yes. Reality today, however, says that nearly 50 percent of all marriages end in divorce, often in the first few years. If the unfortunate happens to you, what recourse do you have? A prenuptial agreement, according to Kervin Simms, Esq., provides protection for each party for any and all possessions that each accumulated *prior* to the marriage. Essentially the agreement serves as a formal listing of your individual assets with an indication of how interest should accrue over time that should revert back to you should your marriage fail. Such an agreement primarily benefits whoever has the greater amount of assets, although it can also apply to assets over the life of the marriage if it is updated from time to time.

What's interesting about this controversial agreement is its similarity to the understood agreement common throughout many Islamic communities in Africa as well as throughout much of traditional West Africa. In these cultures an offering—often called bride price or bride wealth—is presented to the bride's family prior to the formal consummation of a marriage. In some cases, the bride is given plentiful gifts. When the cattle-raising Samburu of Kenya marry, for example, the husband must give his wife at least one cow and one bull to begin her own herd of cattle. Should the relationship end, however, and the bride returns to her family home, she must return the flock of cattle to her husband. If she has no children, her family must also return the items that had been offered to them. Essentially, the woman gets nothing if her relationship fails. The understanding that husbands have exclusive rights over their wives' domestic, sexual, and labor services was historically true among the Gisu of the Kenya-Uganda border, as well as many African regional groups across the Continent, although modern times are seeing more rights evolve for women.

It's not that simple here. Because we live in a society that answers tough questions about property through the court system, some couples choose to protect their legal rights in advance—just in case. Since many more women are finding themselves in positions of economic power, some sisters actually are opting to take this route. If you are interested in securing a prenuptial agreement, you should know certain things. First, be straightforward with your fiancé about your feelings. When you discuss the subject, be able to articulate clearly *why* you feel you want this legally binding agreement and offer honest comfort that you are not feeling that your relationship is doomed before it begins. Should the two of you decide to investigate getting a prenuptial agreement, each of you should have a lawyer representing your interests.

RESOURCE GUIDE

One of the greatest challenges you will face in creating your wedding is finding the best resources to meet your needs. The road will be tough, especially when you are in search of cultural treasures. Although this resource guide is by no means exhaustive, it represents a healthy window into the marketplace of vendors who can assist you.

AFRICAN AND AFROCENTRIC WEDDING ATTIRE

4 W Circle
704 Fulton Street
Brooklyn, NY 11238
718-875-6500
Designers collective of Afrocentric women's and menswear.

Adrienne McDonald Designs
Brooklyn, NY
212-726-8385
By appointment only.
Designs nontraditional bridal ensembles.
  Special detailing with fabric, appliqués, pearls, and glass beads.

Afmeg Enterprise
223 South Boulevard
Oak Park, IL 60302
708-383-1932
1-800-AFRI-MAT (outside Illinois)
Custom African wedding attire for the entire wedding party.
  African and java-printed fabrics sold by the yard.

African Eye, Inc.
2134 Wisconsin Avenue, NW
Washington, DC 20007
202-625-2552
Contemporary African designer fashions for the bride and groom.

African Paradise
27 West 125th Street
New York, NY 10027
212-410-5294
Custom African wedding raiment.

Afrikana
6608 Delmar Boulevard, University City Loop
St. Louis, MO 63130
314-862-1230
Unique African attire, fabric, and accessories.

Ancestral Visions Apparel Art
6925 Willow Street NW, Studio 228
Washington, DC 20012
202-722-4221
Custom-made, hand-dyed, painted silk; specially designed wearable art for the entire bridal party.

Ann Clare Originals
1510 Kingsgate Street
Mitchellville, MD 20721
301-390-9088
Afrocentric men's and women's garments with a Western flair, using European and African fabric. Specializing in Nigerian wedding attire.

Anna Grant Designs
c/o Michelle McKinney Hammond
Chicago, IL
312-337-1476
By appointment only.
Importers of authentic traditional Ghanaian wedding ensembles for the entire wedding party.

Aziza for Elena Braith
P.O. Box 206
Brooklyn, NY 11233
718-723-7589
Custom Afrocentric wedding gowns and headpieces.

Batak
4554 North Broadway, Suite 316
Chicago, IL 60640
312-728-0902
By appointment only.
Ready-to-wear and custom contemporary and traditional African fashions for the entire wedding party.

Carone Crawford
Brooklyn, NY
718-485-8895

By appointment only.
African and traditional custom bridal gowns.

Culturally Correct
580 Vernon, Suite 5
Oakland, CA 94610
510-420-1673
Afrocentric wedding attire and accessories for the entire wedding party.

Heavenly Weddings & Scents
Chicago, IL
312-522-1831
By appointment only.
Royal African bridal, bridesmaids', flower girl's, crowns, and shoe designs.

House of Oosala
235 Washington Avenue
Brooklyn, NY 11205
718-638-2871
Traditional Nigerian bride and groom ensembles made of imported fabrics from Nigeria.

Heritage Gifts
8118 South Albany Avenue
Chicago, IL 60652
312-436-8303
Made-to-order African-inspired attire for the entire wedding party; gifts.

Komplementz Wearable Sculpture by Misha
3647 Broadway, Suite 4E
New York, NY 10013
212-969-0606
By appointment only.
Dyed and hand-painted wraps and other apparel.

Kuumba Place
EE Hale House
12 Morley Street
Roxbury, MA 02119
617-427-8325
Custom African bridal and groomswear.

Lady Mitz
120-24 164th Street
Jamaica, NY 11434
718-949-4298
By appointment only.
Traditional Nigerian and contemporary Afrocentric made-to-order bridal ensembles.

Meh International
Suite 37, Copley Place
100 Huntington Avenue

Boston, MA 02116
617-262-0099
Ready-to-wear and custom African designs for the bride and groom. Instructions on African traditions for the wedding ceremony.

Melonie Lynn Designs
Brooklyn, NY
718-857-4411
By appointment only.
Custom contemporary African-designed fashions with a flair, for the entire wedding party.

Moore Kollection
1720 South Michigan Avenue, Suite 3000
Chicago, IL 60616
312-427-6118
1-800-731-3000 (outside Chicago area)
Contemporary Afrocentric custom fashions for the entire wedding party.

Naana's Boutique
1209 U Street NW
Washington, DC 20009
202-328-7047

Naana's Boutique
41 North Second Street
Philadelphia, PA 19106
215-627-9251
Traditional Ghanaian and West African ensembles for the entire bridal party.

Nigerian Fabrics & Fashions
84 MacDonough Street
Brooklyn, NY 11216
718-230-8060
Servicing the entire wedding party with traditional Nigerian and contemporary bridalwear.

Okoh African Imports & Designs
1511 South Hawkins Avenue
Akron, OH 44320
216-867-3136
Custom, made-to-order, African-inspired wedding attire for the entire wedding party.

Pan-African Connection
300 South Beckley Avenue
Dallas, TX 75203
214-943-8262
Contemporary Western and traditional wear for women and men, made from African fabric.

Phillipa's
3711 Macomb Street NW, Suite 1

Washington, DC 20016
202-686-9488
1-800-358-2271
African-inspired fashions for men and women, made from
authentic African fabrics.

Queen Bilqiy's Spiritual Wear
P.O. Box 289
New York, NY 10031
212-281-5180
By appointment only.
Ethnic, custom spiritual wear with crowns, money bags, and
floral bouquets.

Regene's Custom Originals & African Boutique
109-111 South Lewis Street
Staunton, VA 24401
703-885-3491
Custom African wedding attire for the entire wedding party.

Sandaga Market
1325 Levee Street
Dallas, TX 75207
214-747-8431
Manufacturers of custom Afrocentric and traditional African
wedding attire.

Sayida Hafiz Couture
Philadelphia, PA
215-227-6050
By appointment only.
One-of-a-kind couture, cultural artwear for brides and brides-
maids, and special occasion gowns.

Sesheni Designs
718-369-1635
By appointment only.
One-of-a-kind, African-inspired, ancient Nubian, pedes-sa
bridal gowns and groomswear plus ethnic accessories.

Sunugal African Textiles & Arts
1171 Fulton Street
Brooklyn, NY 11216
718-230-4613
African clothing for men and women.

Tents of Kedar
43 Fifth Avenue
Brooklyn, NY 11217
718-783-6638
718-636-0848 (Fax)
Nigerian and other West African bridal ensembles and groomswear.

Therez Fleetwood
New York, NY

212-714-8058
By appointment only.
Nontraditional Afro-European complete bridal ensembles in
gold and silver; also crowns.

Thony Chukwuemezie Anyiam for Anyiam's Creation
1401 University Boulevard
Langley Park, MD 20783
301-439-1110
Contemporary custom wedding attire using imported West
African fabric for the entire wedding party. Catalog
available.

Two Worlds Art Gallery
3824 Douglas Avenue
Des Moines, IA 50310
515-280-6902
African and Afrocentric wedding attire.

West Afrique International
22795 Watkins Street
Hayward, CA 94541
510-581-3678
Traditional and modern, custom-designed African-American
wedding gowns with flair.

West Fashions
New York, NY
212-289-9182
By appointment only.
Made-to-order bridal and flower girl attire from cotton crochet
lace with Afrocentric detailing.

Wilbourn Exclusives
113 East Lafayette Street
Jackson, TN 38301
404-346-2628
901-424-3815
By appointment only.
Exclusive Afrocentric wedding ensembles with a European
flair, for the entire wedding party.

Yom's Boutique
4904 West North Avenue
Milwaukee, WI 53208
414-444-4833
Imported Nigerian garments, ensembles, and accessories for
men, women, and children.

Zu-Wah
P.O. Box 66057
Jacksonville, FL
904-924-0529
By appointment only.
Custom Islamic-style garments made in African fabric for the
bride and groom.

BRIDAL DESIGNERS AND BRIDAL SALONS

Anthony Mark Hankins
Dallas, TX area
214-520-1697
By appointment only. Nation-wide mail order available.
One-of-a-kind custom bridal ensembles; specializes in garments for the mother of the bride (MOB), and second-time-around brides.

Amsale
347 West 39th Street
New York, NY 10018
212-971-0170
Elegant custom bridal gowns.

Angel Claudio Couture
NJ, NY area
201-345-7616
By appointment only.
Made-to-order unique bridal designs for the bride and bridesmaids.

Annabelle's
2401 ½ Broadway
Anderson, IN 46012
317-643-0107
Contemporary and traditional bridal gowns.

Ask Gwen Bridal & Formalwear
2205 West 95th Street
Chicago, IL 60643
312-881-8800
Couture and Afrocentric bridal and bridesmaids' gowns, special occasion wear, accessories; tuxedo rentals.

Adorning Bride by G
2015 Earl Street
Houston, TX 77098
713-521-1153
Contemporary custom bridal gowns in sizes 4 to 28. Rentals available.

BAB Designs
1130 South Wabash, Suite 202
Chicago, IL 60605
312-427-0284
Custom designs for the entire wedding party.
Specializing in leather and suede, and tailored menswear.

Bettye Downs Fashionable
96 Essex Street
Lynn, MA 01902
617-581-9510
Designer of bridal gowns, and wedding attire for MOB, MOG, and flower girls.

Beverly Olivacce
NJ, NY area
201-869-3515
By appointment only.
Contemporary wedding, black tie, and special occasion gowns.

BJ Sanders Collection
Detroit, MI area
313-273-9622
By appointment only.
Classic bridal gowns with a dash of excitement; special occasion eveningwear.

Bridal Elegance
571 Ritchie Road
Capitol Heights, MD 20743
301-499-7256
Serving the bridal party with custom designs and accessories. Alterations on existing gowns.

The Bridal Outlet
4409 Piedmont Avenue
Oakland, CA 94610
510-653-2877
Vintage, period, and traditional gowns; tuxedo and gown rentals available.

The Bridal Path
306 West 38th Street, #1505
New York, NY 10018
212-868-0626
Contemporary and African-inspired second and third wedding attire; wedding planner.

Bride's Choice
4915 Fulton Drive
Canton, OH 44718
216-493-1500
Traditional and contemporary apparel accessories for the bride, bridesmaids, entire bridal party; tuxedo rentals for men and boys.

Bryan K. Osburn Collection
Brooklyn, NY
718-599-7852
By appointment only.
European-inspired traditional bridal gowns with a touch of fantasy.

Carone Crawford
Brooklyn, NY
718-485-8895
By appointment only.
Made-to-order traditional and African-inspired gowns for brides and bridesmaids.

Cassandra Bromfield
Brooklyn, NY
718-398-1050
By appointment only.
Custom contemporary designs for the bride and bridal party.

Christopher Hunte Designs, Inc.
224 West 35th Street, Suite 1310
New York, NY 10001
212-244-0420
Custom couture bridal and special occasion dresses.

Collection Jean Ralph Thurin
New York, NY area
516-379-7055
212-489-7322
By appointment only.
Made-to-order contemporary couture bridal gowns.

Designs by Edouard
648 South Indian Creek Drive
Stone Mountain, GA 30083
404-296-1931
Specializing in beaded and sequined bridal gowns, and gowns
  for the entire bridal party.

Dyan Nelson
19 Lyons Avenue, #302
Newark, NJ 07112
201-926-3032
Contemporary made-to-order couture bridal gowns.

Evelyn Nelson
15 East 40th Street, #1201
New York, NY 10016
212-545-9504
One-of-a-kind custom traditional bridal gowns, redesigned
  heirloom gowns; gowns for bridesmaids and flower girls.

Harold Clarke
1528 Jackson Avenue
New Orleans, LA 70130
504-522-0777
Couture bridal gowns and special occasion dresses.

IFEOMA COLLECTION by Maggie Obaji
703-729-4416
Ashburn, VA
By appointment only.
Contemporary bridal suits, dresses, and ensembles.

Island Bridal Gown Rentals
148 Broadway
Hicksville, NY 11801
516-681-5816
Bridal gown rentals in sizes 4 to 22.
  (Serving NY, NJ, and CT only).

Joycealyn's Apparel
5619 Forest Hill Drive, #300
Forest Hill, TX 76140
817-483-4735
Full-service bridal salon; tuxedo rentals.

Juliana Fashions & Bridals
7618 Ogontz Avenue
Philadelphia, PA 19150
215-549-0666
Traditional and Afrocentric bridal gowns and gowns for the
  entire bridal party.
Rentals available, sizes 2 to 30.

Kelvin Rice Couture
138 South 8th Street, Studio A
Philadelphia, PA 19107
215-627-1995
By appointment only.
Contemporary to fantasy made-to-order bride's and bridesmaids' gowns.

Laura's Tailor Shop
1902 Martin Luther King Jr. Boulevard
Savannah, GA 31401
912-232-4395
By appointment only.
Made-to-order traditional and contemporary gowns for the
  entire bridal party. Men's tailoring and alterations available.

Lenny Yorke
Baltimore, MD
410-542-2252
By appointment only.

**Leslie Coombs of Heaven's Bride and Nubian
  Expressions**
1375 Broadway, 7th Floor
New York, NY 10018
212-354-6928
By appointment only.
Couture traditional, contemporary, and Afrocentric gowns for
  the bride and bridesmaids.

L.S.O. Designs
20010 Calvert Street
Woodland Hills, CA 91367
818-883-9138
By appointment only.
High-fashion wedding gown rentals in sizes 3 to 14.

Ms. B's
Chicago, IL
312-779-1539
By appointment only.
Custom traditional and contemporary bridal, bridesmaids',
  MOB, MOG and flower girl gowns.

Manale
212 West 35th Street, 5th Fl.
New York, NY 10001
212-760-0121
By appointment only.
Classic, contemporary, sophisticated, elegant wedding gowns
and headpieces.

Nadine J Designs
Manassas, VA
703-369-5847
By appointment only.
Custom designs for brides, bridesmaids, girls, and boys.

Peri
1729 Lynbrook
Flint, MI 48507
810-767-0409
Traditional made-to-order bridal gowns.

Pompey
Brooklyn, NY
718-230-4768
By appointment only.
Made-to-order nontraditional wedding gowns.

Priscy's Design House
1526 Centinela Avenue
Inglewood, CA 90302
310-412-8011
1-800-3-PRISCY (outside California)
Contemporary bridal gowns and headpieces, sizes 2 to 50;
bride gowns and tuxedo rentals.

Raven's Unlimited Formalwear
4912 West North Avenue
Milwaukee, WI 53208
414-444-6888
Traditional and contemporary bridal gowns, specializing in sizes
1 to 30; bridesmaids' sizes 3 to 30; bridal gowns and
tuxedo rentals.

Ruben Zurc for Joelle
237 West 35th Street
New York, NY 10001
212-736-8811
Traditional, contemporary, and nontraditional made-to-order
brides, bridesmaids', MOB, MOG gowns.

Sew-What
Priscilla A. James, seamstress
Orlando, FL area
407-275-6789
Traditional bridal gowns. Nation-wide mail order available.

Sharon Sherry
New York, NY

212-534-3297
By appointment only.
Contemporary made-to-order, special occasion and wedding
ensembles with ethnic touch; second-time-around suits and
dresses.

Sincerely Yours
Eve Holloway, dressmaker
Richmond, CA
510-529-0193
By appointment only.
Specializing in bridal gowns, special occasion dresses.

Tugu De Designs
Brooklyn, NY
718-604-8544
By appointment only.
Made-to-order bridesmaids' dresses.

Vincent Da Mon Collection International
412 West Clay Street
Richmond, VA 23220
804-643-9363
Nontraditional made-to-order bridal gowns.

Vic Jones
New York, NY
212-926-0164
By appointment only.
Fit and flair bridal gowns, special occasion dresses, custom
orders.

CHILDREN

A Matter of Taste
P.O. Box 651
Devon, PA 19333
610-896-9546
Contemporary infants to childrenswear in African fabric.
Catalog available.

Afrika House
19445 Livernois
Detroit, MI 48221
313-341-7423
Specializing in African children's clothing.

Isis World by Athena
San Clemente, CA
714-366-0121
By appointment only.
Fully accessorized, innovative, special occasion dresses for girls
from infants to preteen.

KIMWEAR, Inc.
Brooklyn, NY
718-643-2206

By appointment only.
Funky ethnically inspired childrenswear, sizes newborn to 7
    years.

Jaysson 'n Jourdan, Ltd.
2900 Largo Road
Upper Marlboro, MD 20772
301-627-1966
Special occasion Afrocentric childrenswear.

Missouri, Inc.
Somerset, NJ
908-560-0907
By appointment only.
Made-to-order mother and daughter, brides and little-brides
    gowns, formal and everyday wear. Mother sizes, 4 to 22;
    daughter sizes, infants to 8.

Robin's E.Y.E.
Cambridge, MA
607-492-4843
By appointment only.
Handmade from imported Afrocentric fabric, childrenswear
    from newborn to 5 years.

Rossi B Kids, Inc.
Brooklyn, NY
718-452-5137
By appointment only.
European- and African-inspired, special occasion childrenswear
    sizes 0 to 14.

Tea Cake Kids Originals
P.O. Box 137
Hutchins, TX 75141
214-225-8357
Contemporary childrenswear in imported African fabric. Girls
    sizes, infants to 14; boys, infants to 4.

MENSWEAR AND FORMALWEAR SHOPS

A. Mandella Africa—USA
41 West 45th Street
New York, NY 10036
212-581-3820
Specializing in men's formal Afrocentric wedding attire.

Angela Slate Couture, Inc.
New York, NY
212-696-4229
By appointment only.
Custom-made menswear using natural fabrics.

Club Jes Formalwear
10 East Washington
Petaluma, CA 94954
707-765-5797

Club Jes Formalwear
527 Fourth Street
Santa Rosa, CA 95401
707-571-8343

Club Jes Formalwear
1210 First Street
Napa, CA 94559
707-252-0677
Rental and sales of complete line of men's tuxedos.

Custom Accessories
Detroit, MI
313-893-2454
By appointment only.
Custom-made men's vests, neckwear, and cummerbunds.

Duane Fish Menswear
Woodbridge, NJ
908-855-1731
By appointment only.
Contemporary casual menswear.

Evelyn Nelson
15 East 40th Street, #1201
New York, NY 10016
212-545-9504
Men's custom shirts and furnishings.

Everett Hall Designs
8800 Woodland Drive
Silver Springs, MD 20910
301-608-9578
301-608-9579 (Fax)
Made-to-measure designer formalwear.

Freedom
7428 South Vincennes
Chicago, IL 60621
312-488-FREE
Custom-made men's and women's bridalwear.

Gentlemen's Formalwear
571 Ritchie Road
Capitol Heights, MD 20743
301-499-7256
Complete line of retail, made-to-order designer menswear,
    accessories, and rentals.

The Jass Collection by Duende
Brooklyn, NY
718-230-5201
By appointment only.
Made-to-measure custom suits, eveningwear, and sportswear.

Kevin Dickens
Washington, DC

New York, NY
212-736-2411
By appointment only.
Contemporary upscale menswear made from natural fibers.

Miguel Navarro Inc. Custom Designs
New York, NY
212-736-2411
By appointment only.
High-fashion menswear.

Pompey
Brooklyn, NY
718-230-4768
By appointment only.
Made-to-measure contemporary tuxedos.

Walter Foster Patterns and Designs
New York, NY
212-564-9216
By appointment only.
Made-to-measure European and Western menswear and fur-
nishings, using traditional African and European fabrics.

Shaka King
Brooklyn, NY
718-638-2933
Custom-made menswear in unique combinations of fabrics and
colors.

Tugu De Designs
Brooklyn, NY
718-604-8544
By appointment only.
Made-to-order men's shirts and vests.

ACCESSORIES

African Eye, Inc.
2134 Wisconsin Avenue, NW
Washington, DC 20007
202-625-2552
Wedding bags, garters, photo albums, ring pillows.

Audrey Weaver Designs
New York, NY
212-978-7522
212-772-3504
By appointment only.
Bridal accessories, pillows, headpieces, headbands, bows,
sachets.

Brenda Brunson Bey
Brooklyn, NY
718-638-7624
By appointment only.
Custom headpieces, wrist jewelry, capes, and outer garments.

Broom's by Renee
Baltimore, MD area
301-753-9363
By appointment only.
Custom wedding brooms and favors.

Culturally Correct
580 Vernon, #5
Oakland, CA 94610
Men's furnishings, crowns, anklets, and jewelry.

Earworks by Linda Darnell
Chicago, IL
312-476-5554
By appointment only.
Custom hand-painted earrings, brooches, bracelets, and shoe
clips. Hand-painted shoes.

Heritage Altars
2320 Coloma Street, #2
Oakland, CA 94602
510-530-7837
Customized one-of-a-kind brooms. Write for brochure.

Flowers to Remember
Vallejo, CA
1-800-949-JUMP
Broom favors, brooms, church decorations.

Joyce and Company
880 Thieriot Avenue
Bronx, NY 10473
718-842-6483
By appointment only.
Wedding brooms, albums, picture frames, flower baskets, guest
books, pillows, money bags, garters, party favors, bridesmaids' gifts.

Loving Care by Mar
Orlando, FL
407-855-0044
By appointment only.
Bridal accessories, headpieces.

Poopie Designs
Bronx, NY
718-993-9030
1-800-5-POOPIE
Afrocentric bridal favors, brooms, gifts, jewelry to coordinate
with bridal wear, scented pillows, gift baskets.

Ruth's Creations
Detroit, MI
313-872-2057
By appointment only.
Custom one-of-a kind decorative brooms, gift baskets.

ART GALLERIES

Alitash Kebede Gallery
964 North LaBrea Avenue
Los Angeles, CA 90038
213-874-6269

A.F.T.U./ Bill Hodges Gallery
24 West 57th Street, 6th Floor
New York, NY 10019
212-333-2640
Modern and contemporary African-American and world art,
    $500 and up.

Black Gallery
107 Santa Barbara Plaza
Los Angeles, CA 90008
213-294-9024

Bomani Gallery
251 Post Street,, 6th Floor
San Francisco, CA 94108
415-296-8677
African and African-American artists, $500 and up.

Cinque Gallery
560 Broadway
New York, NY 10012
212-966-3464
Contemporary African-American artists, $300 and up.

G.R. N'Namdi Gallery
161 Townsend Street
Birmingham, MI 48009
810-642-2700
Contemporary paintings and sculpture, $500 and up.

Isobel Neal Gallery Ltd.
200 W. Superior Street, Suite 203
Chicago, IL 60610
312-944-1570
Works by African-American visual artists, $300 and up.

June Kelly Gallery, Inc.
591 Broadway
New York, NY 10012
212-226-1660
Contemporary paintings and sculpture, $500 and up.

Kenkeleba Gallery
214 East 2nd Street
New York, NY 10009
212-674-3939
Contemporary and modern painting, sculpture, and photogra-
    phy by third-world and other underrepresented artists,
    $1,000 and up.

Kumasi Gallery
1353 South Wabash Street, Suite 205
Chicago, IL 60605
312-391-7186
By appointment only.
Imported African art and artifacts, $10 and up.

Malcolm Brown Gallery
20100 Chagrin Boulevard
Shaker Heights, OH 44122
216-751-2955
Contemporary paintings, sculpture, and graphics by regional
    and national artists, $500 and up.

Merton Simpson Gallery
1063 Madison Avenue
New York, NY 10028
212-988-6290
Tribal and modern arts, $1,000 and up.

Museum of African Art
593 Broadway
New York, NY 10012
212-966-1313
African sculpture, tribal art.

Peg Alston
New York, NY
212-662-5522

Porter/Radall Gallery
5624 La Jolla Boulevard
La Jolla, CA 92037
619-551-8884

Robertson African Art Gallery
36 West 22nd Street
New York, NY 10010
212-206-0912
By appointment only.
Collector-quality African sculpture, masks, and artifacts, $500
    and up.

Savacou Gallery
240 East 13th Street
New York, NY 10003
212-473-6904
Prints and posters by African-American artists, $15 and up.

Sherry Washington Gallery
Louis Buhl King Building
1274 Library Street
Detroit, MI 48226
313-961-4500
Works of African-American artists, $500 and up.

Things Graphics and Fine Arts
1522 14th Street NW
Washington, DC 20005
Prints and posters by African-American artists, $25 and up.

Two Worlds Art Gallery
3824 Douglas Avenue
Des Moines, IA 50310
515-279-9591

BAKERS AND CAKE DESIGNERS

A Piece of Cake, Inc.
8236 Cottage Grove
Chicago, IL 60619
312-651-3300
Wedding, special occasion cakes, and party trays.

Bernadette's Inc.
P.O. Box 54
Rumson, NJ 07760
908-530-3344
Traditional West Indian wedding cakes.

Cakeman Raven, Inc.
New York, NY
212-283-0405
By appointment only.
Wedding and special occasion cakes, black cakes, and ice
   sculpture.

Caribbean Cake Connoisseurs
56 Grandview Avenue
Edison, NJ 08837
1-800-322-5452
908-738-6609 (Fax)

Clara and Cheryl Decorated Cakes
Washington, DC
202-829-2726
By appointment only.
Traditional and Afrocentric wedding cakes.

Isn't That Special—Outrageous Cakes
720 Monroe Street
Hoboken, NJ 07030
201-216-0123
Cultural and fantasy wedding and special occasion cakes.

Julia's Bakery
803 East 93rd Street
Chicago, IL 60619
312-488-8200
Specializing in wedding and special occasion cakes.

Moore's Bakery
1235 West 79th Street

Chicago, IL 60620
312-783-6997
312-783-7272

Occasional Tiers
Brooklyn, NY
718-787-4158
By appointment only.
Wedding and theme cakes.

Sauda
614 South 8th Street, Suite 254
Philadelphia, PA 19147
215-923-2551
215-923-4061
Cakes featuring handmade African-American cake-top couples.

CALLIGRAPHY

Darnal Smith
Orange, NJ
201-678-7539
By appointment only.

Napoleon Wilkerson
Savannah, GA
912-236-6714
By appointment only.

Sandra McNeill
New York, NY
212-281-3076
By appointment only.

CATERERS

Alexander's Catering
Chicago, IL
312-783-8262
By appointment only.
Specializing in African/Caribbean cuisine.

Blue Monkey & Lady T's Fine Catering
2915 Harper Street
Philadelphia, PA 19130
215-763-1945
Specializing in vegetarian cuisine.

Catering by Jewels
Brooklyn, NY
718-231-0147
By appointment only.

Catering International Cuisine
P.O. Box 6672
Yorkville Station

New York, NY 10028
212-410-7546
Full-service caterer specializing in southern and Caribbean
cuisine.

Culinary Innovations
Kenneth E. Manley II
Columbia, MD
410-997-1887
410-740-0385
By appointment only.
Continental menu designed to client's needs.

Dee Dee Dailey
Brooklyn, NY
718-615-1654
By appointment only.
Caribbean, vegetarian, and continental cuisine.

Dining Table Restaurant & Catering
1409 Ferndale Avenue
Dallas, TX 75224
214-224-8378
1-800-B-A-GUEST (outside Texas)
Specializing in new southern cuisine.

Elegant Catering International
Orlando, FL
407-648-5062
By appointment only.
Catering for large weddings; specializing in continental,
Polynesian, and Caribbean cuisine.

The Elegant Difference
Cleveland, OH
216-751-4143
By appointment only.
Specializes in Caribbean, African, and southern cuisine.

Fanfares by Faye, Inc.
742 East 95th Street
Chicago, IL 60619
312-568-3293
By appointment only.

Faufauzia Delights
New York, NY
212-283-5905
By appointment only.
Specializing in vegetarian; strict halal meats.

Good and Sweet Catering Services
NJ area
201-783-1204
908-727-6401
Specializing in small to large parties.

In the Mix
NY area
212-592-0084
By appointment only.
Specializing in American continental cuisine.

McCloud & Company Caterers
101 West 22nd Street
Baltimore, MD 21218
410-385-2166
Floral arrangements and decorating services available.

Ms. Georgia's Catering
4436 South Berkeley Avenue
Chicago, IL 60653
312-933-7665
Specializing in southern, American, and continental cuisine.

Obaa Koryoe Restaurant and Cafe
3143 Broadway
New York, NY 10027
212-316-2950
Specializing in West African cuisine.

Point of Rest
Philadelphia, PA
215-223-7645
By appointment only.
Specialty transitional and vegetarian cuisine.

Spoonbread
New York, NY
212-865-0700
By appointment only.
Complete catering service.

State of Hunger Catering
Los Angeles, CA
213-937-9681
By appointment only.
Specializing in gourmet vegetarian dishes for small to large affairs.

Theodora's Catering
Sausalito, CA
415-332-6528
By appointment only.
Catering to client's personal tastes.

Yvonne White & Company
5820 Chariton Avenue
Los Angeles, CA 90056
310-649-6626

CLERGY, STORYTELLERS, SPECIAL CEREMONIES

Bishop Doctor Fola Williams
Brooklyn, NY

718-327-2821
By appointment only.
Interfaith and African interethnic and intercultural weddings,
     healing and prayer circles; spiritual counselling.

David A. Anderson/Sankofa
181 Royleston Road
Rochester, NY 14607
716-482-5192
Storytelling in the tradition by which we have forged the prin-
     ciples of *come-union.*

Donna Washington
P.O. Box 1323
Evanston, IL 60204
708-475-8051
Multicultural folklorist, storyteller; will design folktale for your
     event.

Dr. Larry G. Coleman
2536 Madison Avenue
Baltimore, MD 21217
410-523-4807
Storytelling, drummer, sign language.

Iyalosha Ade Kola Adedapo
Milwaukee, WI
414-483-9892
By appointment only.
Yoruba Shango priestess performs weddings and other tradi-
     tional ceremonies; storytelling and jazz vocalist.

Oyafunmike Ogunlano
212-802-7114
By appointment only.
Performs traditional Yoruba wedding ceremonies, naming cere-
     monies, and storytelling.

Mama Edie
Chicago, IL
312-768-6773
Presentation of tales and songs from the diaspora; rites of pas-
     sage, sign language.

Rev. Willie Wilson
Union Temple Baptist Church
1225 N Street, SE
Washington, DC 20020
202-678-8822
Performs traditional wedding ceremonies accompanied by
     African symbols and readings in Swahili.

Shanta
Chicago, IL
312-994-5554
1-800-249-0863 (outside Chicago area)
Traditional African and spiritual storytelling, and music.

Starspirits
Philadelphia, PA
215-763-4054
1-800-583-9963
Spiritual ceremonies.

DRUMMERS, MUSICIANS, AND DJ'S

BJS Productions
11707 Cromwell Avenue
Cleveland, OH 44120
216-721-1897
Professional DJ

D.K.T. Productions
1727 Martin Luther King Jr. Way, Suite 220
Oakland, CA 94612
510-832-6499
DJ specializing in various music styles from the fifties through
     the nineties.

King Sudiata Keita
Omowale Afrikan Dancers
Detroit, MI
313-393-2393
By appointment only.
Drummers and dancers for weddings and naming ceremonies.

Montego Joe
55 West 184th Street
Bronx, NY 10468
212-933-1989
Veteran master drummer.

Regina Perkins
Chicago, IL
312-221-1076
By appointment only.
Percussionist, drummer, and African chanter.

Saniana
Chicago, IL
312-994-5554
By appointment only.
All woman music group performing before and during wedding
     ceremony.

The Traditional African American Drum Society (T.A.A.D.S.)
P.O. Box 48303
Philadelphia, PA 19144
215-848-DRUM
African drum ceremonies and entertainment; singers, dancers,
     stilt walkers.

Yaffa Productions
The Chelsea Center/YMCA

122 West 17th Street
New York, NY 10011
212-840-1234 (service)
Information on African wedding officiates, drummers, other
  musicians, and dancers across the country.

FLORISTS AND SILK FLOWERS

Barbara's Heavenly Flowers & Balloons
East Orange, NJ
201-675-5327
By appointment only.
Silk and fresh arrangements, balloons.

Bloomers, Ltd.
1216 North Charles Street
Baltimore, MD 21201
410-752-8850
Floral presentations of both domestic and exotic varieties, silks,
  and other synthetics.

Blue Thistle Flowermarket
1060 West Chicago
Chicago, IL 60622
312-829-4100

D' Works
32B Debs Place
Bronx, NY 10475
718-379-6609
Flowers made from African fabrics, floral arrangements for ceremonies and receptions; also brooms, favors, and gift baskets.

Daily Blossom
236 West 27th Street
New York, NY 10001
212-633-9000

Daily Blossom
787 Seventh Avenue
New York, NY 10019
212-554-4600

Designs by Edouard
648 South Indian Creek Drive
Stone Mountain, GA 30083
404-296-1931
Floral arrangements for churches and receptions.

Flowers to Remember
Vallejo, CA
800-949-JUMP
Full-service florist, church decorations, brooms and broom
  favors available.

Gaines & Gaines Florist
15527 Euclid Avenue
East Cleveland, OH 44112
216-268-4700

Gaines & Gaines Florist
8916 Cedar Avenue
Cleveland, OH 44106
216-268-4701

Heaven Sent Floral
1417 East Wood Avenue
Akron, OH 44305
216-784-0588

Heavenly Flowers
4924 West North Avenue
Milwaukee, WI 53208
414-871-2400
Exotic floral, silk, and theme arrangements. Rentals available.

Heavenly Wedding & Scents
Chicago, IL
312-522-1831
By appointment only.
Silk floral arrangements and bridal bouquets, church and recep-
  tion decorations.

Mitchell's Florist
Orlando, FL
407-298-0703
By appointment only.

Ms. Norma's Silk Flowers
P.O. Box 20024
El Sobrante, CA 94820
510-222-1600
Silk flower arrangements.

Renaissance Floral Co.
5333 Wayne Avenue
Philadelphia, PA 19144
215-844-7356
Creative floral arrangements and brooms.

Staircase Florist
844 Copley Road
Akron, OH 44320
216-376-4592
1-800-662-5195

Terry's Enchanted Garden
19338 Livernois
Detroit, MI 48221
313-342-3758

GIFTS

4 W Circle
704 Fulton Street
Brooklyn, NY 11238
718-875-6500
Designers collective of accessories and gifts.

Adrienne McDonald
Brooklyn, NY
718-857-0259
By appointment only.
Custom handmade dolls and accessories.

The African American Museum Shop
3536 Grand Avenue
Dallas, TX 75210
214-565-9026

African Eye, Inc.
2134 Wisconsin Avenue, NW
Washington, DC 20007
202-625-2552
Original African and African-American art, sculpture, and artifacts, fabrics and jewelry.

African Home, Inc.
718-363-1159 (metro NY, NJ, CT)
1-800-D-PILLOW
Made-to-order table top, wallpaper, bed and bath, home products using authentic African textiles.

Afro Mart
3448 Martin Luther King Jr. Highway
Harding Hill Plaza
Des Moines, IA 50310
515-279-9458
Gifts, sculpture, imports from Africa.

The Baobab Tree
1439 Amsterdam Avenue
New York, NY 10027
212-926-0027
Traditional African handicrafts, fabrics, and fashions for men and women, custom-made shoes using African fabrics.

Be A Blessing
Brooklyn, NY
718-398-4850
By appointment only.
Personalized gift baskets for men and women.

Black Images Book Bazaar
230 Wynnewood Village
Dallas, TX 75241
214-943-0142

1-800-272-5027
Gifts, herbs and oils; bridal registry.

Charlotte's Ceramics
Warrensville Heights, OH
216-663-3273
By appointment only.
Black porcelain dolls, made-to-order bride and groom dolls, ceramic wedding plates, attendant gifts.

Craft Caravan
63 Greene Street
New York, NY 10012
212-431-6669
Imported authentic African handicrafts, textiles, jewelry, and furnishings.

Curives' Art & Design
122 Washington Avenue
Brooklyn, NY 11205
718-875-2957
Custom hand-forged, sculptural furnishings and home accessories.

Dorian Webb
New York, NY
212-260-9042
By appointment only.
Handmade Venetian glass vases and jewelry.

Griots
44554 10th Street West
Lancaster, CA 93534
805-948-0411
Specializing in Afrocentric books and gifts.

Hammonds House Galleries Gift Shop
503 Peeples Street, SW
Atlanta, GA 30310
404-752-8730
Fine art, prints, art books, African artifacts, original jewelry.

Harris Design Group
667 West Bethune
Detroit, MI 48202
313-871-4155
Contemporary, ethnic-inspired quilts, pillows, art, and gifts.

House of Oosala
235 Washington Avenue
Brooklyn, NY 11205
718-638-2871
Imported Nigerian handicrafts, musical instruments, and furniture.

The Hue-man Experience
911 Park Avenue West
Denver, CO 80205

303-293-2665
Specializing in African and African-American books.

Jacques Carcanagues
114 Spring Street
New York, NY 10012
212-925-8110
Imported textiles, furniture, jewelry from India, Africa, China,
    and Korea.

Kuumba Place
EE Hale House
12 Morley Street
Roxbury, MA 02119
617-427-8325
Quilts, wall hangings, and tapestries made from traditional and
    custom-woven fabric.

LaVon's Art
Lexington, KY
606-231-9268
By appointment only.
Early African-American wood sculptures.

Okoh African Imports & Designs
1511 South Hawkins Avenue
Akron, OH 44320
216-867-3136

Okoh African Imports & Designs
233½ South Water
Kent, OH 44240
216-677-1498
Arts and crafts, artifacts, pictures, jewelry, and books.

Marrow of Tradition
1706 West Market Street
Akron, OH 44313
216-864-8084
Art gallery, book store, home furnishings, and imported African
    fabric.

Museum of African American Art Gift Shop
4005 Crenshaw Boulevard
Los Angeles, CA 90008
213-294-7091

National Museum of African Art Gift Shop
950 Independence Avenue
Washington, DC 20560
202-786-2147

The Museum of Modern Art Design Store
44 West 53rd Street
New York, NY 10019
212-767-1050
1-800-447-6662
Send $3 for catalog.

Noel Copeland
Brooklyn Navy Yard, Bldg. #62
3rd Floor
Flushing Avenue
Brooklyn, NY 11205
718-852-5487
Handmade ceramic tableware and housewares.

Nu Nubian
132 South LaBrea Avenue
Los Angeles, CA 90036
213-937-5662

Leekan Designs, Inc.
93 Mercer Street
New York, NY 10012
Importers of jewelry, furniture, antiques, and collectibles from
    the Far East, Southeast Asia, and Africa.

Pan-African Connection
300 South Beckley Avenue
Dallas, TX 75203
214-943-8262
Books, arts and crafts, oil paintings, cards, jewelry, and fabrics.

Reflections Museum Shop
California Afro-American Museum
600 State Drive
Los Angeles, CA 90036
213-744-2071

Regene's Custom Originals & African Boutique
109-111 South Lewis Street
Staunton, VA 24401
703-885-3491
Imported African artifacts, paintings, masks, and giftware.

Sarajo
98 Prince Street
New York, NY 10013
212-966-6165
Imported handicrafts, furniture, jewelry from the Middle East,
    Asia, Africa, India, and China.

Shrine of the Black Madonna
Cultural Center & Bookstore
13535 Livernois
Detroit, MI 48238
313-491-0777
Authentic woven and printed African fabric, sculpture, jewelry,
    books, clothing, and gifts; bridal registry.

Small Treasures
51405 East Ponce De Leon
Atlanta, GA 30083
404-292-2801
Black artist's dolls and collectibles. Catalog available.

Studio Museum of Harlem Gift Shop
144 West 125th Street
New York, NY 10027
212-864-4500, ext. 237
Afrocentric gifts. Write or phone for free catalog.

Tarágee Novelty & Decorating Service
NJ, NY area
908-281-0822
By appointment only.
African-American art and prints, custom framing and matting.

Tantau Smith
1353 Abbot Kinney Road
Venice, CA 90291
310-392-9878
Gifts, jewelry, and clothing.

Two Worlds Art Gallery
3824 Douglas Avenue
Des Moines, IA 50310
512-279-9591
Imported African fabric, Afrocentric decorations, oils, and
   books.

Your Heritage House
110 East Ferry
Detroit, MI 48202
313-871-1667
Gifts, art from African-American artists and craftspeople.

Uzoamaka
2047 Walnut Street
Philadelphia, PA 19103
215-569-2400
Multicultural boutique.

HEADPIECES AND CROWNS

Carlos New York Hats
66 West 38th Street, Suite 401
New York, NY 10018
212-869-2207
By appointment only.
Custom-made fantasy bridal hats and headpieces.

Crowns by Marabella
1865 South Millard Avenue
Chicago, IL 60623-2543
312-521-1844
1-800-222-6967 (outside Chicago)
One-of-a-kind exquisite beaded crowns, headpieces, and
   related accessories in African and traditional bridal fabrics.

Cynthiaga's
6927 Plainfield Road

Cincinnati, OH 45236
513-891-6160
Elegant crowns, headdresses, veils, and custom-made
   handbags.

Darlena Goodwin
211-60 90th Avenue
Queens Village, NY 11428
718-740-6738
By appointment only.
Traditional and contemporary headpieces.

Heavenly Flowers
4924 West North Avenue
Milwaukee, WI 53208
414-871-2400
Custom headpieces.

House of Hats
2336½ West 79th Street
Chicago, IL 60620
312-434-3884
Custom-made bridal headpieces and hats.

My Point of View
20001 Greenfield, Suite 5
Detroit, MI 48235
313-835-7717
Made-to-order traditional and nontraditional headpieces.

Sherri Hobson Greene
Brooklyn, NY
718-452-2920
By appointment only.
Custom-made bridal headpieces, hats, and crowns.

Xenobia Bailey
P.O. Box 1114
New York, NY 10156
212-971-1032
One-of-a-kind hand-crocheted African headpieces embellished
   with cowrie shells, lace, tulle, and rhinestones.

JEWELRY

Baxter's Fine Jewelry
138 Southeast 8th Street
Philadelphia, PA 19107
215-627-5050
Custom designer of fine jewelry in 14-karat, 18-karat gold,
   and platinum.

Cameo Designs, Ltd.
New York, NY
800-4-CAMEO-5
By appointment only.

Exquisitely detailed Black cameo collection including earrings, pins, necklaces, bracelets, costume and fine jewelry. Catalog available.

Dorian Webb
New York, NY
212-260-9042
By appointment only.
Handmade Venetian glass and semiprecious stone earrings, chokers, and bracelets.

Earworks by Linda Darnell
Chicago, IL
312-476-5554
By appointment only.
Handpainted and adorned earrings, bracelets, and shoe clips.

Fran Mack
Brooklyn, NY
718-636-1201
Handcrafted beaded earrings, necklaces, bracelets, and rings in precious and semiprecious gems.

Jay Sharpe
1812 West Main Street
Richmond, VA 23220
804-353-4733
Wedding bands uniquely designed in 18-karat gold, platinum, and sterling.

Khamit Jewelers/Studio of Ptah
155 Canal Street, Suite 9
New York, NY 10013
212-226-8487
212-343-9906
1-800-799-PTAH
Appointment preferred.
Handcrafted Khamitic inspired jewelry and African wedding bands and engagement rings.

Komplementz by Misha
3647 Broadway, Suite 4E
New York, NY 10031
212-969-0606
By appointment only.
Handcrafted jewelry fashioned from a lightweight ceramic base embellished with an assortment of contemporary and antique findings, beads, crystals, and semiprecious stones.

Royal Kente Corp.
P.O. Box 130222
Springfield Gardens, NY 11413
718-978-2675 (NY, NJ, CT only)
1-800-722-8285
Sankofa waist beads.

Sandy Baker
New York, NY

212-663-6366
By appointment only.
Contemporary 14-karat, gold-filled, and sterling silver earrings, bracelets, and pins; great attendant gifts.

Shimoda Accessories
New York, NY
212-491-6726
By appointment only.
Hand-beaded bridal waist beads.

Sun Gallery Goldsmith designed by Jamal Mims
2322 18th Street, NW
Washington, DC 20009
202-265-9341
Wedding bands and amber jewelry specially designed in 14-karat, 18-karat, and 22-karat, silver, and platinum.

LIMOUSINES

AAA Limousine
1685 Rogers Avenue
San Jose, CA 95112
408-453-2800
1-800-969-5466

Avanti Limousines
2323 South Voss, Suite 123-E
Houston, TX 77057
713-556-5466

Chuck's Limousine
Chicago, IL
708-535-4776

Classic Tours & Limousine Service
13110 Shaker Square
Cleveland, OH 44120
216-491-0042

Jackson Limousine
Los Angeles, CA
213-734-9955

Magic Touch Limousine Service
Chicago, IL
708-535-4917

Paradise Rolls-Royce & Limousine Service
14896 Bancroft Avenue, Suite 1
San Leandro, CA 94578
510-276-8500
Rolls-Royce and limousine only.

Paramount Limousine Service
2000 Aisquith Street
Baltimore, MD 21218
410-889-3100

Top Hat Limousine
13110 Shaker Square
Cleveland, OH 44120
216-751-8349

MUSIC

Joyce's Wedding Favorites
1-800-525-6923
Supplies CDs and cassettes of traditional and classical organ
music for your wedding ceremony.

P.S.E. Record
P.O. Box 1364
Merchantville, NJ 08109
609-662-2233
Processional song for your wedding, "We're Getting Married"
by Diva Factory, available on CD, cassette, and minialbum.

PHOTOGRAPHY AND VIDEOGRAPHY

BJS Productions
11707 Cromwell Avenue
Cleveland, OH 44120
216-721-1897
Photography, video, and DJ service.

Captured Moments Video & Photography
360 Clinton Avenue, #1F
Brooklyn, NY 11238
1-800-284-4201

Edward Fox Photography
4900 Milwaukee Avenue
Chicago, IL 60630
312-736-0200

In A Flash Photography
3451 Overcross
Houston, TX 77045
713-433-8282

Lang Video Art
1001 Ashmount Avenue
Oakland, CA 94610
510-834-7550
Specializing in videos for weddings and parties.

Lester Seays Videography
Orlando, FL
407-422-1136
1-800-313-4674
By appointment only.

Photographic Elegance
3117-B North Sharon Amity Road

Charlotte, NC 28205
704-536-1991

Photography by Tony
South Euclid, OH
216-291-8740
By appointment only.

Personal Touch Photographics
Orlando, FL
407-578-1824
By appointment only.

Ron Graddy Photography
Chicago, IL
312-278-5094
By appointment only.

Ross Portrait Design
10955 Ettrick Street
Oakland, CA 94605
510-638-6368
Wedding and video photography.

Video Perfection, Inc.
Atlanta, GA area
404-822-9031
1-800-771-2947
By appointment only.

Weddings-R-Us
Jersey City, NJ
201-653-6132
1-800-607-9333 (outside NJ and NY)
Photography and video packages.

TEXTILES

African Paradise
27 West 125th Street
New York, NY 10027
212-410-5294
Wide assortment of imported authentic and printed African fabrics by the yard.

Harlem Textile Works
186 East 122nd Street, 3rd Floor
New York, NY 10035
212-534-3377
Handmade domestic cotton Afrocentric made-to-order fabric
for apparel and furnishings.

Kuumba Place
EE Hale House
12 Morley Street
Roxbury, MA 02119
617-427-8325
Traditional and custom-woven African fabric.

WEDDING INVITATIONS, STATIONERY, CARDS, ETC.

The Arusi Affiliates
Chicago, IL
1-800-800-7759
Customized Afrocentric wedding invitations.

Blacksmiths Card & Prints
P.O. Box 623
Altadena, CA 91103
1-800-736-7778
Cards for all occasions and signed prints.

Carole Joy Creations
107 Mill Plain Road, Suite 200
Danbury, CT 16811
203-798-2060
Custom-designed Afrocentric wedding invitations.

Dynamic Balloons Enterprises
4531 West Sahara Avenue
Las Vegas, NV 89102
702-248-6060
Custom bridal announcements and invitations.

Frederick Douglass Designs
1033 Folger Street
Berkeley, CA 94710
510-204-0950 (SF/Bay area only)
1-800-399-4430
African-American greeting cards. Call for catalog.

Heritage Wedding
P.O. Box 384
Lumberton, NJ 08048-0384
1-800-892-4291
Full collection of African-American wedding invitations. Write for free catalog.

Heavenly Flowers
4924 West North Avenue
Milwaukee, WI 53208
414-871-2400

Jane Evershed Card Collection
P.O. Box 8874
Minneapolis, MN 55408
612-377-6355
Inspirational notes and postcards.

Loving Care by Mar
Orlando, FL
407-855-0044
By appointment only.
Ethnic invitations.

Ona Design
Baltimore, MD
301-891-3645
1-800-381-4019
By appointment only.
Originally designed African-inspired traditional and Afrocentric wedding invitations.

WEDDING PLANNERS, COORDINATORS, AND CONSULTANTS

A Special Time
1135 107th Avenue
Oakland, CA 94603
510-568-6970
Specializing in ethnic weddings, showers, and other special parties.

Adorning Bride by G
3015 Earl Street
Houston, TX 77098
713-521-1153
Specializes in consulting and planning weddings in the United States and worldwide.

The Arusi Affiliates
Chicago, IL
1-800-800-7759
By appointment only.
Complete wedding planner with a personal touch.

Bride To Be
Cleveland, OH
216-348-3072
By appointment only.
Fashion consultant and coordinator.

Carol Hall & Associates
10573 West Pico Boulevard, #147
Los Angeles, CA 90064-2348
213-731-3374
Wedding and event consultant.

CCW, Inc.
Connie Williams
Chicago, IL
312-880-2216
By appointment only.
Complete wedding planning.

Cynthia's Wedding Service
39 Lake Court Loop
Ocala, FL 34472
904-687-0588
Personalized wedding service.

Elegant Moments by Barbara
University Heights, OH
216-321-8010
By appointment only. Wedding consultant, coordinator, and
  party planner.

Elegant Occasions
5310 Arpana Drive
Orlando, FL 32839-2588
407-855-3358
Bridal consultant and coordinator.

Fantastic Celebrations!
569 Ritchie Road
Capitol Heights, MD 20743
301-499-7256
Planner, coordinator for weddings, rehearsals, postcelebrations.
  Bridal workshops.

Fodiva, Inc.
8033 Sunset Boulevard, Suite 916
West Hollywood, CA 90046
310-838-0111
Full-service Afrocentric wedding planner.

Grayphenia Bayles
301 East Burnham
Des Moines, IA 50315
515-285-9573
By appointment only.
Full-service wedding planner and coordinator.

Joanne's
P.O. Box 6672
Yorkville Station
New York, NY 10028
212-410-7546
Consultant and floral arrangements.

Joyous Occasions
9110 Old Palmer Road
Fort Washington, MD 20744
301-248-8027
Full-service wedding planner and consultant.

Nubian Beginnings
Los Angeles, CA
213-957-4900
By appointment only.
Focusing on traditional African customs during the ceremony,
  reception, and honeymoon.

Occasional Tiers
Brooklyn, NY
718-797-4158
By appointment only.
Wedding consultant, party and event planner.

Lynn Allen Jeter & Associates
8530 Wilshire Boulevard, #404
Beverly Hills, CA 90211-3127
213-930-2077
213-930-2366
Full-service wedding planner.

Patricia Hilliard
4924 West North Avenue
Milwaukee, WI 53028
414-871-2400
Wedding coordinator and party planner.

Shayla Simpson Productions, Inc.
Atlanta, GA
404-758-7900
By appointment only.
Wedding consultant.

Shrine of the Black Madonna
Cultural Center & Bookstore
13535 Livernois
Detroit, MI 48238
313-491-0777
African wedding consultant.

Special Occasions & Celebrations
Hayward, CA
510-262-0266
By appointment only.
Consulting, planning, and coordinating traditional Western and
  African-inspired weddings.

Tamala's Unique Designs
P.O. Box 45162
St. Louis, MO 03145
314-995-6226
Arranges your entire wedding.

Things to Be Done. . .
20001 Greenfield, Suite 1
Detroit, MI 48235
313-835-5059
Complete wedding coordination for traditional and Afrocentric
  weddings.

Toni Hazlewood at the Perfect Plan
Hyattsville, MD
301-779-5151
By appointment only.
Specializing in extravagant fantasy weddings from beginning
  to end.

Wialillian Howard
P.O. Box 36482
Charlotte, NC 28236
704-376-9476
Wedding consultant and planner.

Wittlinger's the Signature of Weddings
211 Groveland Circle
Savannah, GA 31405
912-355-8811
By appointment only.
Specializing in elegant and unique weddings.

Weddings-R-Us
Jersey City, NJ
201-653-6132
1-800-607-9333 (outside New Jersey and New York)
Full-service, one-stop wedding planner.

OTHER

Carol Hall & Associates
10573 West Pico Boulevard, #147
Los Angeles, CA 90064-2348
213-731-3374
Kit that enables a bridal couple to turn their wedding into a reunion of family and friends.

Dynamic Balloons Enterprises
4531 West Sahara Avenue
Las Vegas, NV 89102
702-248-6060
Custom balloon designs, sculptures, and decorations.

Golden Ribbon Playthings
P.O. Box 130222
Springfield Gardens, NY 11413
718-978-2675 (NY, NJ, CT only)
1-800-722-8285
Special edition bridal Huggy Bean™ doll in four gown styles.

Hafeezha StressBreaker
New York, NY
212-459-4806
By appointment only.
Ten- to twelve-minute neck and shoulder massage, stress and relaxation workshops for bride, bridal shower, and bridal party.

Heritage Altars
2320 Coloma Street, #2
Oakland, CA 94602
510-530-7837
Chooses personal memorabilia from the bride, groom, and their families, placing it in a setting of symbolic African art, flowers, and candles (available in California only).

International Fabricare Institute
The Association of Professional Drycleaners and Launderers
12251 Tech Road
Silver Spring, MD 20904
301-622-1900
For a free copy of "Wedding Gowns: Caring for Your Fabrics," send a self-addressed business-size envelope to the above address.

Painted Images
Detroit, MI
313-438-1036
By appointment only.
Takes your affair and transforms it into your fantasy.

Party with Balloons
San Pablo, CA
510-235-6852
Providing balloons, bouquets, baskets for showers, wedding receptions.

The Temple Beautiful
155 Canal Street, 2nd fl, Suite 9
New York, NY 10013
212-343-9706
Spiritual consultations, wedding candles, love baths, love oils, spiritual aromatherapy.

Waiting For You
Los Angeles, CA
310-234-3563
Provides waiter and waitress service to caterers.

SELECTED BIBLIOGRAPHY

HISTORICAL REFERENCE

Courtney-Clarke, Margaret. *Ndebele: The Art of an African Tribe*. New York: Rizzoli International Publications, 1986.

Eklof, Barbara. *With These Words . . . I Thee Wed*. Boston: Bob Adams, 1989.

Emery, Lynne Fauley. *Black Dance in the United States from 1619 to 1970*. National Press Books, 1972.

Mbiti, John S. *African Religions and Philosophy*. New York: Heineman, 1969.

Pavitt, Nigel. *Samburu*. New York: Henry Holt, 1991.

Rattray, Captain R.S. *Ashanti*. New York: Oxford University, 1923.

Rattray, Captain R.S. *Religion and Art in Ashanti*. New York: Oxford University Press, 1927.

Ronatree Green, Danita. *Broom Jumping: A Celebration of Love*. Richmond, VA: Entertaining Ideas, Ltd., 1992.

Talbot, D. Amaury. *Woman's Mysteries of a Primitive People*. Fort Lauderdale: Cassell, 1915.

HEALTH

Winikoff, Beverly, M.D., M.P.H., Suzanne Wymelenberg, and the editors of Consumer Reports Books. *The Contraceptive Handbook*. New York: Consumer Reports, 1992.

AFRICAN MUSIC AND DRUMMING

Chernoff, John Miller. *African Rhythm and African Sensibility: Aesthetics and Social Action in African Musical Idioms*. Chicago: University of Chicago, 1973.

Diallo, YaYa, and Mitchell Hall. *The Healing Drum: African Wisdom Teachings*. Rochester, VT: Destiny, 1989.

Kwabena, J.H. *The Music of Africa*. New York: W. W. Norton, 1974.

Wilson, Sule Greg. *The Drummer's Path*. Rochester, VT: Destiny, 1992.

COOKING

Burns, Lamont. *Down Home Southern Cooking*. New York: Doubleday, 1987.

Burton, Nathaniel, and Rudolph Lombard. *Creole Feast—15 Master Chefs of New Orleans Reveal Their Secrets*. New York: Random House, 1978.

Butler, Cleora. *Cleora's Kitchens and Eight Decades of Great American Food*. Tulsa: Council Oak, 1986.

Chase, Leah. *The Dooky Chase Cookbook*. Gretna, LA: Pelican, 1990.

Copage, Eric V. *Kwanzaa*. New York: William Morrow, 1991.

Darden, Norma Jean, and Carole. *Spoonbread and Strawberry Wine*. New York: Doubleday, 1978.

Harris, Jessica B. *Tasting Brazil*. New York: Macmillan, 1992.

Hovis, Gene. *Uptown Down Home Cookbook*. New York: Little, Brown, 1987.

Lewis, Edna. *The Taste of Country Cooking*. New York: Alfred Knopf, 1990.

Odarty, Bill. *A Safari of African Cooking*. Detroit: Broadside, 1971.

Paige, Howard. *Aspects of Afro-American Cookery*. Aspects, 1987.

Pinderhughes, John. *Family of the Spirit Cookbook*. New York: Simon & Schuster, 1990.

Tami Hultman, ed. *The Africa News Cookbook*. New York: Penguin, 1986.

INDEX

ILLUSTRATION CREDITS

PAGE 2: "Jumping the Broom," Bill Pajaud, 1992.

PAGE 12: Crossing Sticks. Photo courtesy of Toone Family Collection, Chase City, VA.

PAGE 17, 18: Courtesy of Ruth Rosedom, Baltimore, MD.

PAGE 22: Courtesy of the Cole Family, Baltimore, MD.

PAGE 30: Heart and hands. Matthew Thomas, 1992.

PAGE 34: "Cool Couple," Lloyd Toone, 1978.

PAGE 44: Khamitic illustration, Sen Ur Semahj.

PAGE 46: Gifts at bride's family home, George Chinsee. Dowry gift on mantel, Robertson African Arts; vase and wooden bowl, Zona (212-925-6750); beaded belt (on mantel), Beads of Paradise; mantel textile, Adrienne McDonald; bark gift box, Zona; gift basket, Beads of Paradise.

PAGE: 47: Porcelain Husband and Wife fruit bowl. Sacred Healing Arts, Atlanta, GA

PAGE 60: Dowry gift, Robertson African Arts. George Chinsee. This cast brass women's dowry treasure from the late nineteenth century was used for royal Owo Nigerian marriage ceremonies.

PAGE 64: Sherri Hobson Greene and Jimmy James Greene with The Spirit Ensemble. Bill Boyd.

PAGE 71: "Untitled," Jimmy James Greene, 1992.

PAGE 78: "As the Ancestors Watched" watercolor, Bill Pajaud. Stationery, George Chinsee.

PAGE 90: "Untitled," Jimmy James Greene, 1992.

PAGE 92: Thank-you note, Carole Joy Creations.

PAGE 94: Bride. Short, fitted linen dress and cropped jacket with reembroidered lace, Kelvin Rice, Philadelphia, PA. Tulle, reembroidered lace and linen crown, Sherri Hobson, Brooklyn NY. Earrings, M&J Savitt. Bouquet, The Daily Blossom.

PAGE 101: Gown sketch, Willie Mitchell at Tents of Kadar, Brooklyn, NY.

PAGE 102: Dress by Willie Mitchell at Tents of Kadar.

PAGE 104: Gown, CD Greene, NY.

PAGE 108: Earrings, Beads of Paradise.

PAGE 111: Crown, hand-beaded earrings and Khamitic pedesa, Seshini, Brooklyn, NY.

PAGE 114: Betty Dubuisson waiting to walk down the aisle. Greg Miller.

PAGE 128: Nigerian dress and crown with reembroidered lace, Lady Mitz, Jamaica, NY. Earrings and necklace, M&J Savitt, NY. Hosiery, Fogal of Switzerland. Shoes, Kinney. Wedding band, Lazarro.

PAGE 148: Brownstone wedding, 1926 by James Van Der Zee.

PAGE 161: Food detail, George Chinsee.

PAGE 164: Wedding gown with headpiece, Leslie Coombs for Heavens Bride and Nubian Expressions. Earrings and necklace, M&J Savitt. Tuxedo, Everett Hall, Silver Spring, MD. George Chinsee.

PAGE 172: Cultural bridesmaid. Bill Boyd.

PAGE 174: The Greenes. Bill Boyd.

PAGE 176: Groom shot, West African robes, Nigerian Fabrics and Fashions, Brooklyn, NY. George Chinsee.

PAGE 186: Bride. Full silk skirt and knit jacket, Twains Twines, NY. Earrings, Sarajo, NY. Gloves, Caroline Amato, NY. Tuxedo, Matsuda. Wedding band, The Studio of Ptah, NY. Child. Lace and cowrie shell dress, Shirley West for West Fashions, NY. George Chinsee.

PAGE 192: Illustration, Jimmy James Greene, 1992.

AN AFRICAN-AMERICAN WEDDING ALBUM

PAGE 1: Bride, Leslie Coombs for Heaven's Bride.

Photography, Jackie Nickerson. All other photographs by George Chinsee.

PAGE 2: Formal garden bridal gown and headpiece, Harold Clarke Designs, NY. Earrings, Fran Mack at Sharon Miller (718)636-1201. Bracelet, M&J Savitt. Gloves, La Crasia. Shoes, Stuart Weitzman.

PAGE 3: Cultural wedding bands, The Studio of Ptah, NY. Flower girl, lace cowrie shells and gold painted dress, Shirley West for West Fashions, NY. Flower basket, The Daily Blossom.

PAGE 4: (Cover shot) Bride. Satin portrait collar wedding column, Amsale, NY. Crown, Lanet at 4W Circle, Brooklyn, NY. Groom. *Asooke* dinner jacket, Franklin Hokett for Hokett Designs, NY. Trousers, Everett Hall.

PAGE 5: Bride. Traditional Ghanaian white lace peplum top and column *kente* skirt, Naana's Boutique, Philadelphia, PA. Earrings, Museum of Modern Art, NY. Bracelets, M&J Savitt. Shoes, Stephanie Kelian. Wedding bands, The Studio of Ptah, NY. Handkerchief, Creative Connections. Groom. *Kente* dinner jacket, Naana's Boutique. Dress shirt, Gittman Brothers. Shoes, Cole Haan. Bride. Gold striped mini-bridal gown with portrait collar and detachable train, Phe Zula Collection, NY. Earrings, Carolee Designs, NY. Gloves, La Crasia. Hosiery, Hanes Stardust. Shoes, Stuart Weitzman. Bride. Crocheted and beaded crown, Xenobia Bailey, Brooklyn, NY. Angora knit beaded top (with long quilted bridal skirt), Anthony Mark Hankins. Wedding band, The Studio of Ptah.

PAGE 6: Bride. Short, fitted linen dress and cropped jacket with reembroidered lace, Kelvin Rice, Philadelphia, PA. Tulle, reembroidered lace and linen crown, Sherri Hobson, Brooklyn, NY. Earrings, M&J Savitt. Gold wedding band, World Gold Council. Hair, Queen N'zinga Goddess Braids, Annu Prestonia for Khamit Kinks, NY and Atlanta.

PAGE 7: Gold and cream Khamitic pedesa with crown and earrings, Seshini, Brooklyn, NY. Hosiery, Pennaco. Shoes, Stuart Weitzman. Wedding band, Hru Ankhra, The Studio of Ptah, NY. Second-time around family. Bride. Full silk skirt and knit jacket, Twains Twines, NY. Earrings, Sarajo, NY. Gloves, Caroline Amato, NY. Groom. Tuxedo, Matsuda. African stole, The Baobab Tree, NY. Wedding band, The Studio of Ptah, NY. Child. Lace and cowrie shell dress, Shirley West for West Fashions, NY. Mature couple: Bride. Silver and white two-piece long gown with reembroidered lace and cowrie shells, Arthur McGee, NY. Headpiece, Sherri Hobson, Brooklyn, NY. Earrings and bracelet, Sun Gallery Goldsmith Designs by Jamal, Groom's ring, The Studio of Ptah.

PAGE 8: Yoruba *bubah* for him and her. House of Oosala, Brooklyn, NY. Earrings and bracelet, Sun Gallery Goldsmith Designs by Jamal. Hosiery, Fogal of Switzerland. Shoes, Kinney. Wedding bands, Hru Ankhra, The Studio of Ptah.

PAGE 9: Crown, Lady Mitz, NY. *Kente* wrap, The Baobab Tree, NY. Four-piece bride. Painted and cowrie-encrusted bustier, slim pant, leg-of-mutton sleeve jacket and crown, Shirley West for West Fashions. Floral staff, The Daily Blossom.

PAGE 10: Bride. Pearl-encrusted lattice work silk jersey gown and veil, CD Greene, NY. Groom. *Asooke* dinner jacket and bowtie and cream wool trousers, Franklin Hokett for Hokett Designs. Bouquet, The Daily Blossom. Inset. Satin and lace bridal gown, Dyan Nelson, Newark, NJ. Earrings, Adrienne Lockett (201) 673-0701.

PAGE 11: Large shot: White dinner coat, Lanvin. *Asooke* vest and bowtie, Franklin Hokett for Hokett Designs. Boutonniere, The Daily Blossom. Small inset. *Asooke* vest, Franklin Hokett. Larger inset. Tuxedo, Everett Hall. *Kente* bowtie, Gents Designer Neck West, Buffalo, NY.

PAGE 12: Dinner spread. Gold and cream embroidered tablecloth, Sarajo (212)966-6156. African mask and wooden trinket, The Studio Museum in Harlem Gift Shop. Wooden spoon, Craft Caravan, NY. Silver plated pedestal, plate warmer, chafing dish, platter and utensils, Oneida Silversmiths, Oneida, NY. Crystal rice dish, Colony.

PAGE 13: Dessert shot. Cowrie shell decorated African textile, Sarajo. Domed animal skin basket and Ethiopian *Agil-Agil* food basket, The Studio Museum in Harlem Gift Shop. Wedding cake. Charmaine Jones for Isn't That Special—Outrageous Cakes, NY. *Asooke* ribbons decorating table, The Baobab Tree.

PAGES 14–15: Gifts, from left. Straw handwoven basket from North Carolina with handle, Patina Prop Rentals. Contemporary candlestick holders, Curives, Brooklyn, NY. Set of dishes with salad and dinner plates, cups and saucers, Maryse Boxer Designs at Avventura. Tricolor stemware, Colony Glass. Large and small iridescent votive candle holders, Vero Vigneri at Museum of Modern Art Design Store. Mini photo album, Joyce and Company, Bronx, NY. Blue glass platter with cultural hand-painted images, Ta-Coumba Aiken, T.B.C. Studio. Espresso Master, Braun, Inc., Lynfield, MA. Silver cocktail shaker, Alessi at Museum of Modern Art Design Store. Broom, The Baobab Tree. Doll, Marcella Welch at Small Treasures, Atlanta, GA. Large painted vases, Noel Copeland. Copper leaf tudor table, Cheryl R. Riley for Right Angle Interiors, San Francisco, CA. Satin hangers, Yvonne O'gara at Metropolitan Design Group. Gold and black bowl, Colony Glass. Green and rust glass dish and crystal platter, Sasaki at Museum of Modern Art Design Store. Picture frame, Martha Sturdy at Metropolitan Design Group. *Harlem Renaissance* by Dr. Mary Schmidt Campbell, The Studio Museum in Harlem Gift Shop. Treasure box, Lee Moody at Metropolitan Design Group. Patchwork hanging textile, Napoleon Jones Henderson. Porcelain bowl with couple painted inside, Sacred Healing Arts, Atlanta, GA. Mesh sachet with potpourri, Vero Vigneri at Metropolitan Design Group. Ethiopian serving tray with legs, wooden spoon and wicker basket, Craft Caravan. Twin Cam 8mm camcorder, Sharp Electronics Corp. *Ndebele* by Margaret Courney Clarke, The Studio Museum in Harlem Gift Shop. Male/female candle holders, Curives. *Shekere* (musical gourd), Bill Simpson at The Studio Museum in Harlem Gift Shop. Napkin rings, Colette Malouf at Metropolitan Design Group. Hand-painted mask, Noel Copeland. Tapestry wedding boxes, Billie Cravens Associates, NY. Sachet and cream lace cowrie-shell trimmed pillow, Maasai African Potpourri Creations. Striped woven Ghanaian fabric pillow, African Home Inc. See Resource Guide for contact information.